THEORIES

OF

BUSINESS BEHAVIOR

PRENTICE-HALL, INC., Englewood Cliffs, N.J.

© 1964, by PRENTICE-HALL, Inc., Englewood Cliffs, N.J. All rights reserved. No part of this book may be reproduced in any form, by mimeograph or any other means, without permission in writing from the publishers. Printed in the United States of America. Library of Congress Catalog Card No.: 64-19002.

PRENTICE-HALL INTERNATIONAL, INC., *London*
PRENTICE-HALL OF AUSTRALIA, PTY., LTD., *Sydney*
PRENTICE-HALL OF CANADA, LTD., *Toronto*
PRENTICE-HALL FRANCE, S.A.R.L., *Paris*
PRENTICE-HALL OF INDIA PRIVATE LIMITED, *New Delhi*
PRENTICE-HALL OF JAPAN, INC., *Tokyo*
PRENTICE-HALL DE MEXICO, S.A., *Mexico City*

THEORIES
OF
BUSINESS BEHAVIOR

PRENTICE-HALL INTERNATIONAL SERIES IN MANAGEMENT

Baumol	*Economic Theory and Operations Analysis*
Brown	*Smoothing, Forecasting and Prediction of Discrete Time Series*
Churchman	*Prediction and Optimal Decision: Philosophical Issues of a Science of Values*
Clarkson	*The Theory of Consumer Demand: A Critical Appraisal*
Cyert and March	*A Behavioral Theory of the Firm*
Greenlaw, Herron, and Rawdon	*Business Simulation in Industrial and University Education*
Hadley and Whitin	*Analysis of Inventory Systems*
Holt, Modigliani, Muth, and Simon	*Planning Production, Inventories, and Work Force*
Kaufmann	*Methods and Models of Operations Research*
Lesourne	*Economic Analysis and Industrial Management*
Massé	*Optimal Investment Decisions: Rules for Action and Criteria for Choice*
McGuire	*Theories of Business Behavior*
Miller and Starr	*Executive Decisions and Operations Research*
Muth and Thompson	*Industrial Scheduling*
Nelson (editor)	*Marginal Cost Pricing in Practice*
Pfiffner and Sherwood	*Administrative Organization*

PRENTICE-HALL BEHAVIORAL SCIENCES IN BUSINESS SERIES

Herbert A. Simon, Editor

Borko	*Computer Applications in the Behavioral Sciences*
Costello and Zalkind	*Psychology in Administration: A Research Orientation Text with Integrated Readings*
Cyert and March	*A Behavioral Theory of the Firm*
Leavitt (editor)	*The Social Science of Organizations*
McGuire	*Theories of Business Behavior*

PRENTICE-HALL, INC.
PRENTICE-HALL INTERNATIONAL, INC., UNITED KINGDOM AND EIRE
PRENTICE-HALL OF CANADA, LTD., CANADA
J. H. DE BUSSY, LTD., HOLLAND AND FLEMISH-SPEAKING BELGIUM
DUNOD PRESS, FRANCE
MARUZEN COMPANY, LTD., FAR EAST
HERRERO HERMANOS, SUCS., SPAIN AND LATIN AMERICA

JOSEPH W. McGUIRE

Dean
School of Business
The University of Kansas

To Marge and the children

PREFACE

A great deal of scholarly interest has been generated during the last two decades in the development of a general theoretical structure to explain and predict business behavior. In part, this interest has evolved as a result of the long-term and gradual blend of economic and management thought, although it has been heightened in recent years through the applications of mathematical techniques and behavioral science concepts in business studies. The evolution of business theory, compounded by recent innovations in interdisciplinary areas and their use in business, is not yet complete. No universally acceptable set of business theories has been forthcoming. Nevertheless, business scholars have been stimulated to work within a variety of theoretical frameworks, and a large number of theories of the firm, administration, management, economics, decision making, organization, and bureaucracy have been constructed. In many instances, the differences between these theories have been more apparent than real. In some cases, these theories have differed primarily in their superficial or semantic details. In still others, of course, the differences have been significant.

The subject of this book is business theory. It is not intended as a final word on the subject. Indeed, there can be no final word without a great deal of further research. However, this book will dispel some of the confusion that surrounds theory in business today by pointing out the similarities and differences between theories and by presenting many highly regarded theories of business behavior in a clear and concise manner. This book also will serve as a benchmark of sorts, because it seeks to summarize the present state of knowledge in the area of business theory.

From the theories presented in this volume, then, further advances in theory should be made—in fact, they are being made. As a survey of theories of business behavior, this book will have some utility for business scholars and, especially, for business students interested in past and current theoretical developments in their discipline. Science is a cumulative process in which we climb upward on the shoulders of our predecessors. It is hoped that in some small way the gathering of theories in this volume, and the clear and accurate account of these theories, may hasten the ascent for those that follow in this area, and may generate still further enthusiasm for careful theoretical work in business.

The author owes a heavy debt to a multitude of scholars, most of whom are acknowledged in the footnotes. In addition, special appreciation is due to Herbert A. Simon for his invaluable editorial comments and suggestions. Professors Fremont E. Kast, Stephen H. Archer, Robert C. Meier, and Scott Walton of the University of Washington read parts of the manuscript, as did Mr. Mitsuo Ono of the University of Hawaii. Of great assistance were the many graduate students in my seminars at the University of Washington who stimulated my thought on business theory, clarified my presentations, and contributed substantially, through their comments, questions, and discussions, to this volume. A final word of gratitude must also be said for my wife and family, who bore so patiently the burden of my unusual writing habits, mumblings, and other eccentricities while working on this book.

Joseph W. McGuire

CONTENTS

1 INTRODUCTION 1

THE METHODS AND MATERIALS OF SCIENCE, 2

THE COMPLEXITIES OF SOCIAL SCIENCE THEORY, 7

    Realism vs. Predictability, 7
    Generalizations in the Social Sciences, 11

THE ORGANIZATION OF THIS BOOK, 12

CONCLUSION, 13

2 THE CONCEPT OF THE FIRM 16

HOLISTIC CONCEPTS, 18

    The Economic Concept of the Firm, 19
    The Concept of the Firm in the Theory of Games, 21
    The Concept of the Firm in Cybernetics, 24
    Other Holistic Concepts, 25

2 THE CONCEPT OF THE FIRM (continued)

BEHAVIORAL CONCEPTS OF THE FIRM, 27

    The Firm as a Bureaucratic Organization, 28
    Organizational Concepts of the Firm, 30
    Other Behavioral Concepts of the Firm, 34

CONCLUSIONS, 37

3 THE ECONOMIC THEORY OF BUSINESS BEHAVIOR   46

THE ECONOMIC THEORY OF THE FIRM, 47

    The Goal of the Firm, 47
    The Theory of Profit, 48
    Profits Per Se, 48
    Profits as a Distributive Share, 52
    Functional Theories of Profit, 54
    Conclusions on Profit Theory, 55
    The Maximizations of Profits and "Rationality," 56
    The Firm as a Transformation Unit, 57
    The Production Function, 58
    The Minimum Cost Mix, 58
    A Digression on Cost Curves, 59
    Economic Environments, 62
    Pure Competition, 62
    Oligopoly, 63

SUMMARY, 66

4 CRITICISMS OF THE ECONOMIC THEORY OF THE FIRM   73

VARIABLES—NUMBER AND PROPRIETY, 74

    The Scitovsky Modification, 75
    Profits versus Control, 77

4 CRITICISMS OF THE ECONOMIC THEORY OF THE FIRM (continued)

Other Variables, 78
Summary, 79

BUSINESS FIRMS DO NOT MAXIMIZE, 80

The Failure to Maximize, 80
Maximization and Uncertainty, 83

THE DEFENSE OF PROFIT MAXIMIZATION, 83

The Methodological Defense, 84
The Traditional Assumptions are Reasonable, 84
Other Defenses, 85

SUMMARY, 85

5 ALTERNATIVE ECONOMIC THEORIES 90

THE MAXIMIZATION OF VARIABLES OTHER THAN PROFIT, 91

Sales Maximization, 91
Liquidity and the Maintenance of Control, 93
A Deliberative Model of Business Behavior, 96

BIOLOGICAL MODELS OF BUSINESS BEHAVIOR, 101

Homeostasis, 102
Viability Analysis, 105
The Critique of Biological Theories, 107

SUMMARY, 108

6 DECISION THEORY IN CERTAINTY, RISK, AND UNCERTAINTY 112

DECISION MAKING UNDER CERTAINTY, 115

DECISION MAKING UNDER RISK, 119

6 DECISION THEORY IN CERTAINTY, RISK, AND UNCERTAINTY (continued)

The Expected Value Criterion, 119
Utility and Money, 121
A Return to Risk Analysis, 123

DECISION MAKING UNDER UNCERTAINTY, 124

The Laplace Criterion, 125
The Maximin Criterion, 126
Maximax Criterion, 126
The Hurwicz Criterion, 127
The Regret Criterion, 128
The Shackle Criterion, 129
Conclusions on Criteria, 132
Subjective Probability, 133

SUMMARY, 134

7 THE THEORY OF GAMES 138

DEVELOPMENT OF GAME THEORY, 139

THE TERMINOLOGY OF GAME THEORY, 140

TWO-PERSON GAMES, 142

Zero-Sum Two-Person Games, 142
Two-by-n Zero-Sum Games, 146

NONCONSTANT-SUM GAMES, 149

Noncooperative Games, 149
Cooperative Games, 151

N-PERSON GAMES, 154

SUMMARY, 156

8 ORGANIZATIONAL THEORIES AND BUSINESS BEHAVIOR 162

FRAMEWORKS FOR ORGANIZATIONAL VIABILITY, 163

Classical Structures, 163
Dysfunctional Elements in Organization, 167
Small Group Theory, 168
Modern Theory: Equilibrium and Viability, 175

RATIONALITY AND DECISION MAKING, 178

Role Theory, 178
Rationality, 180
Satisficing and Maximizing, 182
Organizational Decision Making, 184

SUMMARY, 186

9 PSYCHOLOGY AND BUSINESS BEHAVIOR 193

PERSONALITY THEORY, 195

The Holistic Schema of Personality, 196
Biological, Unconscious, and Hereditary Forces, 196
Common Traits and Unique Individuality, 198
Phenomenological Approaches, 200
n-Achievement, 202
Personality Theory in Retrospect, 204

LEARNING THEORY, 205

Contiguity Theory, 206
Feldman's Problem-Solving Model, 209

9 PSYCHOLOGY AND BUSINESS BEHAVIOR (continued)

BEHAVIORAL DECISION THEORY, 210

>Aspiration Levels, 211

SUMMARY, 214

10 THE INTERACTIONS BETWEEN CULTURE AND BUSINESS 222

CULTURE, SOCIETY, AND ENVIRONMENT: DEFINITIONS, 224

>Definition of Culture, 224
>The Meaning of Society, 225
>The Environment, 226

THEORIES OF CULTURE, 226

>Cultural Evolution, 227
>Historical Theories of Culture, 228
>Functional Approaches to Culture, 229
>Configurational Approaches to Culture, 230
>Other Cultural Approaches, 231
>Cultural Approaches in Review, 232

INNOVATION AND CULTURAL CHANGE, 233

CULTURAL ASPECTS OF BUSINESS BEHAVIOR, 236

>Rationality and Maximization, 236
>The Entrepreneurial Function, 238

SUMMARY, 239

11 BUSINESS THEORIES: AN APPRAISAL — 245

COMMON FEATURES IN THEORY, 246

    Problems in Theory Construction, 246
    Common Elements, 248
    Similarities and Differences: An Overview, 249

BUSINESS THEORIES, 250

    A Managerial Theory of the Firm, 251
    A Behavioral Theory of the Firm, 252

SUMMARY, 254

INDEX — 257

1

INTRODUCTION

Business is a practice in search of a theory. The purpose of this book is to examine the progress of this search and to set forth the variety and scope of the theoretical explanations which have been, or could be, applied to business behavior. Because the theories discussed in this book are drawn from a number of disciplines, they are not original, although in some instances their application to business is unique. The lack of originality and the attempt to focus on a variety of interconnected subjects makes this book a text, in the traditional and, by some scholars at least, despised sense of the term. Nevertheless, it aspires to a certain novelty, because it is an original text—if such a juxtaposition of words is not self-contradictory.

The study of business is basically an analysis of the behavior of the business enterprise as it interacts with its environment. Ordinarily such a study is atomized into its component parts, so that the student is exposed, in varying depths, to such subjects as accounting, finance, marketing, and production. Occasionally these components are joined together in a course, often called "Business Policy," wherein cases are most frequently utilized in a problem-oriented, pragmatic manner. There has been little exploration of the analytical, theoretical, or holistic framework of business. Theoretical essentials customarily consist of somewhat elementary courses in economics, although in recent years students have been exposed increasingly to decision theory and organization theory.

In this book we shall deal with theories. We shall examine these as they help us to explain, and possibly predict, the behavior of business firms. Our interest is in business as an holistic entity, and we shall be concerned only incidentally with specific aspects of business operations. Are there any general patterns of business behavior? Do businessmen, regardless of their particular occupations, have common goals, and do they attempt to act in a common fashion to attain these goals? Are firms and men consistent in their behavior, so that theories might be used to explain past actions and to predict the direction and perhaps even the extent of future changes? These are the kinds of questions to which answers are sought herein. As in all the social sciences, it is not expected that the answers obtained will explain, or prove useful in other ways relating to the behavior of each and every business concern. It is expected that, like all generalizations about human behavior (including this one), there will be exceptions to the rule. Nevertheless, if we know abstractly how firms behave we shall possess information that will greatly increase our understanding of business.

In the following sections of this chapter we shall try to accomplish three objectives. First, we shall discuss the meaning of theories and comment on some related issues of methodology. Second, we shall attempt to indicate some of the complexities involved in constructing a theory of business behavior. And finally, we shall sketch out the sequence of the chapters that follow, and try to give the reader some idea of the organization and flow of the topics we shall examine later.

THE METHODS AND MATERIALS OF SCIENCE

Scientists deal primarily with ideas. So too do businessmen. The ideas that concern scientists, however, are different from those that interest businessmen. Then too, the ideas with which scientists deal vary widely from one area of knowledge to another. The cohesive substance that binds all sciences together, and that separates them from, for example, the work of businessmen, is method, and not ideas or other materials. Scientists use a scientific method composed of rigorous observation and logical interpretation. Needless to add, businessmen who utilize a scientific method may be called scientists, and students who marshal the facts of business phenomena, examine the complex of relationships between these facts, and describe and analyze their sequences in a logical manner which appeals to reason rather than emotion are also men of science. There is no sphere of inquiry that lies outside the legitimate field of science. The scope of science is not limited; its task (old-fashioned though it may sound) is to seek truth in every possible branch of knowledge, including business.

Karl Pearson has written:

> . . . science is in reality a classification and analysis of the contents of the mind; and the scientific method consists in drawing just comparisons and inferences from the stored impresses of past sense-impressions, and from the conceptions based upon them. Not till the immediate sense-impression has reached the level of a conception, or at least a perception, does it become material for science.[1]

Thus, although the facts of science may basically be obtained through our senses, it is only when these facts are arranged abstractly into "constructs" that they become real. Vital to science are abstractions which, in fact, might be conceived to be "reality." Students are frequently bothered by scientific subjects (as often are businessmen) because these are so "abstract" and, therefore, "unreal." Yet, if we examine carefully what we think of as "reality" we find that this consists essentially of the contents of the mind—of abstractions that organize our sense perceptions. An illustration may help us to grasp the meaning of the facts of science. Suppose we examine the characteristics of a close friend—his height, weight, prejudices, weaknesses; his manner of thinking and speaking; the color of his hair and eyes—all those physical, spiritual, and mental qualities of which he is composed. What is it that makes up this person? His physical features alone, or his less tangible attributes too? Was he the same individual when he was a boy or a baby? Obviously, we identify a person by organizing and grouping sense impressions we perceive; the person consists of the organization that resides in our minds. The reality of things may appear differently to different people. The car, an object of love, affection, and status to its owner, may be viewed in quite a different way by the victim it strikes. In order for a conception to have scientific validity, it must be self-consistent, and it must be deducible from the perceptions of a normal and observant person.[2] Thus, a color-blind person who calls a yellow daffodil "a red flower," does not make a daffodil red to a normal individual, and his conception would not have scientific validity. From scientific conceptions, a logical person could draw scientifically valid inferences.

Science, therefore, begins with the observation of facts, but only when these facts are arranged into constructs and conceptions, and when inferences are drawn from them do we approach the real world of science.

Observation, in itself, is meaningless unless it is combined with abstraction. Many factual details are, and should be, ignored because they are irrelevant to the observer's purpose. Thus, a person studying business decision making would hardly be concerned with the fact that the decision maker wore brown rather than black shoes, or that he had blue eyes or a mole on his cheek. The observer would abstract from the decision-making situation those features that compose, for him, an idealized version of the real event. Sometimes the abstraction so created is broken down into its parts, which are treated separately in order to study each component individually. This process is termed analysis; it is the opposite of synthesis, where the parts are combined. A type of abstraction, closely related to analysis, is often called simplification. Here "Not only are certain features abstracted from real events to create idealized events, but also certain aspects of these idealized events are then often altered so as to produce simplified idealized events." [3]

Thus far the discussion has dealt with scientific method and facts, material that appears to be far removed from the realm of business behavior and theory. Furthermore, although we have made certain distinctions above as though they were entirely clear cut, there is actually little unanimity among philosophers of science on the scientific method. Francis Bacon, for example, stressed objective and observable fact as the heart of science. He believed that the scientist should not permit himself to be a part of fact. All preconceived ideas, all hypotheses, all formal logic must be discarded so that the facts stand alone. Empirical evidence is collected in greater and greater volume until, claimed Bacon, it adds up to a generalization. Bacon's method is called inductive empiricism. René Descartes advocated a method known as rationalistic deduction, wherein the scientist doubts all "facts" that can possibly be doubted rationally, and then deduces truth from those facts that cannot be doubted. Darwin was much closer to the position we have taken in earlier paragraphs, for he believed that the facts obtained by observation or by experiment gain significance only when reason is used to build them into a general body of knowledge. He said that: "Science consists of grouping facts so that general laws or conclusions may be drawn from them." [4] T. H. Huxley, Morris Cohen and Ernest Nagel, and John Dewey all go further than Darwin in their emphasis on the need for hypotheses prior to the collection of data.[5]

Hypotheses are propositions that arise from previous knowledge, or that are suggested by the subject matter under investigation. The purpose of a hypothesis is to bring order out of the multitude of facts that confront the investigator. The facts are meaningless until some are judged to be significant and others to be irrelevant. Despite the old saying, facts do not speak for themselves. As Cohen and Nagel have observed, "A hypothesis is believed to be relevant to a problem if it expresses determinate modes of connections between a set of facts, including the fact investigated; it is irrelevant otherwise." [6]

Hypotheses do more than establish the pattern of search for relevant facts. If they are properly formulated it is possible to make deductions from them and to note whether or not they explain the facts observed. Hypotheses often cannot be directly verified because of practical or technical difficulties. However, they are not useful unless capable of refutation. Beveridge has stated:

> Generalizations can never be *proved*. They can be tested by seeing whether deductions made from them are in accord with experimental and observational facts, and if the results are not predicted, the hypothesis or generalization may be *disproved*. But a favourable result does not prove the generalization, because the deduction made from it may be true without its being true. Deductions, themselves correct, may be made from palpably absurd generalizations. For instance, the truth of the hypothesis that plague is due to evil spirits is not established by the correctness of the deduction that you can avoid the disease by keeping out of the reach of the evil spirits. In strict logic a generalization is never proved and remains on probation indefinitely, but if it survives all attempts at disproof it is accepted in practice, especially if it fits well into a wider theoretical scheme.[7]

A hypothesis may originate as an educated speculation. If it holds good in all circumstances it may be called a theory, and if it is sufficiently profound and universal it may be termed a "law." Because a generalization cannot be absolutely proven, it is usually accepted after a number of tests, especially if it is compatible with existing scientific beliefs.

In the above paragraph we defined a theory as an extended hypothesis. However, there is considerable variation in use of these terms. Some authorities define hypotheses and theories to be identical. As defined above, a theory is somewhere between a hypothesis and a law. Karl Popper has written that "Scientific theories are universal statements. Like all linguistic representations they are systems of signs or symbols." [8] Sherman Krupp has extended this definition as follows:

> A theory is a complex of symbols organized to pattern the way we see things, to predict, and explain. It is more than a sum of atomic, empirical hypotheses and observation statements joined together through formal rules of logic and coordinating definitions. True, theories deal mainly with observable matters, but the relationships between the simplifications of a theory and its empirical content are only occasionally clear.[9]

Rather than become involved in definitional controversy, let us look at certain features possessed by theories. First, much of what we have said about hypotheses, of course, also applies to theories. A theory is also an abstraction; it is designed to act as a guide to, or explanation of, real phenomena. Second, a useful theory possesses logical consistency. It is consistent with other laws and theories and facts. An hypothesis which stated: "Businessmen behave as they do because they are, basically, sadistic" would not be acceptable in the light of what is known about mankind in general and businessmen in particular. A theory should also be consistent internally, so that its conclusions follow logically from its assumptions. Third, a theory should be as simple as possible, containing an economy of assumptions. Fourth, it helps if the theory contains a degree of elegance.

Because theories cannot be proven to hold absolutely, it is often difficult to discriminate between them. In an examination of theories of business behavior, for example, how do we know which theory is most appropriate? This, indeed, is an important problem. Stephen Toulmin has used an analogy between theories and maps which is of some help.[10] He notes that maps, like theories, are abstractions designed for the purposes of explanation and guidance. A road map of New York State contains relevant information for the motorist, but it omits many features of the terrain which the cartographer believes are not needed by the typical traveler. Like theories, the map at any future time may not "hold," if there is new construction, a "washout," or other road problems. Furthermore, in New York it is likely that most localities are connected by two or more roads. In the same way, two or more theories may be used to explain a phenomenon, and may actually accomplish this end. As with roads to a community, choice of the best theory often depends upon the direction in which one is traveling. Where two or more roads go between two points, the choice between them may be made on the basis of traffic volumes, scenery, practicable speeds, and similar variables. These features of competing highways are similar to the simplicity, economy, consistency, elegance and other attributes of theories. It may be quite difficult, therefore, to choose between conflicting theories. The best guide is the appropriateness of each for the purpose for which it is to be used. Sometimes, however, it is necessary to consider the secondary aspects of theories (simplicity, and so on) to make a choice among them. It has been suggested facetiously that good theories have often been spoiled by the data. Ultimately, theory must answer to the facts. But when we don't know which is "best" we must often rely upon our personal preferences for one rather than another.

Not all theories possess the same sort of validity. T. B. Roby, for example, has differentiated three major types of validity of theories in the physical sciences.[11] (1) A theory may be valid in a *subjunctive* sense. It may describe the behavior of entities in environments that never exist in reality. Galileo's law of falling bodies is of this type. (2) A theory may hold *locally*—over certain ranges of the relevant variables. Newton's laws of motion, which hold for "middle-sized" phenomena, are illustrative of this type of theory. (3) A theory may hold *statistically*, which means that, although there are local exceptions, it is supported by large numbers of observations. Some of our medical "laws" are of this type.

What has been set forth in this section is applicable to all science and to all theorizing. There are unique problems, however, involved in theory construction in the social sciences and in business. We shall examine these in the next section.

THE COMPLEXITIES OF SOCIAL SCIENCE THEORY

Paul Samuelson has written that:

> According to legend, economists are supposed never to agree among themselves. If Parliament were to ask six economists for an opinion, seven answers would come back—two, no doubt, from the volatile Mr. Keynes! [12]

Economists and other social scientists and business scholars would all find these remarks to apply to their fields of interest, and especially to matters of theory. It is necessary only to suggest a new hypothesis in the behavioral sciences to find oneself embroiled in controversy and conflict. In recent decades, in particular, although there have been many advances in behavior theory, much of the improvement has occurred by narrowing our theoretical scope, so that modern theories seem most often to be addenda to past theoretical systems. There has also been a tendency for traditional theories to remain quite powerful, and for their advocates to adopt an "either with us or you are wrong" attitude, which is often stifling to original and substantially different thought. Thus, in sociology the work of Weber in bureaucracy is still the most frequently cited contribution, and the writings of a Merton, a Gouldner, a Selznick or a Bendix represent basically a chipping away or modification of the original Weberian block. In economics the conventional theory of the firm still forms the cornerstone of most explanations of business behavior. In late years, especially, this traditional theory has been vigorously upheld against counter-theories, with a defense based primarily upon the articulate arguments propounded by Professor Milton Friedman of the University of Chicago.[13] Friedman's work is important as representative of a current and widely held position, then, in the study of theories of business behavior.

Realism vs. Predictability

Friedman has taken the position, not necessarily in opposition to, but narrower than that which we have taken above, that the only relevant test of the validity of a theory is its predictive power. As an economist,

Friedman maintains that traditional economic theory, which holds that firms behave as if they were attempting to maximize expected returns, is substantiated by the evidence.

> An even more important body of evidence for the maximization-of-returns hypothesis is experience from countless applications of the hypothesis to specific problems and the repeated failure of its implications to be contradicted. This evidence is extremely hard to document; it is scattered in numerous memorandums, articles, and monographs concerned primarily with specific concrete problems rather than with submitting the hypothesis to test.[14]

Furthermore, Friedman contends that traditional theory is upheld because it has been used and accepted over a long period of time.[15] He also implies that the economic theory of the firm is most appropriate because it is clear, precise, and economical.[16] Most importantly, a theory cannot be tested by comparing its assumptions directly with reality.

> Indeed, there is no meaningful way in which this can be done. Complete "realism" is clearly unattainable, and the question whether a theory is realistic "enough" can be settled only by seeing whether it yields predictions that are good enough for the purpose in hand or that are better than predictions from alternative theories. Yet the belief that a theory can be tested by the realism of its assumptions independently of the accuracy of its predictions is widespread and the source of much of the perennial criticism of economic theory as unrealistic. Such criticism is largely irrelevant, and, in consequence, most attempts to reform economic theory that it has stimulated have been unsuccessful.[17]

We may sum up Friedman's arguments in the following points: (1) The economic theory of the firm is substantiated by the evidence. (2) It has withstood the test of time. (3) It contains such attributes as simplicity and cohesion to a greater degree than its competitors. (4) All theories are abstractions and as such cannot be appraised by the criterion of the realism of their assumptions. By the accuracy of its predictions alone can a theory be judged.

Point four has aroused the most controversy. The first statement, that the economic theory of the firm has been substantiated by the evidence, is difficult to document. Friedman himself does not specify precisely the source of this evidence, and it is doubtful that it would be acceptable to most observers.

Friedman's second and third points can be dismissed without lengthy comment. There have been many theories in both the physical and social sciences which have been held for years before they were discarded. The test of time is no test at all in science. The third point is obviously of secondary importance. An hypothesis may possess all the lesser attributes of a proper theory and still not be capable of performing its primary tasks. On the other hand, a theory that is much less elegant than the economic theory of the firm may explain and predict the phenomena with which it is concerned.

This brings us to Friedman's last point, which is that the realism of the assumptions of a theory does not matter so long as the theory permits accurate predictions of behavior. It is this view that has resulted in debate.

Eugene Rotwein was one of the first critics of the Friedman position that prediction is the only criterion for the appraisal of theory.[18] He has argued that:

> . . . what we seek in science is not merely "prediction" in the Friedman sense of the term—which is the prediction of the crystal ball—but prediction through "explanation." Only this enables us to construct a deductive system involving the real world which can make this world intelligible to us.[19]

Like most tempests, Friedman's argument has tended to draw attention away from the theoretical teacup that contains it. Obviously, if assumptions do not have to be realistic in order to predict behavior business scholars must either turn to other theories in order to understand the activities and attitudes of the firm, or else assume that micro-economics is irrelevant to the study of business behavior.

Sherman Krupp, for example, has advanced the thesis that the economic theory of the firm is not designed to describe or even to predict its behavior.[20] Instead, from the assumptions of this theory ". . . predictions can be made concerning the patterns of allocation in a competitive society." [21] In other words, economists use their theory of the firm as a means to predict resource allocation among competing uses. The theory of the firm, in this interpretation, forms a part of this larger schema but must not be isolated or studied apart from its larger setting.

Ernest Nagel has observed that the assumptions of a theory may be unrealistic in at least three senses. (1) A statement is not descriptively exhaustive. (2) It is false or improbable on the basis of the evidence available. (3) A statement may hold only in "pure" or "ideal" situations.[22] We have previously discussed conditions one and three. These instances of the lack of realism are understandable. They are common to many theoretical structures. It is only the second case that is a matter for contention, and on this Nagel remarks:

> But in any event, if by an assumption of a theory we understand one of the theory's fundamental statements . . . , a theory with an unrealistic assumption (in the present sense of the word, according to which the assumption is false) is patently unsatisfactory; for such a theory entails consequences that are incompatible with observed fact, so that on pain of rejecting elementary logical canons the theory must also be rejected.[23]

The Friedman hypothesis, as Nagel also observes, contains the expression "the maximum of expected returns" that may provide economists with a set of rules; but it does not provide rules for business behavior.[24] The ambivalent nature of Friedman's arguments, finally, is seen in Nagel's conclusions:

> Is he (Friedman) defending the legitimacy of unrealistic theoretical assumptions because he thinks theories are at best only useful instruments, valuable for predicting observable events but not to be viewed as genuine statements whose truth or falsity may be significantly investigated? But if this is the way he conceives theories (and much of his argument suggests that it is), the distinction between realistic and unrealistic theoretical assumptions is at best irrelevant, and no defense of theories lacking in realism is needed. Or is he undertaking that defense in order to show that unrealistic theories cannot only be invaluable tools for making predictions but that they may also be reasonably satisfactory explanations of various phenomena in terms of the mechanisms involved in their occurrence? But if this is his aim (and parts of his discussion are compatible with the supposition that it is), a theory cannot be viewed, as he repeatedly suggests that it can, as a "simple summary" of some vaguely delimited set of empirical generalizations with distinctly specified ranges of application.[25]

A theoretical system may be conceived as a set—an interrelated grouping between assumptions (A), which are the antecedents of the theory, the theory itself (B), and the complete set of consequences (C) which are implied by, or follow from, (B). Samuelson has argued that (A), (B), and (C) form an integrated whole, and if (C) is realistic (as Friedman claims), then (A) and (B) must also possess the same degree of realism, or the system is not logically consistent.[26] If (A) is the desire of businessmen to maximize profits, (B) is the rational economic calculus of businessmen as they move toward maximum profits, and (C) the profit maximizing prices and quantities as observed in the market, Friedman claims that so long as (C) is valid, it doesn't matter if (A) or (B), or both, are false. Herbert Simon asserts, however, that we do not even know that (C) is valid.[27] He argues that: "no one has, in fact, observed whether the actual positions of business firms are the profit-maximizing ones; nor has anyone proposed a method of testing this proposition by direct observation." [28] Furthermore, we do have a great deal of evidence on (A) and (B), and most of this evidence about (B) indicates that it is false.[29] Simon suggests that through more empirical work at the level of the individual firm and the individual businessman new, accurate, and realistic theories of business behavior may be constructed.

George Katona, in the same vein, has commented:

> At a higher level the goal is the establishment of a theory of social behavior rather than of economic behavior. Integrated principles of motivation, group membership, learning, and decision making must be

developed in several areas of human activity. We need not only more field study of business behavior but also more and better theory.[30]

We would agree with the critics of Friedman's position. The realism of assumptions in theory is important, especially where, as Simon points out, the assumptions themselves are ascertainable matters of fact. The conventional economic theory of the firm assumes that the decision-making processes of businessmen are profit-maximizing processes. This is as much of a prediction of the theory as its predictions for market phenomena. Both on grounds of logical consistency and on the basis of the empirical study of individual decision makers, then, it would appear evident that Friedman's position is untenable.

The introduction of more realistic assumptions about business behavior into our theories does not, of course, automatically enhance their predictive capabilities. Nevertheless, together with Katona, we are interested in this book in theories of business behavior—in understanding, explaining, and predicting business behavior. We want to construct and examine generalizations about the business enterprise. In this context it would seem only appropriate that our theoretical foundations be as realistic (in the sense of truth vs. falsity), as relevant, and as informative as we can make them. The business firm, for our purpose, forms a focal point for theoretical investigation, and is not seen as a means to some further goal such as the allocation of resources in the economy.

Generalizations in the Social Sciences

All scientific investigation is initiated, in somewhat pragmatic fashion, in response to specific problems. In the social sciences the importance of starting with a specific problem, such as the behavior of business firms, is perhaps even more important than in the physical sciences. One reason for this lies in the nature of many behavioral problems, which often are not "objective" in the sense of being based upon physical facts as in the natural sciences, but instead are derived from introspective observations.[31] In the natural sciences, too, introspection may be an important source of discovery. However, in both, the verification of theories may be accomplished by an appeal to empirical data obtained through the senses. Thus, social scientists often claim for their theories the same validity as physical scientists claim for theirs.

Problems in the physical as well as in the social sciences occur as a result of the dual nature of many vital questions. Natural and social sciences both may be concerned with problems such as: (1) How *do* business firms behave? or (2) How *should* firms behave? The first type is called "positive" or factual, whereas the second is termed "normative."

It is important to differentiate positive from normative theory in the social sciences. Positive theory should be capable of refutation, and often the methods of the natural sciences are applicable. Normative theory, on the other hand, by its very nature is not in accord with the facts, and must be treated in a somewhat unique fashion. Throughout most of this book, as we shall see, our subject will be positive and not normative theories of business behavior.

THE ORGANIZATION OF THIS BOOK

In the foregoing pages of this chapter we have examined certain features of the method of science, the construction and meaning of hypotheses, and the complexities of theoretical analyses in the social sciences. In the remainder of this book we shall probe into the intricacies of theories of business behavior, and attempt to ascertain the present state of this abstract area. As we shall observe, there is considerable order among such theories, and although they seem to be going off in all directions, with few tendencies toward synthesis, they in fact are not as divergent as they appear at first glance. In an attempt to systematize our study of these theories we shall examine each group under a number of broad headings.

In Chapter 2 we explore the nebulous concept of the business enterprise. We shall see that, currently, there is no one meaning which should be, or is, attached to the firm. Nevertheless, the concept of the firm is most important, for the firm acts as a catalyst or framework within which behavior takes place.

Chapter 3 begins a three-phased series of studies concerned with economic theory. The amount of space devoted to economics may appear disproportionate to some readers, but it must be understood that the economic theory of the firm is the most fully developed of all the theories of business behavior. It is the "thesis" of business theory—that theory which exists, and as such needs careful attention. It is also the central figure in the theoretical controversy surrounding business behavior. Thus, in Chapter 4 are set forth the criticisms of conventional theory whereas 5 contains alternative economic theories.

Chapters 6 and 7 might be called mathematical theories of business behavior, largely because the methodology employed, but not necessarily the substance, relies heavily upon mathematical concepts. In the first of these, on decision theory, the environmental or informational circumstances in which the firm operates are discussed. The effects of risk and uncertainty on the decision-making process are examined, and the theories of behavior developed to explain decisions under these conditions are analyzed. The second in this sequence deals with the theory of games, wherein the firm is treated as a participant in conflict or cooperative situations in which there exist other opponents or partners.

The following three chapters deal with theories of business behavior that have been attributed largely to—respectively—sociology, psychology, and cultural anthropology. Chapter 8 draws heavily from organization theory, and is focused primarily upon the firm as an organization or as a group. The next chapter, based upon psychology, studies business behavior principally as analogous to, or composed of, the behavior of individuals. Finally, the business enterprise is in many ways a product of its culture, and is certainly affected by it. Thus, in Chapter 10 we note theories of business behavior taken primarily from anthropology.

In the last chapter we attempt to examine those theories which approach business behavior from an holistic viewpoint. Such theories include, for example, a discussion of the firm as a system, drawing upon a variety of social sciences rather than upon any one.

CONCLUSION

This book, like all other texts, is unfortunately a prisoner of its organization. Consequently the brief survey of coming attractions presented above, although helpful in sketching out the general direction we shall follow, tends to conceal more than it reveals. As we shall observe, there are few theories applicable to business behavior that cannot be placed into a relatively small number of theoretical super-structures. For example, many of the theories presented in Chapter 9, which stem primarily from work in psychology, belong to the same general theoretical family as those contained in Chapter 5, which are originated by economists, or to those in the area of organization theory. For indeed, the similarities between theories of behavior are more marked than the differences.

The very fact, therefore, that we have discussed theories of business behavior as imbedded into their disciplinary environments helps to draw attention to the wide spectrum of the social sciences brought to focus on business. On the other hand, this categorization tends to obscure the linkages which exist between theories from different disciplines. The presentation of closely related theories regardless of origin, however, would fail to delineate clearly those differences between them which properly may be ascribed to their origins, and perhaps would dull that unique flavor which is often the hallmark of separate disciplines.

Caught in a dilemma of the need for dual organization, solvable only by writing with forked pen, we have decided to categorize theories primarily by disciplines. Nevertheless, all through this book, and especially in the final chapter, we shall comment on the relationships that exist between theories, to show the areas of communality and agreement between them, and to fit these theories into general classes.

Notes and References

1. Karl Pearson, *The Grammar of Science* (Cleveland: Meridian Books, The World Publishing Company, 1957), p. 52.
2. *Ibid.*, pp. 53-54.
3. E. Bright Wilson, Jr., *An Introduction to Scientific Research* (New York: McGraw-Hill Book Company, Inc., 1952), p. 25.
4. F. Darwin, *Life and Letters of Charles Darwin* (London: John Murray, Publishers, Ltd., 1888).
5. See F. S. C. Northrop, *The Logic of the Sciences and the Humanities* (New York: The Macmillan Company, 1947), especially Chapter 1.
6. Morris R. Cohen and Ernest Nagel, *An Introduction to Logic and Scientific Method* (New York: Harcourt, Brace & World, Inc., 1934), p. 202.
7. W. I. B. Beveridge, *The Art of Scientific Investigation* (New York: Random House, The Modern Library, 1957), p. 118. Reprinted from the edition by W. W. Norton & Company, Inc., New York, 1950.
8. Karl R. Popper, *The Logic of Scientific Discovery* (New York: Science Editions, Inc., 1961), p. 59.
9. Sherman Krupp, "Logic and Meaning in the Theory of the Firm." Paper read before the Southern Economic Association (mimeographed), Memphis, 1961, p. 3.
10. Stephen Toulmin, *The Philosophy of Science,* Harper Torchbooks, The Science Library (New York: Harper & Row, Publishers, 1960), Chapter 4.
11. T. B. Roby, "An Opinion on the Contribution of Behavior Theory," *The American Psychologist,* Vol. 14, No. 3 (March, 1959), p. 131.
12. Paul A. Samuelson, "What Economists Know," in Daniel Lerner, editor, *The Human Meaning of the Social Sciences* (Cleveland: Meridian Books, The World Publishing Company, 1959), p. 192.
13. Milton Friedman, *Essays in Positive Economics* (Chicago: University of Chicago Press, 1953).
14. *Ibid.*, p. 23.
15. *Ibid.*
16. *Ibid.*, p. 41.

17. *Ibid.*

18. Eugene Rotwein, "On 'The Methodology of Positive Economics,'" *Quarterly Journal of Economics*, Vol. LXXIII (November, 1959).

19. Eugene Rotwein, "Some Methodological Questions and the Theory of the Firm." Paper read before the Southern Economic Association (mimeographed), Memphis, 1961, p. 11.

20. Sherman Krupp, *Pattern in Organization Analysis: A Critical Examination* (Philadelphia: Chilton Company, 1961), Chapter 1.

21. *Ibid.*, p. 11.

22. Ernest Nagel, "Assumptions in Economic Theory," *American Economic Review*, Vol. LIII, No. 2 (May, 1963), pp. 211-219.

23. *Ibid.*, pp. 214-215.

24. *Ibid.*, p. 217.

25. *Ibid.*, p. 218.

26. Paul A. Samuelson, "Discussion of Problems of Methodology," *American Economic Review*, Vol. LIII, No. 2 (May, 1963), pp. 231-236.

27. Herbert A. Simon, "Discussion of Problems of Methodology," *American Economic Review*, Vol. LIII, No. 2 (May, 1963), pp. 229-231.

28. *Ibid.*, p. 230.

29. *Ibid.*

30. George Katona, "Appendix A," in Howard R. Bowen, *The Business Enterprise as a Subject for Research*, Social Science Research Council Pamphlet 11 (New York, 1955), p. 43.

31. See Northrop, *op. cit.*, Chapter 13.

2

**THE
CONCEPT
OF
THE FIRM***

Executives generally have found it difficult to keep well-informed on all the latest developments in management science, decision theory, and operations research. Even more bewildering have been the changes that have occurred during recent decades in the disciplines underlying the area of business—in economics, mathematics, and the social sciences.

A wealth of material has become available which makes it clear to most executives that the theoretical foundations of managerial behavior are based securely upon a number of related disciplines. Despite this awareness, the relations between the behavioral sciences and actual management practices are often not fully understood.

For one thing, the sciences are not unified. Then too, each discipline has its own vocabulary which differs from that of the others, and all differ from terms typically employed in business.

Theories of managerial behavior—of decision making

---

* This chapter (with only minor revisions) first appeared as an article in the *California Management Review*, III, No. 4 (Summer, 1961), pp. 64-83.

as they have been termed—are based usually upon hypotheses originating in the social sciences. These theories represent the search for explanations and predictions of the behavior of the basic business unit—the firm. There is a good deal of ferment, however, on what exactly the concept of the firm should be. An examination of this controversy, as we shall observe in this chapter, throws considerable light upon recent studies of behavioral scientists, mathematicians, economists, and others as they pertain to business.

In this chapter we shall try to achieve three objectives: (1) To examine several of the more important concepts of the firm; (2) To reduce somewhat the confusion that results from the existence of a wide variety of notions of the firm by placing these ideas into two broad categories; and (3) To note that, although a profusion of concepts of the firm is probably necessary in the present study of business behavior, it is likely that some sort of eclectic concept, or some new "business" theory of the firm might eventually evolve as business becomes a more significant field for behavioral investigations.

If ever a general theory of business behavior is to evolve, it will be necessary also to derive a concept of the firm as a frame of reference for such behavior. (A frame of reference for a theoretical study is generally shaped by the problems to be solved and the goals to be attained.) Because the problems investigated and objectives sought vary widely among the behavioral sciences, it is evident that the frame of reference suitable to one might differ substantially from that employed in another.

For example, we could speculate that in attempting to derive a concept of the firm the economist might examine only its economic activities; the sociologist might be interested solely in group relationships; the psychologist might be concerned primarily with individual behavior; and the anthropologist might want to study the firm as a cultural institution. The concept of the firm that resulted would probably be different in each case, and each would reflect the frame of reference used.

Criteria for judging the merits of such concepts as the firm do not necessarily include their relation to reality, for obviously each concept is an abstraction of selected facets of business activities. In the medical sciences, to use an analogy, we may distinguish at least three levels of abstraction. The first of these is called phenomenology, which consists of the recording of physically observable facts or events. The doctor looking at a patient's tongue in order to diagnose his illness is an example.

A higher level of abstraction in medicine is pathology. Here the doctor may scrape away some tissue, and examine or test it to ascertain the nature of the patient's disease. In bio-dynamics, on the third level of abstraction, the doctor might examine under a microscope the active forces at work in the patient's cells.

In the study of the firm a start is generally made on the level of phenomenology, but the generalizations and concepts that emerge in theory are often so far removed from the day-to-day workings of any particular firm that they frequently reach the second or third levels of abstraction.

Normally, therefore, the concept of the firm in the behavioral sciences is highly abstract, and its usefulness is judged solely upon its merits as a theoretical container for problems to be examined and upon the assistance it renders in achieving solutions.

In order to organize the concepts of the firm in systematic fashion, we shall group them into two broad classes. The first will be termed *holistic concepts,* which are those that conceive of the firm as a unified acting entity or organism. The second will be called *behavioral concepts,* under which the firm is generally thought to be the "confluence of several streams of interrelated behavior." [1]

Behavioral concepts generally presume individual behavior determined by environment, the actions of others, and personality factors. When the behavior of individuals in a microcosm such as the firm is determined, the behavior of the firm itself also becomes known. The holistic concepts, on the other hand, presume that the firm, or the group, has behavior patterns that may differ from the patterns of the components within it.[2]

Both broad categories are useful to the behavioral sciences. The behavioral approach appears to be logical and consistent, but because most of our data relate to firms or groups rather than to individuals, it is possible to talk operationally about firm behavior; so long as we realize that such behavior is the result of the combined patterns of individual behavior (unknown though these patterns may be) within the organism.[3]

HOLISTIC CONCEPTS

Holistic concepts of the firm are distinguished by at least four major characteristics. They emphasize action by a collective rather than by actors in the collective. They assume predetermined rational behavior patterns. They posit a clear-cut goal for the firms. They assume an external environment that creates the need for action.

The holistic concept has been utilized traditionally in the economic theory of the firm. It is also employed with reference to the firm in the theory of games, statistical decision theory, and cybernetics.[4] Some authorities would in addition include certain sociological and psychological theories in the holistic classification.

The Economic Concept
of the Firm

The traditional economic concept of the firm meets the four specifications of the holistic frame of reference. The concept of the firm in economic theory is centered around the actions of a coordinating unit, termed the entrepreneur, whose behavior is conditioned by its drive to maximize its "incentive function."[5]

Customarily this incentive function is thought of as an amount of profit.[6] The parameters of action for the firm are prescribed by the predetermined assumption of rationality and by the competitive restraints established.

Rationality in economic theory implies that the entrepreneur will choose, from among a relatively limited range of alternatives open to him, the course of action that will maximize profits for the firm. The actions toward maximization are further simplified by taking as given the competitive situations in which choices are made.

Thus, in every economic environment except that of semi-monopoly (where there exists a small group of competitors) the firm can act rationally simply by contemplating its own actions and their results without reference to the actions of its competitors.

At one extreme of the competitive spectrum, for example, lies perfect competition, in which the firm's actions do not significantly affect its competitors or the market; at the other end is monopoly, where the firm is so powerful that it is not affected by the actions of others. In both instances, as in other economically competitive environments, the entrepreneur is aware of the situation that exists, and, by acting rationally, seeks to maximize a determinate and quantitative profit.

The concept of the firm to the economist is in reality the concept of the entrepreneurial role, which is treated as though it were the firm for purposes of theoretical analysis.[7] The entrepreneur, as a person or persons, is generally only a figure lurking in the shadow of his actions, although it is his transformation functions that are studied.

The person of the entrepreneur is seen only through his actions, which are fatalistically guided by his rational incentive function, which in turn is apparently predetermined (although this is not clear) by technical, biological, or institutional forces rarely examined by economists.

Economics has established as one of its goals the prediction of firm behavior with respect to prices and quantities (that is, market behavior), and the entire range of decision-making procedures carried on within the firm is not emphasized.[8] The stress upon market behavior permits economists to substitute the entity of the entrepreneur for the firm and to examine more critically the economic transformations that take place in impersonal exchange or production activities.[9] In this way it is possible for economists to analyze the firm holistically as an acting entity (the entrepreneur) rather than behaviorally as a collective, and to postulate a system of action that is guided unconsciously to the mutual benefit of all parties through the workings of the price mechanism.

For example, new resources are drawn to the firm and to the seller of resources.[10] A quantity of the firm's production is sold when the price of this output is satisfactory both to the firm and to buyers. The economist has evolved a detailed analysis of the entrepreneur unconsciously cooperating with other economic units in market situations which has proved to be extremely useful in explaining firm behavior. However, at the same time, the concept of the entrepreneur as the firm has been so enveloping internally that economists have found it extremely difficult to develop a theory of conscious cooperation.[11]

The economic firm consists, therefore, of a rationally carried out entrepreneurial role in affairs involving prices (costs) and quantities. Finally, the parameters of action for the firm are established by the predetermined assumption that the entrepreneur possesses a rational incentive function, and that all the firm's transformations will be influenced only by the automatic working of the price mechanism and the existing state of competition.[12]

The economist's concept of the firm results in conclusions that are generally unsatisfactory to students of other behavioral disciplines. The very behavior patterns that form the content of these other sciences are obscured by the economic focus on the entrepreneurial role, which tends to pull a cloak of darkness around the conscious interdependence of variables internal and external to the firm.

The economic concept of the firm does, however, possess one great advantage which simplifies the study of business behavior. Because the economist assumes that the firm is the entrepreneur, he is able to discuss its behavior as though it consisted of the actions of a single rational organism. He does not have to become involved in the difficult problems inherent in studying the system of persons in—but still separate from— the firm. Hence, we may conclude that the economic concept of the firm fits well into the holistic framework, which in turn is useful for the examination of many problems; but that this concept is not particularly appropriate for the general purposes of analyzing a wider variety of firm behavior.

The Concept of the Firm
in the Theory of Games

The theory of games is a relatively recent innovation and is useful for studying economic, political, and social phenomena.[13] It is still in the early stages of development, and is continually being enlarged and altered by new applications and new ideas.

One of the useful contributions it has already made, however, is in the construction of a game "terminology" that substitutes a common mathematical vocabulary for many of the difficult and conflicting terms employed in the different social science areas. By examining a part of this terminology we may note the emphasis of game theory, which will help us develop what might be called a "mathematical" concept of the firm.

The theory of games is primarily concerned with the choices and actions of players in a given situation or game.[14] The firm, of course, is designated as a player; and the conflict or cooperative situation in which it finds itself and within which it must move is the game. Any particular game is set apart from all others by its rules. The rules in each game prescribe the number of players involved, the state of information possessed by each player prior to a move, and the set of alternatives (which may include those established by chance or "Nature") from which choices may be made. The nature of the moves, whether they are personal or chance, and their order are also set forth in the rules of each game.

The firm in the theory of games ordinarily is considered to be a rationally choosing player confronted by opponents or cooperators in a game defined by predetermined rules. The firm's prescription for action is set forth by its strategy, which is that set of behavioral rules for all situations that the firm might encounter in the course of the game.[15]

The idea of strategy is one of the important factors that causes the concept of the firm in game theory to diverge from that used in traditional economics. In economics the actions of the firm are limited by impersonal market forces; in game theory strategies also take account of the possible strategies and actions of others, as well as chance.

In classical economics, the rational firm always adapts itself to a given competitive environment. In game theory the firm has to be adaptive to the strategies of others as well as to an impersonal environment. When the conscious actions of others are inserted into the model the payoff (profit) for the firm depends not only upon its own actions, nor only upon those determined by chance; but it also depends upon the conflicting or cooperative actions of others.

The firm in oligopolistic markets (relatively small number of competitors) is a good illustration of a game situation, because the strategies and moves of competitors, as well as the strategy and moves of the firm, will affect the payoff for all players. According to Oskar Morgenstern, in these cases "no maximum problem exists, indeed the notion of a maximum has no meaning."[16] However, if in game theory the notion of maximization in the traditional economic sense fails to apply, what then is it that firms attempt to do?

In one of the most common types of game there are two players, each of whom may select a strategy from a set of alternatives. The total of the payoffs for both players equals a constant sum. However, the division of the total between the players will vary with their actions or because of chance. In this simple game each player would prefer to divide the constant total so that his opponent receives a zero payoff while he gains the entire sum. The practicalities of the situation are such, however, that each participant assumes that this goal is unattainable, for each one believes that his opponent will act to prevent him from reaching it. In this game the logical solution for both players is the selection of that strategy whereby each will obtain the largest possible payoff regardless of the actions of the other. The rational choice for both players, then, is that strategy in which the minimum payoff is higher than (or as high as) that obtainable through any other strategy, for each player must expect that his opponent will strive to make this "highest" minimum payoff as low as possible.[17]

Because through this strategy each player minimizes his maximum loss or risk of loss, this solution is usually termed the "minimax" principle. The firm confronted with this game, therefore, would not necessarily attempt to maximize its profits in the traditional manner but rather would strive to obtain the greatest profit within the confines of a strategy which minimized its losses. The goal of the firm, even in this simple game, is more limited, and yet more complex than the goal of maximum profits set forth in classical economic theory.

In certain games, other than the constant-sum game described, the element of uncertainty may be enhanced or lessened, and this in turn may cause the firm to strive toward a goal other than the minimaxing of its profits.[18] Unfortunately, there is at present a lack of agreement upon the usefulness and propriety of other goals in more complex games. For example, some game theorists have argued that the firms participating in games involving uncertainty or ignorance should minimax regret—the difference between actual payoff and maximum payoff which might have been obtained through perfect foresight—rather than loss.[19] In some circumstances firms might maximize a weighted average of the minimal and maximal payoffs expected.[20]

The firm that emerges from an examination of the theory of games is different from, and yet similar to, that which evolves in classical economic theory. The assumption of rational behavior still remains, but the relationships that exist between the firm and its competitors or cooperators, its goals, and the state of its information may be substantially different.[21] Yet, over-all, the theory of games may properly be considered as an extension and broadening of the analysis of market conflicts found in the traditional stream of economic thought. Antoine Cournot in 1838, for example, explored the duopoly problem wherein two entrepreneurs, each seeking to maximize his profits, make their price and output decisions on the basis of information about costs and demand elasticities. Cournot, however, assumed that a duopolist did not have to consider the reactions of his rival. F. Y. Edgeworth, in his article on the "Pure Theory of Monopoly" in 1897 severely criticized this assumption, and introduced the notion of the uncertainty resulting from mutual reactions, finally concluding that there was no determinate solution in duopoly. Interest in reaction patterns was extended to still other economic variables in the 1920's. The well-known books by Edward Chamberlin and Joan Robinson on imperfect competition, published in the early 1930's, were part of this general theme, as are the many papers on oligopoly theory that have appeared during the last twenty-five years. The theory of games is closely allied to this tradition in economics.

More than this, game theory, because it is a conceptual device designed to treat conflict, can be utilized in the investigation of a broad range of problems. Thus, the theory of games can be employed to analyze competition between firms, and also to examine bargaining among competing interests within the firm.[22]

For example, the entrepreneur may be considered as the host of a countless number of strategies for dealing with a vast variety of business, personal, or chance games that occur endlessly within the firm. At times these games may involve labor disputes, or the allocation of resources to their most efficient destinations, or any situation in which money may be gained as the result of the moves that follow upon the proper choice of strategy.[23] Although the theory of games may be considered as an extension of the traditional stream of micro-economic theory, then, it also represents a broadening of this theory to a wider variety of business situations.

The concept or concepts of the firm that may eventually emerge from game theory will include a greater number of variables than that contained in the purely economic model. However, although the promise of the future is bright, the present stage of experimentation with the theory of games has resulted in considerable confusion and ambiguity in the definition of rational strategy, except in the zero-sum, two-person game,[24] wherein the firm evolves as a rational player acting to minimax its profits in a personalized duopolistic duel.

In other situations, game theory has not yet crystallized solutions, although it has clarified somewhat the issues involved in extending the ideas of economic firm behavior beyond traditional boundaries. At the same time, game theory has made the concept of the firm more complex, for it requires that the firm be conceived as possessing remarkable and possibly unattainable reasoning powers.[25] The emphasis upon rational strategies, payoffs, the game, and moves in the game does conform exceedingly well to our category of holistic concepts of the firm, however.

The Concept of the Firm in Cybernetics

Cybernetics has recently become an established region of research and study, and several of its concepts and terms have been found to be useful by scholars who have attempted to apply them to the behavior of the firm.[26]

Cybernetics, which originated in the physical sciences, has contributed substantially to the theory of coding and transmitting messages in electrical engineering. Because it is primarily concerned with communication and control, however, its possibilities for application to the firm soon became evident.

Most of the theories of the firm that use cybernetic ideas and terms describe the enterprise essentially as a "closed-loop" control system.[27] Schematically this kind of system includes a number of interdependent variables. It usually possesses some sort of "feedback" process whereby the mechanism is instructed by informational governors that it has missed or reached its goal.[28] The most common applications of cybernetics to the firm have also borrowed heavily from—and become merged with—the notions of homeostasis, which were originally employed to describe the processes by which an organism attained the relative stability it needed for survival.[29]

One of the simplest illustrations of an electrical system with feedback contains the following components: (1) An enclosed space; (2) A heating device (for example, an electric space heater); (3) A thermostatic control which operates to turn the heater on or off whenever the temperature in the space exceeds certain theshold limits. The thermostat's task is to act as a feedback system which compares the actual heat in the room with the heater's input (the *desired* range of warmth), and which becomes operative as a result of differences between actual and desired temperatures.[30] However, there will customarily be some oscillation or "overshooting" because of the time lag between the output of heat and its actual delivery to the enclosure—even with the most efficient thermostat. Cybernetic devices, therefore, always involve a cycle, the amplitude and length of which are dependent upon the design of their feedback loops.

There are many ways in which this concept of a servosystem may be applied to arrive at a "cybernetic" view of the firm.[31] For example, the firm may be considered as a "hunting" mechanism, analogous to the thermostat, which is either at, or is consciously searching for, equilibrium. The "command" or equilibrium position for the firm may be described by the desired quantity or value of each balance sheet item.

Any movement away from "ideal" figures sets up conscious (perhaps even habitual) forces that tend to return the firm to equilibrium. When machinery becomes obsolete it is replaced; if raw materials are consumed they are replenished—so that the picture of the firm is one of a continually correcting servomechanism that constantly attempts to maintain a balance in the midst of forces of varying intensity which are striving to lead it astray.[32]

Its success, furthermore, is dependent upon the efficiency with which it corrects for disequilibrating forces. The firm thus becomes an active combatant in a perpetual conflict situation; but it always plays the conservative role of advocating the status quo of equilibrium, even though it may—because of haste or ignorance—actually overshoot the positions desired. Finally, although the firm in this conception does not have to maximize, it does have to perform rationally in order to attain its equilibrium status most efficiently.[33]

Cybernetics as applied to the firm may take several forms, only one of which has been discussed. In all its forms, however, it retains the one big disadvantage which all borrowings from the physical to the behavioral sciences possess: That man's behavior and his institutions are considered to be analogous with the behavior of machinery or matter.

The concept of the firm as a response mechanism is not, of course, limited only to cybernetics and homeostasis, for to some extent this idea prevails even in traditional economic theory. However, by itself the notion of a self-adjusting or deliberately adjusting organism is meaningless, for even in the case of the thermostat it is evident that outside forces must establish the command position toward which the mechanism tends.

So too in the firm, the equilibrium position of all balance sheet items must be established. Unless the explanation is given of how the command position itself originates it must of necessity be incomplete. Thus, the application of cybernetics to the concept of the firm, although providing a framework that may be useful, omits what many behavioral scientists would consider the most salient feature of the firm in this context—namely, how equilibrium is established.[34]

Other Holistic Concepts

Our discussion of holistic models of the firm is not intended to be all-inclusive, but merely to illustrate a certain type of concept. In all these the common thread of a single acting organism, of depersonalization, and the threads of other mutual ideas combine to form at least a thin strand that holds all holistic concepts of the firm together.

It is not essential, furthermore, that a concept be holistic originally for it to be included in this category. Papandreou, for example, believes that the concept of the firm in economics reflects the action frame of reference developed by Talcott Parsons and others.[35] We would tend to think that Parsons would consider his theory to be behavioral, for although the emphasis in this frame of reference is placed upon action—the relationship between the organism and things external to it,[36] he has stressed:

> It is actors in situations who act . . . ; organisms in environments have activity. In other words, that which impinges upon our senses and which our measuring instruments record are the activities of organisms in environments; what we deal with on the scientific level are the actions of actors in situations, which are abstractions in terms of principles of relationship.[37]

This statement implies that although it is action upon which the focus of social science should center, action cannot be examined effectively without reference to personalized actors and a broad environmental field for action. The Parsonian action frame of reference is more behavioral than holistic, for it involves needs which a cognitive, cathectic, and evaluative actor attempts to satisfy by striving toward goals.

It uses as parts of its structure the essentials of culture, personality, and social studies. The economic concept of the firm was not built to "Fit the specifications of this frame of reference," [38] although there is nothing inherently wrong with trying to make it fit into this superstructure.[39]

Through the construction of the action edifice to hold the economic concept of the firm we do, however, pour a behavioral concept into the holistic mold. Kurt Lewin's field theory,[40] or more specifically, the terms and methodology of his behavioral theory, also appears on the verge of being used to forge a holistic concept of the firm.[41] Other theories that originally were conceived as behavioral have been, or may eventually be, applied holistically.[42]

Although there is nothing basically unscientific about this procedure, it does indicate some of the problems of categorization of concepts that exist, and the multiple uses that might be made of certain theories.

The physiological theories of the scientific management school, founded by Frederick W. Taylor, produce a concept of the firm that conforms to the patterns established by our holistic framework. The firm in these theories is conceived primarily as a relatively simple machine process oriented rationally toward the goals of profit maximization.[43]

However, the scientific management school of thought did have behavioral overtones, for it was not interested specifically in the actions of the whole firm: rather its attention was directed internally toward the tasks performed by the human and mechanical machines that make up the components of this entity.

The elements in each sub-set (whether human or mechanical or both) were delineated chiefly in neurophysical terms to ascertain their efficiencies in performing specific acts. The worker (especially in the early years of the study of scientific management) was regarded as a muscular bundle of energy, defined in terms of his effort, speed, cost, and susceptibility to fatigue.

In the same way that all of the other concepts of the firm came to exist as a convenience for specific areas of study, so too was the scientific management concept the result of problems that Taylor and his cohorts attempted to solve. The engineering approach to efficiency, however, so limited investigation and research to mechanical and physiological variables that it has been almost abandoned today by persons with an interest in behavior.[44] The failure of the laws of physical science to be applied in their entirety to the actions and behavior of persons has been recognized more fully in this area than in perhaps any other field where such analogies prevail.[45]

BEHAVIORAL CONCEPTS OF THE FIRM

The concepts of the firm discussed under the general heading of "holistic" contain common themes, because they stress the impersonal movements of an organism operating toward a specific goal in an environment that is objectively defined. In this section we shall present illustrations of alternative formulations of the idea of the firm, to which we have attached the term "behavioral."

The behavioral frame of reference usually consists of concepts which have the following features in common: (1) The assumption that it is actors within the firm, rather than the firm itself, that act; (2) That behavior is conditioned by personality as well as environmental factors; (3) That, as a minimum, the behavioral processes examined must take into account the cognition, perception, beliefs, and knowledge of the actor(s); and (4) That rewards, or goals, are oftentimes complex.

The behavioral framework, therefore, encompasses a much wider area within which concepts of the firm may be established. However, it is not always separated completely from holistic notions. For example, it is possible to construct a behavioral model of the firm that utilizes the theory of games or of cybernetics, although the variables that would be included in such a model would range beyond the parameters noted in the concepts of the firm discussed earlier. Perhaps the most satisfactory method of bringing out the differences between holistic and behavioral concepts is to present illustrations of the latter. Before this material is introduced, however, we should attempt to clarify one source of confusion that might arise.

We have already pointed out that the principal difference between the holistic and behavioral categories is that the former considers the firm as being an acting entity, whereas the latter conceives of the firm as being composed of actors.

This is not to imply, however, that behavioral concepts cannot treat of the group or the total firm. The essential difference between the two concepts is not that one is limited to an examination of individuals and the other to a study of aggregates; rather it lies in the manner in which the aggregates are analyzed. The holistic approach attributes to the aggregate a type of Gestalt quality; it creates a group mind, a singleness of character, an additional entity.

The behavioral category includes no such mystical quality when it considers aggregates such as the group or the firm. Behaviorists may describe the group and talk about its common features (its leadership, sub-groups, interactions, and so on), but only on a nonmystical, empirical, and testable basis. As such they may describe the firm and its goals and nature as different from those of the individuals in it, but not as a rational entity with its own mind, as seems to be the case in holistic studies of the firm.[46]

The Firm as a Bureaucratic Organization

Students of bureaucracy have formulated several theories which, when related to business activities, result in a number of closely allied concepts of the firm. We shall examine briefly the works of three of these scholars, Max Weber, Robert K. Merton, and Philip Selznick, abstracting from their remarks on bureaucratic organizations those ideas which appear most germane to our production of concepts of the firm.

These concepts contain the common notion that firms are adaptive, or functional, organizations, although two of the theorists (Merton and Selznick) postulate dysfunctional elements that retard the tendency of firms to adapt themselves to their environment.

Weber's theory of bureaucracy is based upon his efforts to ascertain and abstract those elements that he believes are essential to all bureaucratic organizations, regardless of the time or culture in which they exist.[47] The "ideal-type" bureaucracy that emerges as Weber's universal, and which we may consider as his basic concept of the firm, is one of functionally linked offices arrayed in hierarchical order.

In each office are occupants whose behavior is restricted and directed toward common goals by general rules.[48] Important to Weber's theory is the existence of rules that codify behavior in each office of the organization.[49] Although Weber does devote some of his discussion to individuals within the bureaucracy, and to their relationships to each other and especially to their offices, he is primarily interested in the bureaucracy (firm) as a functional structure, which he considers to be bound together by rational laws into an organization that is superior to other organizational types and to individuals.

The efficient ranking of administrative offices autocratically controlled by functional rules, filled with specialists who are highly skilled, and operating continuously with traditional principles of the division of labor, free selection process, and so on, represents to Weber the highest type of organization. Thus, to some extent Weber's concept resembles that advanced by F. W. Taylor, for he considers the firm as the ideal framework within which specialized skills are most satisfactorily adapted to attain the goals of precision, reliability, and efficiency.

Robert K. Merton's theory of bureaucracy, in many of its features, follows closely the concepts advanced by Max Weber.[50] The emphasis on the desirability of functional relations among actions, offices, and organization goals; the hierarchy of offices; pre-existing rules; formality of relationships—all these are similar to the ideas set forth by Weber. Merton extends these concepts, however, by dividing functions into two classes: (1) manifest functions, which are intended adjustments recognized by persons in the organization; and (2) latent functions, which are neither intended nor recognized.[51]

He also stresses the dysfunctional aspects of bureaucracy: those consequences that reduce the adaptability of the organization. The firm that results from this elaboration is not as "ideal" as that perceived by Weber. The rules established by the top hierarchical offices to effect reliable and predictable behavior among those of lesser status lead to an increase in conformity, impersonality, and ritual; and to a decrease in innovation.[52]

In other words, Merton emphasizes that an organization in which functionalism is the goal will produce dysfunctional and latent functional by-products which will tend to create barriers to the achievement of goals. The firm in Merton's image becomes a field for conflict and rebellion. This picture is carried one step further in Phillip Selznick's concept.

Selznick also views the firm as a formal organization attempting to mobilize its human and technical resources toward stated objectives.[53] The individuals employed by the firm are conceived as means to an end. They resist this role strongly, and attempt to substitute their own purposes and problems for those of the firm. The internal conflicts that occur between organizational sub-units are paralleled by the pressures bearing upon the firm from external environmental (for example, political, legal, social) forces.

One obtains from Selznick the picture of the firm as a sort of an organizational bathysphere, moving through the water-like environment which presses upon it from without and filled with air-like pressures that tend to explode or collapse its organization, or at least to alter its symmetrical shape. Under such conditions the firm, to survive, must adapt itself to hostile situations fraught with dangers.

One way in which it does so (apparently after resisting strongly) is to follow the dictates of the adaptive individuals within it, who form informal groups with informal lines of communications. As Selznick points out, organizations may be examined within a framework of needs and self-defensive mechanisms.[54] The entry of fresh needs into the firm and the development of systems for self-defense result in alterations to the organization.[55]

Common to all of these bureaucratic descriptions of organization is the view that the firm (or more specifically the large corporate organization) is a highly organized functional institution that in some way has an existence apart from the individuals that populate it. The attempt to advance the purposes of the organization, which in Weber's schema brings about a harmonious structure, in Merton's and Selznick's theories results in unintended and undesired individual and group behavior.

Organizational Concepts of the Firm

During the years since 1940 an ever-increasing stream of ideas has been forthcoming from authors who belong to what we may loosely classify as the "organizational" school of thought. This stream is by no means completely united, but rather has been diffused by such interrelated tributaries as human relations, administrative science, and organization theory.[56]

Furthermore, the source of this stream springs from a coalescence of the behavioral sciences, with some stress upon economics, anthropology, and political science but with the major emphasis upon psychology and, in particular, sociology.

Organizational concepts of the firm, therefore, vary considerably in their details. The majority of these, however, appear to possess at least three features in common: (1) The concept of the firm as a complex *pattern* of personal relationships rather than a framework in which actors perform; (2) The omission of the traditional assumption of strict rationality, and its replacement with any one of several types of qualified assumptions of rationality;[57] (3) The assumption, often only implicit, that the firm is a homeostatic socio-economic organization with the underlying goal of survival.

In order to illustrate how the organizationalists view the firm we shall in this section present three concepts: the first constructed from the work of Chester Barnard, who is representative of what we might call the "traditionalist" school; the second based upon the writings of Burleigh Gardner, who is principally a human relationist; and a third represented by Herbert Simon, who is a prominent scholar of the science of administration. Although each of these concepts of the firm will differ somewhat from the others, they will also contain many similarities, for they are all part of the mainstream of organizational thought.

Chester Barnard regards the firm as a cooperative system, which he defines as "a complex of physical, biological, personal, and social components which are in specific systematic relationships by reason of the cooperation of two or more persons for at least one definite end." [58] The elements basic to every firm (and, for that matter, to every organization) are (1) communication (2) willingness to serve and (3) common purpose.[59]

From the nature of these three essentials it is evident that Barnard conceives of the firm as a system of conscious cooperation wherein components act and react upon one another and upon the environment in communicative patterns. It is recognized that in all organizations the willingness to serve of most participants will be positive, but slight, and that this willingness will be a function of the net inducements offered to each participant.

The common purpose of the firm is not necessarily identical with the motives of individuals within it. However, although each individual may be motivated by different forces and to different degrees, the purpose of their *act of cooperation* is common to the organization and vital for its survival.[60] Common purpose is the coordinating and unifying force of the firm, and is dispersed through communications to those with a personal willingness to serve in the firm.[61] The executive, or executives, of the firm becomes the center of communications, coordinating the components of the organization, and exercising authority to weld these components into the cooperative system that is the firm.

Finally, underlying Barnard's thesis is the idea that a firm requires a proper combination of the three elements of communications, willingness to serve, and common purpose in order to survive. An equilibrium state must exist both externally, between the firm and its environment, and internally, between the organization and individuals.[62] Barnard points out that these external and internal equilibria may vary with the environment, and that "when one is varied, compensating variations must occur in the other if the system of which they are components is to remain in equilibrium, that is, to persist or survive." [63]

Burleigh Gardner conceives of the firm as a miniature social organization reflecting, and operating in, the environment of a larger society.[64] His emphasis, like Barnard's, is upon the pattern of relationships that tie the actors in this microcosm together, rather than upon the organization or the actors themselves. It is this pattern and its fluidity, which affects both individuals and the totality, that is the firm. The total pattern is composed partly of formal relationships, and in part made up of diversified informal patterns of relationships. These informal patterns, which emerge spontaneously, exercise a powerful control over individuals in the firm.[65]

The total pattern that is the firm also includes a complicated set of status systems established formally, and by sex, age, position, pay, kind of work, and so on.[66] Most of these status systems are reinforced by symbols of superiority. There exist also complex boss-man relationships. This whole societal complex is held together by an imperfect system of communications.

As an externally static but internally fluid organism the firm is difficult to comprehend in its complex entirety. This difficulty, moreover, is compounded by the external environment and by internal shifts and changes which bring pressures to bear upon the firm for further changes. Gardner presents a homeostatic notion of the organization resisting these pressures to change, or in some cases adjusting to change, in an effort to maintain its social equilibrium.[67]

Closely related to Gardner's—and especially to Barnard's concept—is the notion of the firm advanced by Herbert Simon. Simon, however, has extended, revised, and altered Barnard's thesis, and has elaborated upon it in a number of ways. The firm still remains a "complex pattern of communications and other relations in a group of human beings." [68] This pattern still affects the goals, informational flows, and attitudes of each participant, and shapes for each a set of stable and understandable expectations of interactions within the firm.[69] Simon, like Barnard and Gardner, remains interested in viable solutions which permit survival of the firm.[70] He also believes that the willingness to serve of each member of the firm (and thus the glue that holds the firm together) is dependent upon the net inducements offered to each member, which must be positive.[71]

However, much of Simon's unique contribution to organization theory has been directed toward the question of rational behavior and maximization. He rejects the notion of omniscient rationality attributed to the entrepreneur by economists, and substitutes for this an idea of limited or bounded (but intended) rationality. This concept Simon has set forth in the following passage:

> Administrative man recognizes that the world he perceives is a drastically simplified model of the buzzing, blooming confusion that con-

stitutes the real world. He is content with this gross simplification because he believes that the real world is mostly empty—that most of the facts of the real world have no great relevance to any particular situation he is facing, and that most significant chains of causes and consequences are short and simple. Hence, he is content to leave out of account those aspects of reality—and that means most aspects—that are substantially irrelevant at a given time. He makes his choices using a simple picture of the situation that takes into account just a few of the factors that he regards as most relevant and crucial.[72]

Simon has elaborated upon these points in a variety of publications, and from them has constructed his own concept of the firm.[73] Briefly, this firm may be described as a pattern of relationships among individuals, none of whom acts with perfect rationality, but all of whom attempt to be as rational as possible within the limits set for them by their personalities and by the environment.

The firm becomes an imperfect decision-making machine, forced to choose from alternatives continually without knowing exactly what the results of each choice will be. Under such conditions it becomes evident that men in business cannot *know* the best alternative in all cases where choices must be made: they cannot, therefore, maximize. What business men must strive for is not maximum profits, but rather for behavior patterns that produce satisfactory conclusions. In other words, the firm (or rather that organization of decisions and actions that is the firm) cannot maximize profits; it can only satisfice.[74]

The work of Simon is constructed more explicitly upon the postulates of psychology and biology than are the writings of either Barnard or Gardner, and thus, the notion of the homeostatic firm is brought out more clearly. Simon, for example, has compared the firm to the rather blind probing of an animal in a maze to satisfy his minimal requirements for survival. He has also been influenced by communications theory to incorporate the importance of the number, nature, and behavior of relay points (decision-making units) as factors significant for his concept of the firm.

The importance of organizational theories, and their application to the business concern, has become widely recognized during the past decade, and more work has been, and is being, conducted in this area of business theory than in any other. At present, however, the field is not highly organized, and the concepts that have been forthcoming are diverse and somewhat conflicting.

It is evident that these concepts rest more securely upon a base of reality than do, for example, the economic notions of the firm. In addition to the problems that exist among the organizational theorists because of their lack of agreements on several issues, there are also other difficulties with their concepts of the firm.

To mention only a few of these: it is evident that these theories are relatively complex, and include a large number of variables which, although making them more realistic, tend to make them intractable for prediction purposes. It is also apparent that these concepts make the firm a less systematic organization than is frequently found in real life.

Finally, the goal of "satisficing" (or even of viability) is not clearly delineated, nor is it backed by a great deal of empirical evidence of firm behavior. Nevertheless, it is possible that these studies of organizational behavior may help to bridge the gap between traditional theories and more satisfactory concepts of the firm which are as yet unknown.

Other Behavioral Concepts of the Firm

There are many, many variations of sociological, psychological, and other concepts, most of which encompass the variables and follow the same general themes that we could apply to the firm in order to note the framework or background in which theories of behavior operate. A few deserve mention here, either because they have been influential, introduce a different terminology, or reflect in some way an important school of thought. Even with the addition of these, however, our list of behavioral concepts still remains far from complete.

In recent years a number of articles have tried to mingle the economic and various behavioral theories of the firm. One of these, advanced by Professor Margolis, University of California, is illustrative, and is of interest because of the debate that followed its publication.[75] Briefly, Margolis rejects the economic concept of the firm, stating that "it does not explain nonprofit maximizing goals and business rules observed in practice which arise in part because of the existence of uncertainty."[76]

His concept of the firm, which is termed a "deliberative" model, assumes limited knowledge and profits satisfactory to management's "aspiration level," which means essentially that profits in each period must be equal to or greater than current profits. Furthermore, firms will prefer alternatives which tend to minimize uncertainties; for example, within a "satisfactory" profit constraint they will produce differentiated products rather than manipulate prices.[77] Margolis, then, is seeking a framework within which the decision-making process may be understood.[78] This framework, it may be noted, is quite similar to that used by Simon and others.

Professor Bodenhorn of the University of Chicago has criticized Margolis' paper because economic theory concerns market behavior, not decision making, and Margolis' statements are, therefore, irrelevant.[79] In so doing, Bodenhorn points out that traditional economic theory actually consists of alternative theories, each of which is only "sometimes" applicable.[80] However, there is little reason, if one broadens this argument, why Margolis' theory (or any other—or every other, for that matter) cannot be also "sometimes" applicable, and all, therefore, become trivial.

Role theory is an area in which the analysis of behavior of groups by sociologists and the analysis of the motivation of individuals by psychologists have overlapped. As applied to the firm, role theory resembles in many respects the bureaucratic and organizational concepts already discussed. For example, the following quotation from Clyde Kluckholm and Henry A. Murray's *Personality in Nature, Society, and Culture*, which defines the firm and explains the notion of the "role," brings out these similarities:

> (The firm is) . . . a series of integrated offices, in which are a number of obligations and privileges closely defined by limited and specific rules. Each of these offices contains an area of imputed competence and responsibility. Authority, the power of control which derives from an acknowledged status, inheres in the office and not in the particular person who performs the official role.[81]

Although the idea of a role was originally attributed to dramatic parts, it is evident that these men "perform" according to their positions. Thus, if we consider the firm as an aggregation of roles, and if we can understand the wide band of behavior forced upon actors by these roles, then we may be able to understand the behavior of the firm.

For example, through the use of a modified "role" analysis, Everett C. Hughes has speculated that executives tend to conform to expected rituals placed upon them by their roles.[82] In this way they escape judgments and seek "stable and safe" solutions rather than those alternatives which might increase profits substantially.

Neal Gross and others in *Explorations in Role Analysis* have evolved a theory of roles which may be useful for predicting firm behavior.[83] Under role theory, therefore, we would have to consider the firm as a complex of "roles," with the emphasis upon relationships between offices rather than between individuals, quite similar to the bureaucratic concept of Weber. Unfortunately, there appears to be considerable latitude for individual behavior within the framework of a "role," and it is doubtful that this type of analysis will ever be sufficiently refined to enable us to use it for detailed predictions.

A concept of the firm resembling that set forth by Talcott Parsons and others is the idea of small groups in the work of George C. Homans.[84] We could conceive the firm, in Homan's terms, as possessing three major attributes. These are: activity, which is what the members of the firm do as members; interaction, the relationships between members of the firm; and sentiment, which is the additive total of the individual group member's feelings toward the group's activities. The three elements of group behavior, furthermore, are directed toward any situation by a "norm," which is a code of behavior, and take place within "external and internal systems," which are the relationships between the group and its external environment and toward one another.

Bernard De Voto, in his foreword to Homans' *The Human Group*, has summarized this succinctly:

> What the small group reveals when thus studied is a social system reacting with its environment as a self-adjusting organization of response whose parts are mutually interdependent. What acts, and what reacts, is not any single part or function of the social system, nor any combination of parts or functions, but the system as a whole, a totality whose mutual interdependence *is* the system. Cause and effect disappear; what must be looked for is the resultants of complexes of interacting forces. The group is a dynamic social equilibrium. It sets up its own responses organically, determines its own measures of control, derives its own possibilities of adaptation, elaboration, and change.[85]

Homans' notions of the firm, therefore, are also much like those of the organizational theorists. Although his remarks are confined only to small groups, and are based upon the empirical studies made of five such groups, it would appear that they could be applied to firms of any size, at least in their essentials.

Common to many students of business, and especially to those with a psychological bent, is a concentration upon the individual and his motivations rather than upon the group or the total firm. The concept of the firm that often arises from the writings of these individuals is that of an organization in conflict.

Persons within organizations all have ego wants that are formulated in early training and by the social mores of a culture. These include prestige wants and domination wants which presumably enable the individual to attain more satisfactory id goals of a more fundamental nature.

On the other hand, the individual also has superego wants which dictate that he submerge himself in the group with which he is identified. The conflict between the ego, which demands prestige, and the superego, which desires conformity, tends to lead to a multiplicity of goals, to insecurities and a feeling of entrapment.[86]

Frequently, however, such conflicts between the ego and the superego endow the individual with an enlarged ego which has as its goal the success and prestige of the group. Thus, the successes and failures of the group become the successes and failures of the individual.[87] The firm, in these circumstances, becomes primarily a symbol of relationships between men who are identified with it; and the participants then work toward a common end that is established for them by society.

In this chapter we have tried to point out that there are many concepts of a business firm, and that these concepts depend primarily upon the purpose for which they are used. Whether we consider the firm holistically or in behavioral terms, whether we regard it as an economically productive unit or a social organization, or in some other fashion is contingent upon the type of business behavior in which we are interested, and what we are trying to explain or predict. The firm is not the only institution, nor the only thing, that may be viewed differently from a variety of angles by people with different backgrounds and different skills.

For example, there is a passage in one of Theodore Dreiser's novels, in which the following fictional conversation between a man and a little girl is recorded:

> "What's water?" he would ask; and being informed that it was "what we drink," he would stare and say, "That's so, but what is it? Don't they teach you any better than that?" "Well, it is what we drink, isn't it?" persisted Vesta (the little girl). "The fact that we drink it doesn't explain what it is," he would retort. "You ask your teacher what water is"; and then he would leave her with this irritating problem troubling her young soul.[88]

CONCLUSIONS

In almost the same way we shall have to leave the concept of the firm, for the proper or correct concept still remains an irritating problem. We may, however, point out a few of the features that these notions possess that are significant for further investigations.

First, as we go through the various explanations of firm behavior, we can understand them more satisfactorily if we are aware of the frame of reference that they employ, and of the concept of the firm that they utilize.

None of these concepts has general validity, none of them is perfectly realistic. Their virtue lies not in these features, but rather in their usefulness in providing a model within which the theory of behavior that is expounded may be best set forth. How useful each concept of the firm is for the theory it contains and how helpful it is in solving the problems postulated are matters which the reader must judge for himself.

Second, none of the concepts of the firm we have examined in this chapter is eminently suitable for the student of business—and yet, at the same time, all are important. If we are ever to produce business scholars (not economists, sociologists, psychologists, and so on, with an interest in business) then it is possible that someday some sort of eclectic model of the firm will evolve. In the meantime, however, we must be satisfied with looking at the firm in a more noncohesive manner, from all angles, so that we may better be able to understand it and to explain its behavior.

The problem of the "proper" concept of the firm need not be troublesome, however, for it is analogous to a type of problem which confronts persons every day, one in which there may be more than one correct solution. As Harold L. Johnson has written: "With this approach to the basic nature of theorizing, the error of pseudo-simplicity is avoided wherein it is stated that if one model is useful or "true" others are thereby "false" or unnecessary. In view of the great diversity of business behavior, "both-and" rather than "either-or" appears to be the most valid conception of theory construction." [89]

Finally, as we look back upon the concept of the firm presented in this chapter, the parallels and similarities between many of the theories gleaned from diverse disciplines stand out. Economic theory, especially that part of micro-economics which deals with oligopoly, closely resembles the theory of games, and in other respects both stress variables common to decision theory, cybernetics, and homeostasis. Behavioral concepts, too, contain many parallels. Bureaucracy, role theory, organization theories, small group theory—all these emphasize closely similar, and in many cases identical, variables. Furthermore, there are links between holistic and behavioral theories, concepts such as homeostasis, viability, satisficing, and equilibrium. Thus, the concepts of the firm and the theories of business behavior connected to these concepts, are not as diverse and scattered as they might at first appear. We shall continue to point out similarities, as well as differences, in the chapters that follow.

Notes and References

1. Terminology is similar to that used in: William J. Gore and Fred S. Silander, "A Bibliographical Essay on Decision-Making," *Administrative Science Quarterly*, 4, No. 1 (July, 1959), 101.

2. For further comments on these differences see the debate between Rutledge Vining and Tjalling C. Koopmans in the *Review of Economics and Statistics*, XXXI (1949), 77-94. Also of interest in this regard are the remarks by Kenneth J. Arrow, "Mathematical Models in the Social Sciences," in Daniel Lerner and Harold D. Lassewell, eds., *The Policy Sciences* (Stanford: Stanford University Press, 1951), especially pp. 133-134.

3. Arrow, *op. cit.*, p. 134.

4. Gore and Silander, *op. cit.*, pp. 112-120.

5. This term originates in work carried out under the auspices of the Cowles Commission and is used, for example, by Jacob Marschak, "Organized Decision-Making," *Cowles Commission Discussion Paper, Economics*, No. 2034, Feb. 29, 1952; and T. C. Koopmans, *Activity Analysis of*

Production and Allocation, Cowles Commission Monograph No. 13, New York and London, especially pp. 93-95.

6. In recent years some economists have substituted preference-function maximization for profit maximization. For example, Gerhard Tintner in several articles, including "The Theory of Choice Under Subjective Risk and Uncertainty," *Econometrica*, IX (July-October, 1941), 298-304, has presented a strong case for the substitution.

7. See especially, James H. Stauss, "The Entrepreneur: The Firm," *The Journal of Political Economy*, LII, No. 2 (June, 1944), 112-127.

8. D. Bodenhorn, "A Note on the Theory of the Firm," *Journal of Business*, XXXII, No. 2 (April, 1959).

9. Cf. Kenneth E. Boulding, *Economic Analysis*, 3rd edition (New York: Harper & Row, Publishers, 1955), Chapter 25.

10. Cf. Andreas G. Papandreou, "Some Basic Problems in the Theory of the Firm," in Bernard F. Haley, ed., *A Survey of Contemporary Economics*, Published for the American Economic Association, II (Homewood, Ill.: Richard D. Irwin, Inc., 1952), p. 183.

11. See the comments by R. H. Coase, "The Nature of the Firm," *Economica*, New Series, IV (1937), 386-405. Reprinted in: G. J. Stigler and K. E. Boulding, eds., *Readings in Price Theory*, Published for the American Economic Association, VI (Homewood, Ill.: Richard D. Irwin, Inc., 1952), 331-351.

12. The "linear-programming" concept of the firm is not too different in its essentials from that employed by economists, and therefore will not be treated in this chapter. For a description of this concept see: Robert Dorfman, Paul A. Samuelson, and Robert M. Solow, *Linear Programming and Economic Analysis*, The RAND Series (New York: McGraw-Hill Book Company, Inc., 1958), pp. 130-133.

13. See John Von Neumann and Oskar Morgenstern, *Theory of Games and Economic Behavior* (Princeton: Princeton University Press, 1944). This book is generally regarded as the innovating contribution on the theory of games. Like every other new theory in the social sciences, however, it had apparently been anticipated by someone else—in this case by Emile Borel in the 1920's. See: M. Fréchet, "Emile Borel, Initiator of the Theory of Psychological Games and Its Application," *Econometrica*, 21 (1953), 95-96.

14. Game theory may also be employed in a variety of ways that differ from the way it is described here, but still be pertinent to firm behavior. It may, for example, be concerned with individual behavior under uncertainty, and with allied matters. As an illustration see: Leonid Hurwicz, "What Has Happened to the Theory of Games," *American Economic Review*, XLIII, No. 2 (May, 1953), 398-405. For an example wherein the terminology of game theory has been most useful, see: Karl-Olof Faxen,

Monetary and Fiscal Policy Under Uncertainty, Stockholm Economic Studies, New Series I (Stockholm: Almquist & Wiksell, 1957), especially the use of partition trees and strategies in Chapter 3.

15. A strategy may be thought of as the set of rules for one player wherein he takes into account all contingencies in planning all his moves during the course of the game. For example, if you were in charge of public relations for a political candidate in a two-man election race, your opponent's campaign manager would have a possible set of responses to your first move. You in turn would plan alternative actions depending upon his response to this first move, and so on. Obviously strategies can be statistically ascertained only in the simplest games.

16. Martin Shubik, *Strategy and Market Structure* (New York: John Wiley & Sons, Inc., 1959), Foreword by Oskar Morgenstern, p. viii.

17. Von Neumann and Morgenstern, *op. cit.,* Chapter 3 and especially Chapter 4, pp. 169-178.

18. When uncertainty is introduced in varying degrees into the theory of games, the line of demarcation between this theory and statistical-decision theory becomes extremely tenuous, so that the concept of the firm as used by students of statistical-decision theory will not be considered separately herein. For example, the classic reference to statistical-decision theory is Abraham Wald, *Statistical Decision Functions* (New York: John Wiley & Sons, Inc., 1954), in which the formulation of statistical-decision theory is very similar to the playing of a game against nature.

19. L. J. Savage, *The Foundations of Statistics* (New York: John Wiley & Sons, Inc., 1954). "Regret" is the difference between the actual payoff and the payoff that might have been obtained with perfect foresight.

20. Leonid Hurwicz, "Some Specification Problems and Applications to Econometric Models" (abstract) *Econometrica,* XIX (July, 1951), pp. 342-344.

21. In games where there is a lack of communication among players, rationality might be sacrificed. See: J. F. Nash, "Non-Cooperative Games," *Annals of Mathematics* (1951), pp. 286-295.

22. One of the first explorations of administration using the terminology of the theory of games, although he later denied that he consciously utilized game theory in this book, was made by Herbert A. Simon, *Administrative Behavior,* 2nd Edition. (New York: The Macmillan Company, 1957).

23. Ward Edwards, "The Theory of Decision-Making," *Psychological Bulletin,* 51, No. 4 (July, 1954), 406.

24. Discussed previously as a constant-sum game. It is customary to establish the constant sum as zero, hence the alternate terminology.

25. For a statement similar to this, see: Herbert A. Simon, "Theories of Decision-Making in Economics and Behavioral Science," *The American Economic Review*, XLIX, No. 3 (June, 1959), 266.

26. The founder of cybernetics is generally regarded to be Norbert Weiner although, as is customary, this science did have several forerunners. See: Norbert Weiner, *Cybernetics* (New York: John Wiley & Sons, Inc., 1948). A much more simple idea of cybernetics on a broader plane may be found in: Norbert Weiner, *The Human Use of Human Beings: Cybernetics and Society*. 2nd ed. rev. (New York: Doubleday Anchor Books, Doubleday & Company, Inc., 1956). Applications of cybernetics to the firm have been made by Kenneth Boulding, H. A. Simon, W. W. Cooper, S. Enke, and others.

27. R. G. D. Allen, *Mathematical Economics* (London: Macmillan & Co., Ltd., 1957). Chapter 9 contains an interesting discussion of closed-loop control systems applied to macro-economic models of the economy.

28. Weiner, *The Human Use of Human Beings, op. cit.*, pp. 58-59.

29. Walter B. Cannon, *The Wisdom of the Body* (New York: W. W. Norton & Company, Inc., 1932), p. 24. The term "sociostasis" has been suggested where the application is to social systems, see: G. A. Lundberg, "Human Social Problems as a Type of Disequilibrium in a Biological Integration," *American Sociological Review*, XIII (December, 1948), 689-699.

30. Cf. H. M. James, N. B. Nichols, and R. S. Phillips, eds., *Theory of Servomechanisms*, M. I. T. Radiation Laboratory Series (New York: McGraw-Hill Book Company, Inc., 1947), p. 62.

31. W. W. Cooper, "Theory of the Firm: Some Suggestions for Revision," *American Economic Review*, XXXIX, No. 6 (December, 1949), contains several interesting ideas in which the firm is perceived as a servomechanism affected by feedbacks from profit and liquidity positions.

32. Cf. Kenneth E. Boulding, *A Reconstruction of Economics* (New York: John Wiley & Sons, Inc., 1950), especially Chapters 2 and 17.

33. This picture of the firm borrows both from homeostasis and cybernetics. For an article in which servomechanisms are discussed in output and inventory control systems, without recourse to the idea of homeostasis, see: Herbert A. Simon, *Models of Man* (New York: John Wiley & Sons, Inc., 1957), Chapter 13. Reprinted as *Cowles Commission Paper*, New Series, No. 59.

34. Several behavioral scientists do incorporate the establishment of equilibrium into their systems. For example, see: James G. March and Herbert A. Simon, *Organizations* (New York: John Wiley & Sons, Inc., 1958), pp. 48-50.

35. Papandreou, *op. cit.*, p. 183.

36. See Talcott Parsons, *The Structure of Social Action*, 2nd ed. (New York: The Free Press of Glencoe, Inc., 1949), especially pp. 43-51 and 732-733 for his position on the theory of action.

37. Talcott Parsons and Edward S. Shils, eds., *Toward a General Theory of Action* (Cambridge: Harvard University Press, 1952), p. 31.

38. Papandreou, *op. cit.*, p. 183.

39. Parsons and Shils, *op. cit.*, p. 28. The authors point out that although economic theory has its conceptual foundations in action theory, in effect its differences are substantial.

40. It is difficult to give the best reference by, or to, Lewin in this context. Possibly R. W. Leeper, *Lewin's Topological and Vector Psychology: A Digest and A Critique*, University of Oregon Monographs, Studies in Psychology, No. 1 (Eugene: University of Oregon Press, 1943) presents the best over-all summary of those aspects of Lewin's theory referred to here.

41. Lewin's theories have apparently been of special interest to marketers. See the essays by Joseph Clawson and Wroe Alderson in: Reavis Cox and Wroe Alderson, eds., *Theory in Marketing* (Homewood, Ill.: Richard D. Irwin, Inc., 1950), pp. 41-89.

42. It would not be surprising, for example, to find Freud's psychoanalytic theory applied holistically as a concept of the firm in the future—with the study being perhaps limited to the differentiation of the matrix within which the firm as the id commands its reflex actions and primary processes as it seeks to fulfill its wishes of profit maximization; perceiving its environment through the focus outcomes presented to the entrepreneur acting as its ego, and being confined by parameters defined as its superego.

43. Frederick W. Taylor, *Scientific Management* (New York: Harper & Row, Publishers, 1947).

44. Cf. Gore and Silander, *op. cit.*, p. 113, for qualifications of this statement.

45. This results largely from the work of Elton Mayo and his followers, which swung the pendulum of research in this area away from "science" and into the rather vague field of "human relations."

46. Cf. Kurt Lewin, "Experiments in Social Space," *Harvard Educational Review*, IX (1939), 22-24. Reprinted in: Kurt Lewin, *Resolving Social Conflicts* (New York: Harper & Row, Publishers, 1948), pp. 72-74.

47. An interesting discussion of this point may be found in: H. H. Gerth and C. Wright Mills, eds., *From Max Weber: Essays in Sociology* (New York and London: Oxford University Press, 1946), pp. 204ff.

48. For a full discussion of Weber's view on the "ideal-type" of bureaucracy, see: Max Weber, *The Theory of Social and Economic Organization*.

Translated by A. M. Henderson and Talcott Parsons, edited by Talcott Parsons (New York and London: Oxford University Press, 1947).

49. Cf. Alvin W. Gouldner, "Discussion of Industrial Sociology," *The American Sociological Review,* XIII (1948), 396-397.

50. See Robert K. Merton, "Bureaucratic Structure and Personality," *Social Forces,* XVII (1940), 560-568.

51. Robert K. Merton, *Social Theory and Social Structure,* revised and enlarged edition (New York: The Free Press of Glencoe, Inc., 1957), Chapter 1, especially pp. 50-54.

52. *Ibid.,* pp. 139-160.

53. See Philip Selznick, *TVA and the Grass Roots,* University of California Publications in Culture and Society, Vol. III (Berkeley: University of California Press, 1949). More complete for our discussion is Philip Selznick, "Foundations of the Theory of Organization," *American Sociological Review,* XIII (February, 1948).

54. Philip Selznick, *TVA and the Grass Roots, op. cit.,* pp. 251-252.

55. March and Simon, *op. cit.,* Chapter 3, especially pp. 34-47. This chapter contains some interesting comments and diagrams on these and other theories of bureaucracy.

56. Cf. Gore and Silander, *op. cit.,* pp. 101ff. These authors appear to divide organizational theories into the two classes of traditional and behaviorist.

57. Often rationality is attributed to executive members of the firm, and the qualities of passivity or manipulability are given to all other firm members.

58. Chester I. Barnard, *The Functions of the Executive* (Cambridge, Mass.: Harvard University Press, 1956), p. 65.

59. *Ibid.,* p. 82. Compare Barnard's essential elements with those set forth by Alderson, *op. cit.,* pp. 68-74, where (1) componency, (2) seriality, and (3) concurrence are basic to every organization.

60. *Ibid.,* pp. 86-89.

61. *Ibid.,* pp. 94-95.

62. *Ibid.,* p. 83.

63. *Ibid.*

64. Burleigh B. Gardner, "The Factory as a Social System," in William Foote Whyte, ed., *Industry and Society* (New York: McGraw-Hill Book Company, Inc., 1946), Chapter 2.

65. One of the best studies on informal groups is summarized in: William Foote Whyte, "Corner Boys: A Study of Clique Behavior," *American Journal of Sociology,* 46, No. 5 (March, 1941), 647-664.

66. See Chester Barnard's chapter in Whyte, *Industry and Society, op. cit.*, pp. 46-83, for a good discussion of status systems in the firm.

67. Gardner, *op. cit.*, pp. 14-15.

68. Herbert A. Simon, *Administrative Behavior,* 2nd Edition (New York: The Macmillan Company, 1957), p. xvi.

69. *Ibid.*

70. Herbert A. Simon, "A Comparison of Organization Theories," *Review of Economic Studies,* 20, No. 1 (1952-53). Reprinted in Herbert A. Simon, *Models of Man* (New York: John Wiley & Sons, Inc., 1957).

71. *Ibid.*

72. Simon, *Administrative Behavior, op. cit.*, pp. xxv-xxvi.

73. See, for example, a number of the articles in Part IV of Simon, *Models of Man, op. cit.;* and *Administrative Behavior, op. cit.*, especially Chapters 4 and 5; and his article in the *American Economic Review, op. cit.*

74. Several scholars agree, more or less, with Simon's ideas on the firm. For two examples, see: William J. Baumol, *Business Behavior, Value and Growth* (New York: The Macmillan Company, 1959), Part I; and Neil W. Chamberlain, *A General Theory of Economic Process* (New York: Harper & Row Publishers, 1955).

75. J. Margolis, "The Analysis of the Firm: Rationalism, Conventionalism, and Behaviorism," *The Journal of Business,* XXXI, No. 3 (July, 1958).

76. *Ibid.*

77. *Ibid.*

78. J. Margolis, "Traditional and Revisionist Theories of the Firm: A Comment," *The Journal of Business,* XXXII, No. 2 (April, 1959).

79. Bodenhorn, *op. cit.*

80. *Ibid.*

81. Clyde Kluckholm and Henry A. Murray, *Personality in Nature, Society, and Culture* (New York: Alfred A. Knopf, Inc., 1948), p. 282.

82. Everett C. Hughes, "Institutional Office and the Person," *American Journal of Sociology* (November, 1937).

83. Neal Gross, Ward S. Mason, Alexander W. McEachern, *Explorations in Role Analysis* (New York: John Wiley & Sons, Inc., 1958).

84. George C. Homans, *The Human Group* (New York: Harcourt, Brace & World, Inc., 1950).

85. Foreword by Bernard De Voto, *ibid.*, p. xv.

86. Albert Lauterbach, *Man, Motives and Money, Psychological Frontiers of Economics* (Ithaca: Cornell University Press, 1954), pp. 18f.

87. E. C. Tolman, "Psychological Man," *Journal of Social Psychology*, XIV (1941), 208.

88. Theodore Dreiser, *Jennie Gerhardt* (Cleveland: The World Publishing Company, 1911), pp. 270-271.

89. Harold L. Johnson, "A Behavioral Approach to the Business Enterprise," *The Southern Economic Journal*, XXVII, 1 (July, 1960), 1-2.

3

THE ECONOMIC THEORY OF BUSINESS BEHAVIOR

Economics essentially is the study of the process of economizing. As such it can encompass a variety of human activities where persons are confronted by choices involving two or more alternatives. If the choice is to be made on an economic basis, however, the criterion must always be in terms of what is least costly, or conversely, what is most profitable. Mankind, in fact, is never entirely economic, although in theory it is possible to imagine an "economic man." In any realistic situation the concepts of costs and profits are confined implicitly within cultural limits, and must involve judgments, although some economists insist that societal values do not (or should not) form part of the framework of decision. Nevertheless, very few businessmen decide that their most profitable alternatives include the murder of competitors, largely because they take the legal (cultural) and moral costs of such actions into account, and find them exhorbitant. In the same way, a battle which might be too costly in terms of human sacrifice to an

American general may not be too costly to a Chinese Communist general.

On the other hand, culture assists in the definition as well as the limitation of costs and profits, for in a general way it indicates what is least costly and what is most profitable. In a society where salvation is a prime goal, men may still economize but the accumulation of material goods may be considered to be too expensive a means to spiritual ends. In most modern societies ethereal objectives are divorced from the pursuit of worldly possessions, or else the latter are believed to be compatible with the former, or even to be of assistance in helping man reach his eternal goals. The emphasis on materialism has unquestionably affected economic thought, and has caused economists to direct their attention almost exclusively to problems in which costs and rewards are conceived and measured in pecuniary terms.[1]

Thus, although economizing actions in general include all those which move most efficiently toward their goals, economic actions customarily have been interpreted more narrowly to encompass only those in which the production, exchange, and consumption of economic goods and services occur. Production and distribution usually are carried on in organizations while both individuals and organizations consume. The key organization in business is, of course, the firm or business enterprise, which produces, exchanges, and consumes.

THE ECONOMIC THEORY OF THE FIRM

Although the business concern has been central to much of economics for decades, and although a formal economic theory of the firm has existed for thirty years, there still is not complete agreement among economists as to the precise features of this theory. However, although there is no universality of economic opinion, there does appear to be a fairly broad consensus with which many economists would agree. The principal components of this consensus may be summed up in the following fashion:

1. The firm has a goal (or goals) toward which it strives.
2. It moves toward its objectives in a "rational" manner.
3. The firm's function is to transform economic inputs into outputs.
4. The environment in which the firm operates is given.
5. The theory concentrates particularly upon changes in the price and quantities of inputs and outputs.[2]

The Goal of the Firm

Economists traditionally have stated that the maximization of profits is the objective of the firm.[3] In recent years this goal has often been challenged and frequently has been qualified, but like the Rock of Gibraltar, has remained firmly imbedded in the sea of economic thought, although its surface may be somewhat eroded and stained.

At this point, however, it is not our intent to criticize, but to analyze. The flat statement that firms tend to maximize profits obviously needs further explanation. We must understand the concept of profits, and the fashion in which profits are maximized. Let us first look at profits.

The Theory of Profit

Frank H. Knight, the famous economist from the University of Chicago, has written "Perhaps no term or concept in economic discussion is used with a more bewildering variety of well-established meanings than profit." [4] There are a number of theories of profit, then, and as we shall see, an investigation into these is somewhat "profitless," although the study of profit does produce an interesting maze of semantic and economic problems about which economists have been debating for decades. In order to simplify our investigations, we shall try to segregate profit concepts into three major categories (which, unfortunately, often overlap): (1) Those that stress the manner in which profits arise. The theories in this class are sometimes termed "functional" profit theories, for they emphasize the function for which profits are the reward. (2) Those theories that classify profits according to recipients. Here, profit is examined as an income share from economic activities which is given to a certain type of individual or to a particular class in the population. (3) Finally, there is a school of economic thought which is primarily interested in the nature and definition of profits *per se*, and only incidentally concerned with how profits arise or how they are distributed. We shall begin our discussion with the third view of profits, and work back toward the first.

Profits *Per Se*

Most modern economists, when writing on the theory of the firm, discuss only the nature of profits, rather than their origin or distribution. The simplest definition of profits, and perhaps that most commonly utilized by economists is $\pi = pq - C$, where π represents profits, pq is total revenue (price times quantity), and C is total cost. It is evident that in this definition π may be positive or negative, and that its magnitude is a residual dependent upon the relative size of revenues and costs. Even in this simple exposition, however, several terms are sufficiently ambiguous and complex as to warrant further comment. One matter of some importance is the meaning of costs. Another concerns the element of time: in $\pi = pq - C$ both pq and C must be measured over some interval—but which interval is the pertinent one?

Economists are concerned with only economic goods and services. These are goods and services that are demanded at a price and which would at zero price be demanded in greater quantities than they could be supplied.[5] Economic goods and services, therefore, are priced because they are scarce, and because not enough of the aggregate quantity of such items is available to satisfy all the wants of all the people in a society. Because economic goods and services are scarce, if they are used in the production of certain items they cannot be used in the production of others. Economists define the costs of production in these terms. Costs are those payments that must be made (by business firms) to retain resources, and to keep them from flowing into alternative productive uses. All resources employed by the firm may also be utilized in the production of alternatives. Scientists, for example, may be looked upon as an economic resource. By employing them to work on hydrogen bombs rather than in similar work on life-saving medical devices it may mean that society necessarily is foregoing life for death; or less poetically, that the output of medical inventions is reduced in order to increase the production of hydrogen bombs.

The prices paid for raw materials and the wages paid to labor must be just high enough to attract these resources to their productive uses in the firm. These prices, then, are costs to the firm, and are measured in terms of the prices that would be paid to these factors should they be committed to alternative opportunities. The types of items included in "accounting" costs, in the normal sense, are considered also by economists to be costs. In addition to these, however, economists also include certain "implicit" costs in their totals which accountants customarily do not. For example, if the owner of a firm could obtain an equal income by working for another his alternative cost would be the same as his income, and economists would say that he is not making a profit. Furthermore, the alternative (or "opportunity") cost doctrine insists on valuing resources in terms of present alternatives, whereas accountants ordinarily value resources at original purchase prices less depreciation, which may produce entirely different results.

If, then, economists state that $\pi = pq - C$, it is immediately apparent that π and C are quite different from what is usually meant in business. Costs must always be measured in terms of alternatives, and the alternatives available to *all* resources (entrepreneurial services, labor, capital, and so on) must be included in arriving at total costs and, in turn, at profit.

Time is a variable contained implicitly in the formula $\pi = pq - C$. Economists, however, have shrewdly by-passed the problems inherent in time by establishing certain timeless environments in which a firm operates and makes profits or losses. In order to understand how economists can discuss profits made during a precise but yet indefinite time period it is necessary to return to a further examination of inputs and costs.

The inputs in the production process of a business enterprise may be categorized in a number of ways. One common classification (and the one useful in this instance) is to divide inputs into those that are variable and those that are fixed. Fixed inputs, as the descriptive title implies, are those that do not vary with every change in output. Factories, machinery, and other fixed assets are of this type. On the other hand, variable inputs are those that vary with every increase or decrease in output. Quantities of labor, raw materials, and power are commonly variable inputs. Now, a period of time during which only the input of variable factors changes is termed a short-run period. If the fixed inputs are altered during a period the period is long-run. Given a sufficiently long period of time, of course, all inputs are variable. The short-run is an interval long enough to permit outputs to be produced, but not long enough to permit changes in the quantity or quality of fixed inputs. In the long run, changes in the quantity or quality of fixed inputs occur.

Economists, then, generally discuss profits in the short run or in the long run, and in so doing avoid problems of time, although the intervals with which they are concerned are rigidly delimited. It would be possible, therefore, to alter the profit formula to read $\pi_s = pq - S_s$, or $\pi_l = pq - C_l$, where s refers to the short run, and l to the long. However, because the principal difference between the two is the number and type of inputs that are variable, the analysis takes much the same form in both cases.

This, then, is the simplest and also the most commonly used definition of profits, as the concept is employed by economists. After all costs, computed in terms of their alternative uses, are subtracted from total revenues during the short run (or long run), the remainder is profit. This increment is known as "pure" profit, because it is over and above all the alternative costs of all the factors of production.

Not all economists would agree that "pure" profits constitute the most convenient profit concept. One small group argues that profit theory should be constructed to be useful for businessmen, and that by atomizing the gross revenue to the entrepreneur into wages for his labor, interest on his invested capital, and pure profit, economists neglect reality. "Our observation of the real world then shows us only gross profit or entrepreneurial income," it is said.[6] Economists who take this point of view believe that the gross amount received by entrepreneurs is significant, and not only the fraction called "pure profit." It is this gross quantity with which entrepreneurs are concerned, it is claimed, and they receive it as individuals and not as a schizophrenic threesome (capitalist, laborer, and entrepreneur) artificially constituted by the whim of "ivory-tower economists." [7]

Despite the fact that profit is most commonly defined as a sum of money, there is still some confusion that remains, for economists sometimes discuss the "rate" of profit, or the "rate" of return. Now, it is evident that the rate of return which matters is not the rate per unit of output. Maximizing this rate would result in the production of only very small quantities of commodities in order to yield the highest return per unit, through the operation of the forces of supply and demand.[8] Furthermore, the total sum of profit over a long time period would be smaller if the rate of return per unit of output were the criterion quantity, for surely the public reactions to such profit behavior would soon prove detrimental to the rate of return, and reduce it over time. Thus, the rate of return that is of interest is the return per unit of assets to the owners of the firm after the deduction of all costs.[9]

The firm, as we previously noted, is a mechanism having the task of transforming inputs into outputs. For example, an automobile manufacturer will take many types of materials—chemicals, steel, aluminum, glass, cloth, plastics, rubber—and transform these into cars. In order to perform its transformation function a firm has to possess assets: such things as land, machinery, cash, buildings, inventories, and the like. Each asset has a varying number of alternative uses. In order to operate a business concern in the most economical fashion, management must select the best possible alternative use for each of its assets. This may involve the productive utilization of an asset (as in the case of machinery) or the exchange of one asset for another (as when cash is reduced to purchase additional raw materials). The best utilization or exchange of assets is measured by the stream of income returns that will eventually be realized by the owners of the firm. If we assume with economists that this profit stream should be as large as possible, then it is evident that that combination of assets should be maintained which will have the greatest present worth.[10] The firm will continually attempt to find the combination of assets that will create the maximum income stream. This maximum stream will flow from the combination of assets that has the greatest present worth, that is, the discounted value of its future income.[11]

The notions of profit as an amount or as a rate of return are not incompatible in the long run. It is possible, of course, that a firm seeking profits in the short run may jeopardize the size of its long-run income stream. For this reason many economists agree that profit maximization in the short run is meaningless unless the actions undertaken to obtain this goal also happen to maximize long-run profits.[12] If then, it is desired to maximize the present value of the enterprise, that combination of assets will be selected which will produce this result. However, this same decision will maximize the long-run amount of profit as well as the rate, for assets will be combined (by definition) most efficiently.

Economists, for various reasons, are much more interested in future (*ex ante*) profits rather than those which have been realized (*ex post*). Economists are concerned primarily with evolving a theory of the firm that will assist them to predict business behavior. They regard profit, therefore, as a goal which influences managerial decisions. *Ex post*, or past, profits are relevant to behavior only insofar as they may influence future expectations of profits. Thus, *ex post* profits are significant only as they may serve as a historical guide to the future. *Ex ante* profits, in the end, act as the goal for managerial actions, for these actions are based inherently upon future expectations rather than past records. It is these future profits, then, which are of greatest importance to economists, and which play such a vital role in their theory of the firm.[13]

To sum up this brief section on profits *per se*, then, we can generalize that most economists would consider these to be that *ex ante* pure return which is in excess of all alternative costs. This return may be expressed either as a rate of profit resulting from asset combinations, or as a long-run amount of profit. It is permissible to discuss profit in the short-run, but this concept must be related to long-run rates or amounts. Finally, there are some economists who view profit as gross entrepreneurial income, but this viewpoint is not commonly held nor highly regarded.

Profits as a Distributive Share

Profits are often defined according to the persons or institutions to which they accrue.[14] Profits, in this context, are the *ex ante* pure return that is allocated to, rather than originated by, specific persons, classes, or institutions. In this section we shall examine the concept of profits as a share of income defined by the recipients to whom it is distributed.

One question that has caused some confusion concerns the distribution of profits between institutions and persons. Is it possible for profits to be allocated to institutions as well as to persons? In accounting parlance, reference is often made to undistributed profits, or to retained earnings, which would imply that profits may be withheld from individuals and accrue to the corporation. This matter has also been clouded by economists who discuss the enterprise and the entrepreneur as one and the same, and who sometimes term profits the returns to the firm, and at other times talk about profits as the return to the firm's owners.[15] This distinction may be quite significant in certain instances, as when the firm is a corporation owned by a number of persons. Situations may arise, for example, wherein one owner, by maximizing his profits, may actually reduce the profits of "the firm" as an abstract entity, or of the owners.[16] Yet, there appears to be little unanimity among economists on the proper answer to the question: are profits a return to individuals or to business units? [17] If we agree that the firm is the entrepreneur and profit is the net income of the enterprise, as advocated by Stauss and Davis, we sidestep certain conceptual difficulties; for example, we do not have to worry about the segregation of factor costs or the problems of the entrepreneurial population.[18] Yet, it appears that, for our purposes, it is difficult to accept the convenient fiction of the impersonal institution—the firm—as an ultimate income recipient separated completely by convention from the people who inhabit it.[19] However, until economists arrive at a definitive answer to this debate on firms versus persons, we shall escape the problem with Triffin, who writes: "Pure theory has often ruled too blindly on the formula that 'each firm tries to maximize its profits.' The traditional analysis of the firm depends, for its validity, on this methodological postulate. In fact, however, the firm is a mere abstraction: profit maximization is the concern, not of the legal entities called firms, but of human beings." [20] This, then, seems to be our answer. If we want to consider firms as intermediate recipients of profits, this may be a satisfactory convenience for certain theoretical purposes. However, in the last analysis, profits are received by persons and not by institutions.

If profits are to be, in the end, considered primarily as returns to persons, these persons should be described more precisely. Are profits the amounts (net above all costs) received by owners of a business enterprise? Or do executives receive profits? Or do both? In partnerships and sole proprietorships, and even in many small corporations where managerial duties are performed by owners, there are no problems, for these are the persons who receive profits. However, in large corporations management and ownership are frequently separated, and the definition of profits as a return to one or the other, or both, becomes more confused, especially if (to jump briefly into the next section) profits are considered to be the returns received by entrepreneurs. For who are the entrepreneurs in the large corporation? Management? Or stockholders? In the case of separation of ownership and control, a few economists claim that profits should include the income of the nonowner entrepreneur.[21] It would seem that many economists, however, would agree with Professor Knight: "The *crucial* decision is the selection of men to make decisions." [22] In this view, even in the modern giant corporation, with widespread ownership, the stockholders make the final decision to hire, fire, or retain the management, and, thus, are in reality the entrepreneurs.[23]

The definition of profits according to recipient has certain advantages; namely, it delineates a definite sum that is realized *ex post,* and in this way proves more agreeable and tractable for certain accounting purposes. Nevertheless, as a concept for students of business behavior, it is far from satisfactory. Although most economists would perhaps define profits in this sense as the net income stream flowing to the owners of the firm (above all costs), there is little unanimity on this point. Furthermore, the concept of profits as *only* a distributive share is relatively uninformative analytically, for it describes simply the result, and does not tell us anything about causation.[24] To say that profits are a distributive share is merely descriptive, when analysis is desired. A profit concept that discloses how profits can be made is of greater use to the theory of the firm than knowledge of their distribution, although, of course, the latter information may also be helpful for many purposes.

Functional Theories of Profit

What do persons (or firms) do to obtain profits? Or, to put the question more generally, how do profits result? Although the majority of profit theories have inquired into this problem, there is a wide variety of answers.

Many of the important functional theories of profit have their roots in the work of Professor F. H. Knight.[25] Knight pointed out that under perfect competition there would be no profit, because profit is the noncontractual residual remaining to the entrepreneur after the deduction of all alternative costs. In perfect competition there would be no such residual for, as we shall observe later, all plans are realized, and under this condition it would be impossible for residuals to arise.[26] Thus profits, according to Knight, arise because of the presence of uncertainty, which causes results to differ from plans.[27] Uncertainty is defined as immeasurable and uninsurable risk that arises because of the unpredictability of demand and supply functions.

Knight's theory has been carried to its extreme by Professor J. Fred Weston, who writes that profit is the difference between *ex ante* and *ex post* incomes.[28] Decision makers, even under conditions of uncertainty, must plan for the future, must decide upon certain courses of action, and must expect certain outcomes. In the face of the unpredictable, however, such outcomes are realized only by chance, and if they are realized, profits are zero.[29] In other words, such a realization of expectations is "normal," and not profit. It is the *ex post* deviations from *ex ante* normal that are to be reckoned as profits or losses.

The relation between uncertainty and functional theories of profit has been set forth by A. C. Pigou, who looks upon profit as a return to the entrepreneur for his burden of decision making under uncertainty.[30] This theory assumes that profits are associated functionally with uncertainty bearing, and it is implied that the greater the uncertainty, the greater the profit. Because intuition and the little empirical evidence available do not appear to justify this conclusion, Pigou's theory has not become very popular among economists.

Profits are often regarded as payment for the performance of the entrepreneurial function under conditions of uncertainty. Although there is considerable support among economists for this view, there is little agreement on the meaning of entrepreneurial functions. One concept, for example, brings to mind a picture of the entrepreneur as a business dentist, prying apart as far as possible jaws composed of consumers and suppliers of productive factors in order to extract the optimum rewards for this action.[31] In another instance the entrepreneurial function has been defined as the organization of productive factors.[32] A third authority regards this function as synonymous with business leadership.[33] The entrepreneur has also been regarded as the innovator, with profits resulting from innovation.[34] Innovation may be defined as new ways of doing things, or new combinations of the factors of production, or more broadly, changing production functions or products.[35]

There is also a school of economic thought that considers profits as resulting from positions of advantage in business. For example, monopolists may obtain surplus revenues from the sale of their outputs at a price higher than that which would prevail in competitive markets. There are also "windfall" profits, which may occur for short periods as the result of circumstances that cause demand to exceed supply. Finally, profits may arise because of market imperfections, as when new firms are unable to enter certain industries because of various obstacles.[36] Most economists today conceive profits arising from positions of advantage to be in fact "rents" or "quasi-rents," and to occur because a firm can sell its output so as to bring in a total revenue above that which it would have been willing to accept. This situation, in theory at least, is usually regarded as temporary.

Conclusions on Profit Theory

For purposes of describing the concept of profit most useful to a study of the firm, we may limit ourselves to the following: (1) Profit is that *ex ante* "pure" amount or return in excess of all alternative costs. Although it is permissible to discuss profit in the short run, long-run profit is most significant to the firm, and business enterprises are primarily interested in the latter. (2) Profit is allocated ultimately to individual owners of the company, although its distribution may be delayed by the firm in its journey to the final recipients. (3) Profits arise primarily through the performance of a host of entrepreneurial functions in an environment of uncertainty. To state that profits arise solely because of uncertainty is to reduce the profit motive to an absurd and meaningless statement which is certainly not consistent with the economic theory of the firm.[37]

The Maximizations of Profits and "Rationality"

The economic theory of the firm does not merely postulate profits as the goal of the business concern. It states explicitly that the goal is maximum profits, and that entrepreneurs will try to move toward this objective in a rational manner.

Rationality, in the economic theory of the firm, implicitly assumes no action will be undertaken by the business enterprise that will move it away from its goal of maximum profits. Furthermore, it assumes that the decision maker, faced with two or more alternatives that will result in various outcomes, will invariably select the alternative that will tend to move the firm to (or closer to) profit maximization. In order to accomplish changes in the proper direction, and to insure that their magnitudes will be neither too large nor too small, it is customary for economists to postulate that decisions be made on the basis of marginal values. In the economic theory of the firm, then, rational action is normally understood to mean action wherein the pertinent variables are weighed at the margin, and changes are in the direction of increasing net profits. The logic of the economic entrepreneur is thus based upon marginal analysis, which is a process for finding a maximum.

Marginal functions may be defined generally as the first derivative of any continuous function, dy/dx, where $y = f(x)$. If we state that profits are $\pi = pq - C$, let us see how they may be maximized through the use of marginal analysis. Total costs include both variable costs, which change with changes in output, and fixed costs, which continue at the same level (at least in the short run) independent of output changes. We can write the total cost formula, then, as $C = f(q) + k$, where (q) represents items of output produced per unit of time and k is fixed costs. The marginal cost of production, then, is $dc/dq = f'(q)$, the derivative of costs (c) with respect to the quantity (q), or, less formally, the incremental change in C which occurs with a change in output. Marginal revenue is the change in revenue which accompanies changes in sales, so that $dr/dq = f'(pq)$. It is usually assumed, furthermore, that the revenue and cost functions are continuous, and that their derivatives exist at any point. We know that it is necessary, if profit is to be at a maximum, that $d\pi/dq = 0$. We can write this also as:

$$\frac{d\pi}{dq} = \frac{dr}{dq} - \frac{dc}{dq} = 0$$

It is evident, then, that when profits are at a maximum, $dr/dq = dc/dq$, or, in other words, that marginal costs equal marginal revenue. Finally, in order to insure that profits are maximized and not minimized when $d\pi/dq = 0$, we must meet the sufficient condition for a maximum, which is that $d^2\pi/dq^2 < 0$, so that

$$\frac{d^2r}{dq^2} - \frac{d^2c}{dq^2} < 0 \quad \text{and} \quad \frac{d^2r}{dq^2} < \frac{d^2c}{dq^2}$$

Profits are maximized in the economic theory of the firm, therefore, when marginal costs are equal to marginal revenues, and when, at the point of intersection of the two marginal curves, the marginal cost function cuts the marginal revenue function from below. Entrepreneurs, when making their output decisions, weigh the expected costs of producing additional units of output against the expected revenues from the sale of these additional items. If the additional revenues (marginal revenues) are larger than the additional (marginal) costs of production, output will be expanded and simultaneously (as the sufficient condition above requires) total revenues will expand more than total costs. Production will continue to expand as long as $R_m > C_m$. Additional production will not be contemplated if $C_m > R_m$, for at such an output position net revenues would be reduced by additional production.[38]

The Firm as a Transformation Unit

In order to attain maximum profits, which in economic theory constitute the goal of the business firm, certain variables must be manipulated, or changed, or transformed. In our discussion above of profit maximization, output quantities were altered to attain the firm's objective. Although the most customarily exploited variable in economics is output, other variables also must either change or be changed (ordinarily) in order to achieve a maximum. However, the firm's existence, even in economic theory, is justified not merely because it succeeds or fails in its goal of maximum profits. Rather, it is justified because it performs an economically useful task. This task consists of altering or transforming valued inputs to outputs of a higher order of value. If the firm performs this task in a perfectly efficient manner, it will, in the ordinary course of things, also maximize profits. In order to understand the firm's "productive" activities as well as its money-making ambitions, we must examine briefly the concept of the production function, minimum cost mixes, and prices.

The Production Function

The production of any output requires a certain specific combination of inputs. This combination of inputs is affected by the state of technology which exists at any time. For example, in order to produce a ton of steel today a firm has to combine a minimum amount of labor, management, and other resources in certain ways. A hundred years ago the output of a ton of steel depended upon a different combination, and different quantities, of these resources, and even on somewhat different inputs. The production function, therefore, summarizes the relationships existing between the rates of inputs and the rate of output, given the state of technological knowledge. It tells us that, by using a specific amount of input x_1, and input x_2, and input . . . x_n, the firm can produce a maximum output, q. The production function for a firm may be mathematically stated as

$$q = f(x_1, x_2, x_3, \ldots, x_n)$$

where q is a certain amount of output, and the x's refer to the amounts of different inputs technologically necessary to produce q. Implied in the production function is the assumption that input units will be combined most efficiently so that the maximum output will result.[39]

One last point on the mix of inputs is of vital importance in the economic theory of the firm; this is the law of diminishing returns, which states that there will be diminishing marginal products after some point if more and more of some input is added while all other input quantities are held constant. It is from this law that some of the most basic concepts of the shape of output and cost curves in economic theory are derived.

The Minimum Cost Mix

If the objective of the firm is to maximize profit, it will produce any given output at minimum cost. Costs of production may be defined here as the values of inputs included in a cost function, assuming fixed prices. Businessmen must know not only the technological mix of inputs; they must also be aware of the values of these inputs—of their costs of production. If C represents the costs of production, the cost function is defined as:

$$C = p_1 x_1 + p_2 x_2 + \ldots + p_n x_n$$

where the x's are again the quantities of specific inputs and the p's the prices of these inputs. All that this tells us, of course, is that the costs of production are equal to the sums of all the products of individual input quantities times their prices. The cost function does not, however, inform us that the p's and x's are combined most efficiently. What we must do, therefore, is to define the least costly combination of productive factors.

Inputs are most efficiently combined if it is not possible to increase the total output by redistributing expenditures between them. This optimum combination of inputs is assured if the ratio of their marginal product is equal to the ratio of their prices.[40] This may be written:

$$\frac{MP(x_1)}{p_1} = \frac{MP(x_2)}{p_2} \quad \text{or} \quad \frac{MP(x_1)}{MP(x_2)} = \frac{p_1}{p_2}$$

where $MP(x)$ is the marginal product of x. The rule of equality of the ratios of marginal products to their prices makes it possible for us to observe how costs may be minimized in the production of a specific quantity of output. Suppose that x_1 is machine time, and input x_2 is labor. By running a particular machine one additional hour we can increase output by 5 units at a cost of \$1. $MP(x_1)/p_1$ is thus $5/1 = 5$. If an additional man-hour of labor increases output by 6, at a cost \$2,

$$\frac{MP(x_2)}{p_2} = \frac{6}{2} = 3$$

Thus, if output can be increased by 5 through the expenditure of one more dollar on machine time, and only by three through a dollar increase of spending on labor, it obviously pays to redistribute expenditures until the ratios of the last dollar spent for every productive factor are equal. In this way costs to the firm will be minimized.

A Digression on Cost Curves

It is extremely useful (although not directly part of this skeleton of economic firm theory) to depict costs in terms of continuous curves or functions. We have already discussed the meaning of the pertinent costs—total, average, and marginal. Total cost (C_t) is a function of output, of course, but it is also the locus of points established by (1) the prices paid for inputs at each level of output, (2) the efficiency of inputs at each level of output, and (3) the technological state of the arts.[41] If an entrepreneur is rational (and he always is in economic theory) the heights of the total cost curve at any level of output will always be the minimum C_t for that level of q, that is, the function will follow that path which conforms to the expression,

$$MP(x_1)p_1 - MP(x_2)p_2 = 0$$

at every level of output.[42] The total cost function, furthermore, is drawn usually so that its configuration conforms to the law of diminishing returns. This means, in the short run, that output is usually depicted as increasing at a greater rate than costs as variable inputs are added to existing fixed inputs, but that after some output level is reached additional increments of variable inputs increase costs more than proportionately with the corresponding increase in output.

Figure 1 illustrates certain total cost concepts typically used in economic theory. C_f is the fixed cost curve, which is drawn as a horizontal line, indicating that it is a constant, unaffected by changes in output. The C_v curve is the total variable cost curve (or function), which varies with changes in output. Because the total cost curve, $C_t = C_v + C_f$, and because its slope at any level of output equals $dC_t/dq = dC_v/dq$, so that it has the same slope as the total variable cost curve, we may discuss the C_v curve together with the C_t curve, for they will both change in the same way and for the same reasons. First, it is assumed output will increase initially at a relatively slow rate in relation to the increases in variable inputs, that is, the slopes of both C_t and C_v curves are more vertical in the first stages of production expansion than they are at immediately following outputs. The economic reasoning behind this assumption is that at low levels of output there will be more inefficiencies in input combinations than at higher output levels. For example, increased increments of labor as a variable resource may lead to specialization, and thus to enhanced efficiency. Second, as these remarks imply, after some early stage of output expansion, increased efficiencies in input combinations will cause output to grow at a relatively rapid rate as more variable inputs are added. Finally, after some point the law of diminishing returns

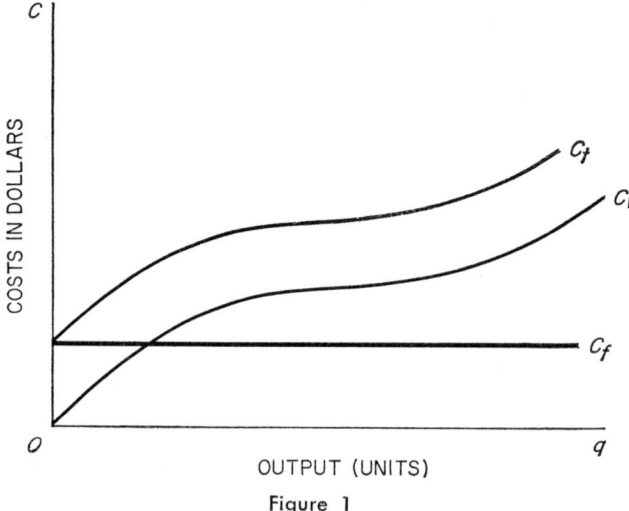

Figure 1

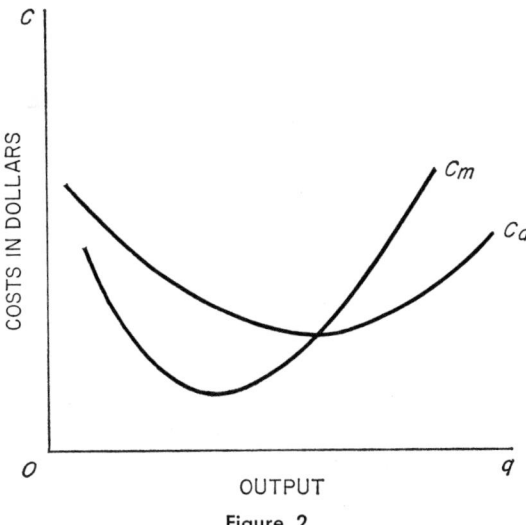

Figure 2

operates, and the C_t and C_v curves both begin to increase rapidly with relatively small changes in output.[43]

Unit cost curves are utilized more frequently for economic analysis than are total cost curves, and are also more useful, for the relationships between revenues, costs, and prices are more readily evident when the former are employed. The unit cost curves of primary interest and significance are two, the average cost (C_a) and marginal cost (C_m) curves. Both of these are derived from the total cost curve, which can be written to show fixed costs as a constant in the short run, and all other (variable) costs as a function of output, so that $C_t = f(q) + K$. Average costs, then, are simply total costs divided by the level of output and the C_a curve describes the total cost at each level of output divided by the corresponding level of output, that is,[44]

$$C_a = \frac{f(q) + K}{q}$$

The marginal cost function is the first derivative of the total cost curve, so that $C_m = dc/dq$. These relationships are illustrated in Figure 2, where average and marginal cost curves are drawn.[45]

The average and marginal curves are of value in our analysis, for they remain as given in Figure 2 regardless of the environment in which the firm operates. To attain the point of maximum profit in any theoretical environment, we know that C_m must equal marginal revenue R_m. The knowledge that the C_m curve is as depicted above thus solves at least half the problem of profit maximization.

Economic Environments

The individual firm in economic theory operates in a given economic environment, or state of nature, or market structure. There is a continuum of such environments (each one of which, however, is discrete) ranging from perfect competition to monopoly. Usually, these discrete states are differentiated by the slope of the demand function confronting the firm, over feasible ranges of output. In general, as we move from perfect competition through monopoly the slope of the demand curve confronting the firm is altered to distinguish the changed environment. This change in the slope of the demand curve is the distinguishing mechanical mark of the different conditions under which the firm operates. We shall, in the following paragraphs, explore two of these environments: pure competition and oligopoly.

Pure Competition

The conditions under which pure competition exists are: (1) a large number of firms, none of which is able to affect the prices at which its output is sold; (2) a large number of buyers who are indifferent in their purchases among firms in any industry, for each concern produces goods identical to those produced by all others in that industry.[46] Structurally, the market environment of pure competition hinges on the fact that the individual firm is confronted by a price that is given to it, and which it cannot alter by increasing or decreasing its output. Thus, its average revenue (demand) function must be horizontal, that is, $R_a = pq/q = p$, where p again is price and q is quantity of output.

Under the market conditions prescribed by pure competition, wherein it is possible for the firm to produce any amount and still sell each item of its output at the same price, the essential problem is to determine that output at which profit is maximized. This maximum is attained at the intersection of the C_m and R_m curves. At this point the R_m curve is the same as the R_a curve, for the revenue from the sale of an additional item will, like R_a, equal price.

As Figure 3 is drawn the C_a function is tangent to the horizontal R_a curve at its minimum point, where it also intersects the C_m function. With the R_a curve at this particular level, the firm in pure competition is at long-run equilibrium. There is no reason for output to change from OA. If the R_a curve is lower than that depicted in Figure 3 the firm will not be able to remain long in existence, for its per unit costs will be higher than its per unit revenues, and it cannot affect (raise) prices to alleviate its distress. On the other hand, if the R_a curve lies above the C_a

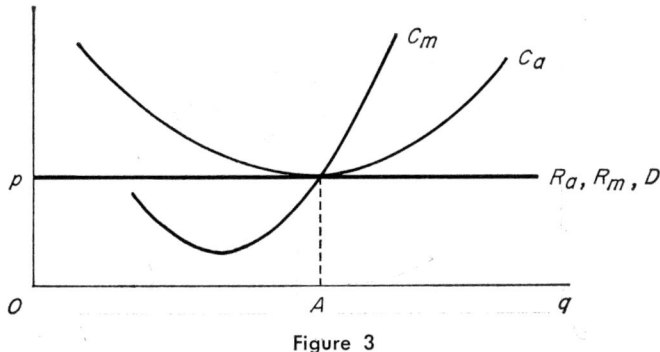

Figure 3

curve at its minimum point, the firm would earn more than "normal" profits, and new business enterprises would soon enter the industry, which would eliminate this surplus through changes in the revenue and cost functions. It is possible in the short run for the R_a curve not to be tangent to the C_a curve at its lowest point, but as long as there is freedom of entry and exit—as there is under conditions of pure competition—this lack of tangency is only temporary. Finally, at output of OA, where $C_m = R_m$, profits are "normal," meaning that they are just sufficient to repay entrepreneurs as much as they could obtain in other occupations.

Oligopoly

Oligopoly is a market structure in which there are only a few sellers, all of whom may affect prices, and all of whom must take into account the reactions of competitors when adjusting prices or output. Because of the interdependence among competitors it has been difficult for economists to treat oligopoly through traditional analysis.[47] It is possible in oligopolistic situations for a number of outcomes to develop. For example, oligopoly could result in conflict or collusion among rivals, in price leadership, basing point systems, extensive advertising campaigns, independent actions, and so on. There is little unanimity as to how oligopoly should be treated.

One model of oligopoly which has drawn considerable attention is that described by kinked demand curves. This model employs the concept of "imagined" demand: the demand envisaged by Firm A for its output at all relevant prices except the prevailing price. The demand at the present price is real, of course. The entrepreneur of Firm A, in his efforts to anticipate the reactions of his rivals to any movements in his price, imagines that his competitors will also lower their prices should he lower his, and will not raise their prices should his price be raised. This means, in effect, that the entrepreneur of Firm A imagines his

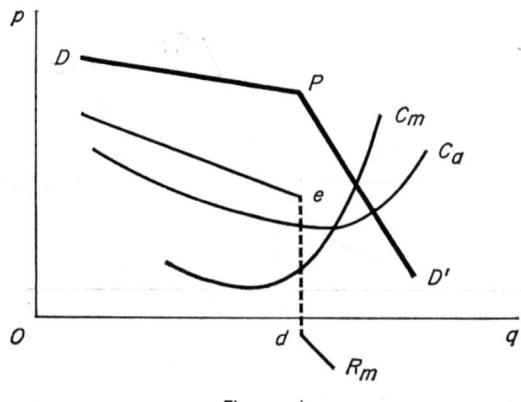

Figure 4

demand curve to be kinked at the prevailing price, so that any increase in his price will result in a rather substantial reduction in his sales (because his rivals will not follow his price increase), and any decrease in his price will not gain much in additional sales (because his rivals will follow his downward price changes). Thus, the entrepreneur of Firm A imagines his demand curve to look like the curve DPD' in Figure 4.[48]

This analysis seeks to explain why oligopolistic firms tend to maintain prices, and why they are reluctant to alter them. The R_m (marginal revenue) curve is depicted in Figure 4 as discontinuous between c and d. Because the R_m curve is the derivative of the demand curve, at point P on the curve DPD', dp/dq is undefined, as shown by the dashed vertical line, since at this point the demand function is not differentiable. Should the C_m curve pass through the section of the R_m curve, cd, C_m would equal R_m at price P, and there would be no reason to increase or decrease output or price, because profits would be maximized at this output level, as shown in Figure 4

Variations on this basic kinked demand curve theme are illustrated in Figure 5(a) and 5(b). Figure 5(a) depicts a situation where rivals are

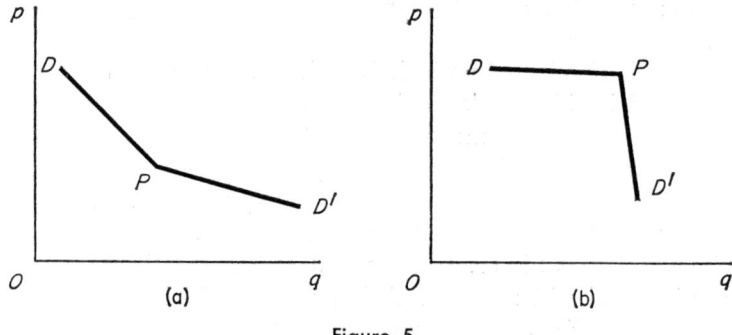

Figure 5

not expected to react to price reductions, but will increase their prices should the price of Firm A be increased.[49] This curve might be imagined if Firm A would secretly grant lower prices to its buyers, and if its rivals were not aware of these reductions. It might also occur if the entrepreneur of Firm A believes that his competitors are operating at or near capacity, so that he imagines they will follow his price increases, but they will not lower their prices when he lowers his. The kinked demand curve that results in this sort of situation has been termed a "reflex" curve. We shall discuss it more fully below. Figure 5(b) indicates what the entrepreneur of Firm A might imagine in a period of depression, when his rivals are eager for business. Any reduction in price in this case would lead to very few additional sales, and any increase in price to a substantial loss in sales. DPD' in Figure 5(b) is drawn so that it approaches a right angle at point P, to illustrate this situation.

We may make a few more remarks to indicate some of the problems involved in the analysis of oligopoly with traditional economic tools. We can begin by examining Figure 6, in which the reflex demand curve of Figure 5(a) is reproduced along with the pertinent marginal curves. We assume now that the entrepreneur of Firm A believes that price reductions will not be followed, but that price increases will, for rivals are at or near full-capacity operations.[50] Recall that P is the actual price for which Firm A is selling the amount of output OA. The remainder of the DPD' curve is as the entrepreneur of Firm A imagines it. Point P, furthermore, is always at the kink in DPD'. If actual price should shift, P would again be at a new kink, and the MR curve would reflect this kink by its discontinuity.

Now, how will the C_m curve intersect the marginal revenue curve, so that the point of maximum profits may be obtained? Obviously, the C_m curve can cut the AP vertical line at three significant points: (1) The C_m curve can intersect AP above point R, in which case C_m will meet MR_b to the left of AP. (2) It can intersect AP below point S, and C_m will

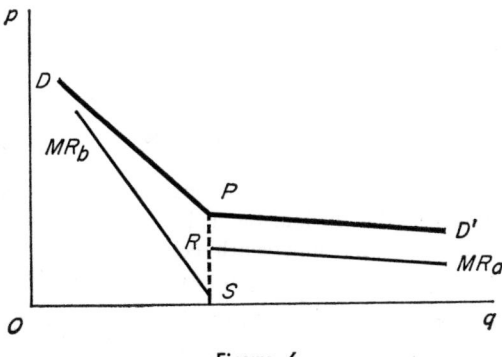

Figure 6

cut MR_a to the right of AP. (3) Or, most likely, the C_m curves will cut the AP line between R and S, in which case it will intersect both MR_b and MR_a, and profits will be maximized on both sides of AP.[51]

If the entrepreneur, in situation (3) moves either left or right to maximize profits, the kink at point P moves also, and profit maximization never is attained, for the intersection of C_m and R_m is always out of reach. This instability can cease only when the entrepreneur of Firm A believes that his rivals are producing at less than capacity, at which time the DPD' curve becomes obtuse.[52]

The variety of possible alternative outcomes and courses of action confronting the firm in oligopolistic situations is of concern to the economic analyst. The problem is that entrepreneurs can never be absolutely sure of their rivals' reactions to their moves. Even the kinked demand curve analysis may not lead to satisfactory results, as noted above. Finally, there is some evidence that the picture of oligopolistic behavior presented by kinked curves is not appropriate.[53]

SUMMARY

This then, in brief, is the economic model of the business firm. It is one of the most highly elaborate, yet simple, theories constructed in any social science discipline. Economists assume that business firms, operating in carefully defined environments, attempt to move toward their objectives of long-run profits by transforming inputs into outputs, and principally by adjusting prices and quantities of inputs and outputs. Although basically the economic theory of the firm is clearly defined, there are areas wherein concepts are vague, or not universally accepted by economists. The notion of profits, for example, is fuzzy, and there are conflicting opinions as to their proper nature. Oligopolistic situations also have presented problems. The economic theory of the firm is most definite, and most generally acceptable, when it is mechanistic, that is, when economists present their refinements on the hedonistic calculus—the processes through which movements toward a goal are accomplished.

Notes and References

1. Although the philosophical bases of economic thought extend at least to Ancient Greece, the hedonistic (pleasure-pain) writings of Jeremy Bentham in the early nineteenth century form the most influential philosophical foundation for explorations in economics.

2. Substantially different, but equally brief, descriptions of the economic theory of the firm may be found in: D. W. Bushaw and R. W. Clower, *Intro-*

duction to *Mathematical Economics* (Homewood, Ill.: Richard D. Irwin, Inc., 1957), p. 144; and R. M. Cyert and J. G. March, *The Embryonic Corpse: Being an Inquiry into the Possible Existence of a Theory of the Firm*, Behavioral Theory of the Firm Project, Working Paper No. 17, Carnegie Institute of Technology, December, 1959, pp. 2-4.

3. Recent, and widely used, textbooks which set forth profit maximization as the firm's goal include the following: Richard H. Leftwich, *The Price System and Resource Allocation* (New York: Holt, Rinehart & Winston, Inc., 1955); James M. Henderson and Richard E. Quandt, *Microeconomic Theory* (New York: McGraw-Hill Book Company, Inc., 1958); Diran Bodenhoren, *Intermediate Price Theory* (New York: McGraw-Hill Book Company, Inc., 1961); George J. Stigler, *The Theory of Price*, Revised Edition (New York: The Macmillan Company, 1952).

4. Frank H. Knight, "Profit," in the *Encyclopedia of the Social Sciences*, Volume XII (New York: The Macmillan Co., 1934), p. 480. Reprinted in: American Economic Association, *Readings in the Theory of Income Distribution* (Homewood, Ill.: Richard D. Irwin, Inc., 1949), pp. 533-546. F. W. Taussig once referred to profits as "that mixed and vexed income," in "The Employer's Place in Distribution," *Quarterly Journal of Economics*, Vol. X (1895), p. 86.

5. See Diran Bodenhoren, *Intermediate Price Theory* (New York: McGraw-Hill Book Company, Inc., 1961), pp. 257ff. for a discussion of this and similar points. Also George J. Stigler, *The Theory of Price*, Revised Edition (New York: The Macmillan Company, 1952) pp. 96-106 for an excellent discussion of costs.

6. Jean Marchal, "The Construction of a New Theory of Profit," *The American Economic Review*, Vol. XLI, No. 4 (September, 1951), 550. A profit concept similar to Marchal's, wherein it is argued that the compensation of certain executives of the firm should be included by economists as part of profit, is advanced by W. L. Crum, "Corporate Earnings on Invested Capital," *Harvard Business Review*, Vol. XVI (Spring, 1938) pp. 336-350. Reprinted in: American Economic Association, *Readings in the Theory of Income Distribution* (New York: McGraw-Hill Book Company, Inc., 1949) pp. 571-595.

7. Marchal, *op. cit.*, p. 550.

8. Cf. P. J. D. Wiles, *Price, Cost and Output* (Oxford: Basil Blackwell & Mott, Ltd., 1956), Chapter 2, especially pp. 183-184.

9. It must be remembered that we are here discussing "pure" profit even when we talk about rates of return. Thus, the rate of profit would be that rate of return over and above the rate of interest that could be obtained on—say—Government bonds. Cf., F. H. Knight, *Risk, Uncertainty and Profit* (Boston: Houghton Mifflin Company, 1921). (London School of Economics, Reprints of Scarce Works, No. 16), p. 304ff.

10. This does not mean that any one particular combination of assets should be continuously maintained. Instead, it is most probable that the combination will be continuously altered as the firm strives to maintain that changing asset structure which will produce the maximum income stream. The general formula for finding the present worth of a stream of future payments is:

$$A = \frac{P_1}{(1+i)} + \frac{P_2}{(1+i)^2} + \frac{P_3}{(1+i)^3} + \cdots + \frac{P_n}{(1+i)^n}$$

where P is receipts at end of periods 1, 2, 3, ... n, and i is the prevailing discount rate.

11. Cf. Norman S. Buchanan, *The Economics of Corporate Enterprise* (New York: Holt, Rinehart & Winston, Inc., 1940), Chapter 7 for an excellent discussion of the profit stream.

12. See William Fellner, *Competition Among the Few* (New York: Alfred A. Knopf, Inc., 1949), p. 158ff.

13. See Charles E. Johnson, "A Case Against the Idea of an All-Purpose Concept of Business Income," *The Accounting Review*, Vol. XXIX, No. 2 (April, 1954) especially pp. 224-243.

14. See the discussion in: P. L. Bernstein, "Profit Theory—Where Do We Go from Here?" *Quarterly Journal of Economics*, Vol. XLVII, August, 1953.

15. Cf. Buchanan, *op. cit.*, pp. 179-181; Robert Triffin, *Monopolistic Competition and General Equilibrium Theory*, Harvard Economic Studies, Vol. LXVII (Cambridge: Harvard University Press, 1940), pp. 179-187; J. Fred Weston, "Enterprise and Profit," *Journal of Business*, Vol. XXII, No. 3 (July, 1949), pp. 141-159.

16. Wiles, *op. cit.*, pp. 177-178.

17. To mention but two recent articles in which this controversy appeared: R. M. Davis, "The Current State of Profit Theory," *American Economic Review*, Vol. XLII, No. 3 (June, 1952), pp. 246-264; and J. Fred Weston, "The Profit Concept and Theory: A Restatement," *The Journal of Political Economy*, Vol. LXII, No. 2 (April, 1954), pp. 152-170.

18. Davis, *op. cit.*, pp. 251-252. James H Stauss, "The Entrepreneur: The Firm," *The Journal of Political Economy*, Vol. LII, No. 2 (June, 1944), 112-127.

19. Weston, *Journal of Political Economy, op. cit.*, pp. 162-163.

20. Triffin, *op. cit.*, p. 186.

21. See R. A. Gordon, "Enterprise, Profits, and the Modern Corporation," *Explorations in Economics* (New York: McGraw-Hill Book Company, Inc., 1936), pp. 306-316. Reprinted in American Economic Association, *Readings in the Theory of Income Distribution* (Homewood, Ill.: Richard D. Irwin, Inc., 1949), pp. 558-570.

22. Knight, *op. cit.*, p. 300.

23. Cf. John F. Due, *Intermediate Economic Analysis*, Revised Edition (Homewood, Ill.: Richard D. Irwin, Inc., 1951), p. 415, and M. M. Bober, *Intermediate Price and Income Theory* (New York: W. W. Norton & Company, Inc., 1955), pp. 425ff. However, Martin Bronfenbronner, "A Reformulation of Naive Profit Theory," *The Southern Economic Journal*, Vol. XXVII, No. 1 (July, 1960), writes: ". . . the attempt to locate within a corporate body any 'entrepreneur' with paramount claim to profit is to look in a dark room for a black cat which is not there," p. 301.

24. See H. S. Ellis, ed., *A Survey of Contemporary Economics* (New York: McGraw-Hill Book Company, Inc., 1949), Chapter 1, "Value and Distribution" by B. F. Haley, especially pp. 45-48.

25. Knight, *Risk, Uncertainty and Profit, op. cit.*

26. This can be, and has been, proved mathematically by Euler's theorem. See, for example, R. G. D. Allen, *Mathematical Analysis for Economists* (London: Macmillan & Co., Ltd., 1938), pp. 317-320.

27. Knight's theory is not properly a "functional" theory of profits, because profits are not considered a reward for doing something, but rather as a gift from the environment. It does, however, fall into the category of answers to our question: How do profits arise?

28. J. F. Weston's "A Generalized Uncertainty Theory of Profit," *The American Economic Review*, Vol. XL, No. 1 (March, 1950), pp. 40-60.

29. *Ibid.*, p. 49.

30. A. C. Pigou, *The Economics of Welfare*, (London: Macmillan & Co., Ltd., 1932), p. 771ff.

31. Marchal, *op. cit.*

32. C. A. Tuttle, "The Function of the Entrepreneur," *American Economic Review*, Vol. XVII (1927), 13-25.

33. R. A. Gordon, *Business Leadership in the Large Corporation* (Washington: Brookings Institution, 1945), especially Part III.

34. Joseph A. Schumpeter, *The Theory of Economic Development*, translated from the German by Redvers Opie (Cambridge: Harvard University Press, 1934).

35. Triffin, *op. cit.*, pp. 168-169.

36. F. Machlup, "Competition, Pliopoly and Profit," *Economica*, IX (February and May, 1942), pp. 15-17, 154-156; also E. H. Chamberlain, "Monopolistic or Imperfect Competition?" *Quarterly Journal of Economics* (1937).

37. See Anatol Murad, "An Uncertainty Theory of Profit: Comment," *The American Economic Review*, Vol. XLI, No. 1 (March, 1951), pp. 164-169.

38. If $C_m = R_m$ over a range of outputs the proper specific output is indeterminate, but we do know that businessmen should not reduce production to a point below $C_m = R_m$, where $R_m > C_m$, nor increase output to a position in excess of $C_m = R_m$, where $C_m > R_m$. See R. L. Bishop, "Cost Discontinuities, Declining Costs, and Marginal Analysis," *American Economic Review*, Vol. XXXVIII, No. 4 (September, 1948), pp. 607-617.

39. If we have a production function $q = f(x_1, x_2)$, this assumes that the amounts of x_1 and x_2 are so combined as to produce a maximum q. The marginal productivities of x_1 and x_2 are $\partial q/\partial x_1$ and $\partial q/\partial X_2$ respectively. For q to be a maximum, $\partial q/\partial x_1 = 0$ and $\partial q/\partial x_2 = 0$; that

$$\begin{vmatrix} \dfrac{\partial^2 q_2}{\partial x_1} & \dfrac{\partial^2 q}{\partial x_1 \partial x_2} \\ \dfrac{\partial^2 q}{\partial x_1 \partial x_2} & \dfrac{\partial^2 q_2}{\partial x_2} \end{vmatrix} > 0$$

and that $\partial^2 q_2/\partial x_1 < 0$; and $\partial^2 q_2/\partial x_2 < 0$.

40. We can *approach* the minimum cost mix through the use of Lagrange multipliers. We want to find the minimum expenditures on inputs needed to produce a certain output. However, this minimum must be obtained within the technological limits set by the production function. The production function, it will be recalled is:

$$q = f(x_1, x_2, x_3, \ldots x_n)$$

By transposing the q and multiplying that equation by our artificial variable λ, we have our constraint

$$\lambda[f(x_1, x_2, x_3, \ldots x_n) - q] = 0$$

To obtain our Lagrangian expression, we simply add this constraint to our cost function:

$$C_t = p_1 x_1 + p_2 x_2 + p_3 x_3 + \ldots + p_n x_n + \lambda[f(x_1, x_2, x_3, \ldots x_n) - q]$$

and minimize each expression in turn by setting its partial derivatives equal to zero, for example,

$$\frac{\partial c_t}{\partial x_1} = p_1 - \lambda \frac{\partial q}{\partial x_1} = 0, \ldots \frac{\partial c_t}{\partial x_n} = p_n - \lambda \frac{\partial q}{\partial x_n} = 0$$

These equations can be solved simultaneously to obtain minimum values of the x's and of the Lagrangian constraint λ. This, in turn, can be expressed as

$$\frac{\partial q/\partial x_1}{p_1} = \frac{1}{\lambda}, \ldots, \frac{\partial q/\partial x_n}{p_n} = \frac{1}{\lambda}$$

It is, therefore, evident that because all $\partial q/\partial x/p$ are equal to $\frac{1}{\lambda}$ they are equal to each other:

$$\frac{\partial q/\partial x_1}{p_1} = \frac{\partial q/\partial x_2}{p_2} = \frac{\partial q/\partial x_n}{p_n}$$

where $\partial q/\partial x_1$ is the marginal product of x_1, and so on.

41. The total cost function, therefore, is merely the production function with each input valued by multiplying it times its price. Thus,

$$C_t = p_1 x_1 + p_2 x_2 + p_3 x_3 + \ldots, + p_n x_n$$

as stated earlier.

42. This is often called the "expansion path." If costs at any level of output are minimized where

$$\frac{MPx_1}{MPx_2} = \frac{p_1}{p_2}$$

then a line drawn through all output points where $MPx_1 p_1 - MPx_2 = 0$ will be a minimum cost function for all output levels.

43. As usually drawn, the C_t function may be divided into three stages, from the vertical axis and moving to the right. In the first stage the first derivative dc_1/dq_1 is greater than the first derivative in the second stage

$$\frac{dc_2}{dq_2} \left(\frac{dc_1}{dq_1} > \frac{dc_2}{dq_2} \right)$$

which in turn is also smaller than the first derivative of the C_t curve in the third stage

$$\frac{dc_3}{dq_3} \left(\frac{dc_2}{dq_2} < \frac{dc_3}{dq_3} \right)$$

and dc_3/dq_3 is usually drawn as eventually greater than 1. ($dc_3/dq_3 > 1$). We could then write the slope of the C_t (or C_v) curve as:

$$\frac{dc_1}{dq_1} > \frac{dc_2}{dq_2} < \frac{dc_3}{dq_3}$$

44. Average variable costs, $C_v = f(q)/q$, and average fixed costs, $C_f = K/q$. There is an extensive literature on the "real and pertinent" shape of the average cost curve. To cite just a few articles on the "proper" shape of this function: A. H. Hansen, "Cost Functions and Full Employment," *American Economic Review*, Vol. XXXVII, No. 4 (September, 1947), pp. 551-565; W. J. Eiteman, "Factors Determining the Location of the Least Lost Point," *American Economic Review*, Vol. XXXVII, No. 5 (December, 1947), pp. 910-918; and H. Apel, "Marginal Cost Constancy and Its Implication," *American Economic Review*, Vol. XXXVIII, No. 5 (December, 1948), pp. 870-885.

45. The relationship between the C_a and C_m curves is specific, for the C_m curve always intersects the C_a curve from below at minimum C_a. If $a_1 = C_a$ for a specific q, take a to be the C_a for $q - 1$. As long as the C_m added at

$q-1$ is $<a$, $a_1 < a$, and C_a falls, with the C_m curve below the C_a curve (because $C_m > a$ at all such points), if C_m added at $q-1$ is $> a$, $a_1 > a$, and the C_a curve rises. Thus, $C_m = C_a$ at the minimum level of C_a.

46. Pure competition is much like perfect competition, with one most important difference. In perfect competition it is assumed that both buyers and sellers possess perfect knowledge.

47. Even though economists have puzzled over oligopolistic problems of at least two competitors (duopoly) for over 100 years. See: A. A. Cournot, *Researches into the Mathematical Principles of the Theory of Wealth*, first published in French in 1838, English translation (New York: The Macmillan Company, 1897).

48. This analysis of the kinked demand curve is based on: Paul M. Sweezy, "Demand Under Conditions of Oligopoly," *Journal of Political Economy*, Vol. XLVII (August, 1939). Reprinted in American Economic Association, *Readings in Price Theory* (Homewood, Ill.: Richard D. Irwin, Inc., 1952).

49. This has been termed a "reflex" demand curve, in contrast to the "obtusely" kinked curve illustrated in Figures 4 and 5(b).

50. These remarks are based on: C. W. Efroymson, "A Note on Kinked Demand Curves," *American Economic Review*, Vol. XXXIV, No. 1 (March, 1943), pp. 98-109. Reprinted in: Richard V. Clemence, editor, *Readings in Economic Analysis*, Vol. II (Cambridge: Addison-Wesley Press, Inc., 1950), pp. 218-229.

51. *Ibid.*, pp. 105-106.

52. *Ibid.*, p. 107.

53. George J. Stigler, "The Kinky Oligopoly Demand Curve and Rigid Prices," *Journal of Political Economy*, Vol. LV (October, 1947). Reprinted in American Economic Association, *Readings in Price Theory, op. cit.*

4

CRITICISMS OF THE ECONOMIC THEORY OF THE FIRM

The economic theory of the firm has been presented in its customary form in Chapter 3. Although most economists would agree that this sketch accurately portrays the traditional economic theory of business behavior, many would argue that it does not accurately reflect their own thinking on this subject, for there can be no question but that many economists have been highly dissatisfied with tradition, and have criticized this theory harshly. In this chapter we shall examine several of these criticisms and, for the most part, shall limit our study of criticisms of the economic theory of the firm to those made by fellow economists. As shall be seen, this limitation is not excessively confining, and in fact the boundaries set by proper chapter length rather than the paucity of economic criticisms will bring this chapter to an end.

It is possible to criticize the traditional economic theory of the firm within a variety of frameworks. For example, it could with some justification be stated that as a theory—*per se*—it does not lend itself to empirical testing for predictive purposes, and thus fails to possess one of the major attributes of any good theory. Such a methodological attack, however, although useful, would fail to come to grips with the behavioral problems inherent in this theory. Thus, it would also appear suitable that the economic theory of the firm be criticized on its economic content.

As Professor Boulding has observed, the two principal areas of criticism have been: (1) The failure to include in the theory either a sufficient number of variables or the proper variables, and (2) that firms do not, in fact, maximize profits.[1] Although a number of criticisms have been directed toward the first point, many of these are actually alternative theories of the behavior of the firm, and as such will be discussed principally in Chapter 4. The second prong of the attack, and perhaps the more basic criticism, has been directed along two major themes: (a) that firms, in reality, do not maximize profits and (b) that firms cannot maximize profits, even if they desired this goal, because of uncertainty.[2] These criticisms, of course, may be summarized simply by stating that many economists feel that economic theory is not sufficiently realistic. To be sure, all theories are simplifications—abstractions from the real world, but the point of complaint is that the traditional theory does not in fact abstract from reality. It has not been built upon empirical research, but instead is based upon the activities of imaginative individuals whose interests lie in the realm of theory construction rather than the observation of business behavior.

VARIABLES—NUMBER AND PROPRIETY

Human nature is variable, even in business situations. The examination of external business activities and appearances offers a variety of clues to a variety of observers about internal motivation and goals. It is little wonder, therefore, that some economists, observing business operations, have reached conclusions which differ from those established by tradition. Many critics have, for example, stressed the need for a theory of business behavior that contains a wider range of goals and other variables than the single goal of profit maximization and the assumption of rationality. The notion of multiple goals, furthermore, seems to correspond to the findings of many psychologists, who would consider a single-goaled individual to be, in fact, most unusual.

In this section, then, modifications of traditional economic theory are discussed wherein either different variables are utilized or the number of variables is increased, or both. Because the addition of new or more variables to the theory in effect produces a different theory, several of the major contributions along these lines will be postponed until the next chapter, in which alternative economic theories are presented. However, we shall discuss several points here.

The Scitovsky Modification

A modification of the traditional economic theory of the firm which is illustrative of a model with a small increase in the number of variables is that presented by Tibor Scitovsky.[3] In Scitovsky's alteration the second variable introduced is leisure or business inactivity. The entrepreneur, depending upon his character, may elect to maximize his profits and forgo his leisure, or to choose total business inactivity and give up all profits, or he may decide on some combination of the two.[4]

Figure 7 below illustrates how total receipts and costs may increase

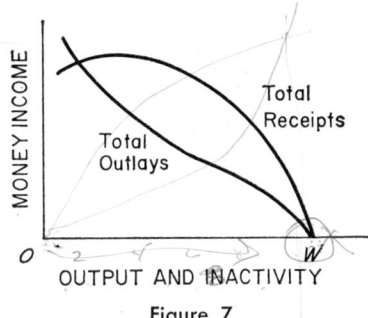

Figure 7

as an entrepreneur becomes more active. The entrepreneur's money income is measured on the vertical axis, and output and leisure on the horizontal axis. "W" indicates that point where the entrepreneur is completely inactive in his business, output is zero, and where his income from it is zero. As we move toward the origin from W, where output is zero, and as the entrepreneur becomes more and more active, total outlay, receipts, and output increase. Entrepreneurial activity is, of course, measured in terms of units of output.

Figure 8 below shows the relationship between the entrepreneur's net

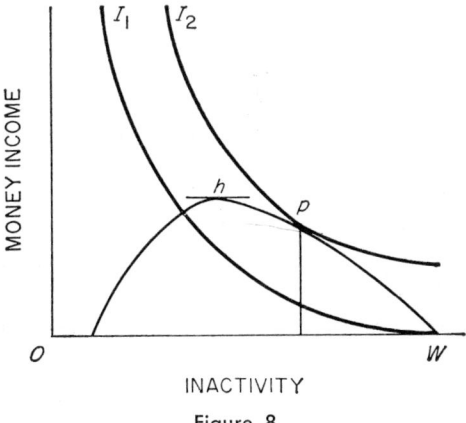

Figure 8

income, derived from the difference between total receipts and outlays in Figure 7, and his indifference map between leisure and income. The p, where the entrepreneur's indifference curve I_2 is tangent to the net income curve, represents the entrepreneur's point of maximum satisfaction. However, it may be observed in Figure 8 that "p" is not, and "h" is, the point of maximum profits. In order for an indifference curve to be tangential to "h" it would have to be horizontal or almost horizontal at this point. This would mean that the entrepreneur would have to have indifference curves which sloped differently from those presented in Figure 7. In effect, if the entrepreneur is to maximize profits, his interest in work must be so intense that it is unaffected by his income level. He must be willing to put forth a continued and sustained effort even after his standard of living has risen substantially. He must desire success—measured in terms of money income—for its own sake.

Scitovsky points out that early capitalist entrepreneurs probably possessed the psychological attributes which enabled them to maximize profits.[5] He also argues that the modern day entrepreneur probably also maximizes profits, and thus profit maximization is a useful hypothesis.[6]

Critique of the profit-leisure dichotomy. The Scitovsky modification of the profit maximization motive assumes that only the unique entrepreneur will maximize profits. Other men, possessing more "normal" indifference curves, will attempt to maximize their satisfactions from both leisure and money income at a level which will not coincide with the level where profits are greatest.

There have been many criticisms of the hypothesis advanced by Professor Scitovsky. For example, leisure need not be directly in conflict with money income for many businessmen. The extended holidays in Florida or Europe taken by these men may not necessarily reduce the profits obtained by their concerns. Even more significant, the amount of leisure may have become of less importance in our modern society than "better" (more expensive) leisure.[7] There is danger in equating leisure with idleness. There are quality differences in leisure time activities that complicate Scitovsky's simple comparisons. A rise in leisure today may imply an increase in monetary expenditures on leisure goods and activities rather than longer leisure time. This may mean, further, that the size of entrepreneurial income may be contingent upon expenditure patterns, rather than the other way around.[8]

Finally, Nettl has argued that if the consumption of profits is divorced from the making of profits, it is more likely that these may be maximized.[9] This occurs most frequently in the large corporation, where salaried executives are interested in making, but not having profits, so that their leisure is not substitutable for their money income.[10]

Profits Versus Control

Let us examine one more alternative theory at length, prior to setting forth more briefly a number of criticisms. Like Scitovsky's hypothesis, this alternative too is based upon the premise that at least some businessmen do not maximize profits because they have another goal which is desirable, and which acts as a restraint upon their maximizing behavior.

Assume that an entrepreneur has two objectives: (a) to maximize profits and (b) to maintain his financial control of the firm.[11] If his control is in jeopardy, the entrepreneur will do all in his power to retain his position of power. Figure 9 below illustrates this situation. The point

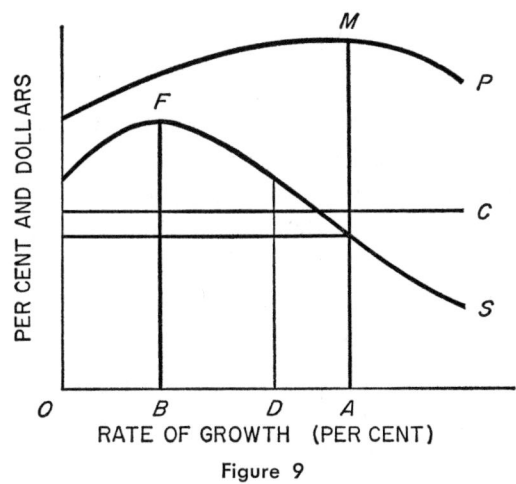

Figure 9

of this diagram is essentially this: if the firm is to grow at its maximum rate (so that the present value of the firm's net worth is maximized) the entrepreneur will be forced to lose control, because he will have to obtain large amounts of loan or equity capital from external sources. Therefore, he will not maximize profits, but rather will sacrifice this rate of growth for a slower one that will permit him to finance the firm's expansion from his own funds or from retained earnings.

In the diagram above, the vertical axis measures both the percentage of the firm's total assets that will be owned by the entrepreneur at some time (t_1) in the future, assuming growth between now (t_0) and t_1, and the present value of the firm's net worth at t_1. On the horizontal axis the average rate of growth, measured by the percentage increase in the firm's assets between t_0 and t_1, is given.[12] Reder assumes there will be some average growth rate, OA (imagine this to be, say, 10 per cent) which will maximize the present value of the firm's net worth at t_1, as illustrated by the line AM. The S curve indicates the percentage of the firm's assets to be owned by the entrepreneur at t_1, as a function of the average rate of expansion between t_0 and t_1. At a rate of growth OB (imagine perhaps 2 per cent), this percentage of ownership will be at a maximum, as the entrepreneur invests his slowly accruing savings and retained earnings. At any more rapid rate of growth than OB the rate of increase in the entrepreneur's ownership share will decrease, for funds are needed from external sources for more rapid rates of expansion. The horizontal line C indicates the minimum percentage of ownership which the entrepreneur feels he must maintain in order to retain his control over the firm.[13] The height of C is determined, says Reder, by a number of forces, among which are:

> (1) the ratio of equity capital to debt; the greater this ratio, the greater will be the height of C; (2) the distribution of the ownership of the equity capital; the smaller the percentage owned by any one person or group (other than the entrepreneur) the lower will be C; (3) the greater the likelihood of losses sufficient to bring the firm to the verge of bankruptcy, the greater will be C, and so on.[14]

Thus, if the entrepreneur, faced with the situation detailed in Figure 9, must choose between profit maximization and a loss of control, or a slower rate of growth, positive (but not maximum) profits, and control; Reder assumes that the entrepreneur will select the latter alternative.

This analysis is, of course, not without its flaws. Among other things, this alternative theory applies only in somewhat unique circumstances where profit maximization conflicts with entrepreneurial control.[15] There is also the problem of determining the proper height of C—the line of minimum desired control. Although Reder's comments, quoted earlier, are helpful in establishing C, they are not adequate in pinpointing this level. Finally, an aura of omniscience surrounds the entrepreneur in this model: the assumptions of knowledge of proper rates of firm growth, minimum control levels, conflict of growth rates and control, and so on, which are rarely descriptive of real life business situations with their attendant uncertainties and confused information flows.

Other Variables

K. W. Rothschild has argued that the desire for secure profits is probably as strong a motive as profit maximization for businessmen operating in oligopolistic industries.[16] As one piece of evidence substantiating the secure profit motive, Rothschild points to the reinvestment of profits in the firm, even though more profitable investment opportunities exist elsewhere. A similar alternative has been suggested by William Fellner, who claims that firms are interested more in "safety margins"—the difference between unit price and average unit costs—than in optimizing profits.[17]

By maintaining the largest possible gap between unit prices and costs the firm minimizes the harmful effects of possible price declines or cost increases. Because prices in this case will be higher than in the traditional firm, not as many units will be sold, and profits will not be maximized.[18]

Other variables, similar to those discussed above, include such items as the maintenance of the firm's share of the market;[19] liquidity sufficient to assure the firm's financial position;[20] growth;[21] and a perfectionist efficiency which interferes with the attainment of maximum profits.[22] On another level are such variables as "satisfactory" profits, an objective which ordinarily is considered to be diametrically opposed to profit maximization. This variable will be discussed at greater length in following chapters.

There are a number of variables which, observers have claimed, supersede or modify the profit motive because of the human qualities of entrepreneurs. Managers, for example, may desire economic power as exemplified by size, and may push output beyond the point of maximum profits.[23] Or the desire for "empire building" may lead departmental managers to expand the size of their staffs unnecessarily, thus complicating the organization, and rendering it unable to maximize profits.[24] It has been suggested, furthermore, that a businessman has motives which may be summed up as a bundle of satisfactions which he tries to maximize, and which he may obtain from pecuniary profits, security, craftsmanship, independence, and similar variables.[25] However, if he maximizes any one of these he cannot maximize the others. Along these lines, it is also quite possible that the growing interest in the "social responsibilities" of businessmen (although it has sometimes been argued that such interests are intended to further long-run profits) may actually deflect executive actions from profit-making.[26] Certainly, as Richard Eels has observed, it is difficult to determine whether corporate gifts to educational institutions constitute altruism or long-run profit maximization.[27]

Summary

These, then, have been some of the alternative goals suggested by economic revisionists. None of these alternative hypotheses have been widely accepted, and most of them resemble burned out Christmas-tree bulbs—their brief and transitory moment of glory lost in the glow of the star of profit maximization which remains bright and secure at the top of the tree.

It should be noted that not all these alternatives operate with profit maximization in the same manner. Some of these theories do not seek to deny the importance of the profit motive, but they do deny its primacy, and set forth other objectives as being of equal importance. Still other alternatives are utilized to replace the profit motive, or to discard it or relegate it to a position of lesser importance. Finally, there are those critics who would prefer to see profits placed in proper perspective as part of the businessman's preference function, with its position subjectively ascertained through introspection, but not to be questioned by the observer.

Still, the search for alternative objectives for business behavior is by no means a worthless or lost cause. There is little evidence, of course, that these are "better" for predictive purposes than traditional theory; but then again, profit maximization has not proved to be as convincing a predictor of business behavior as one might desire. The very unrest and dissatisfaction with the goal of optimum profits, and the development of alternative objectives is a healthy sign in any scientific endeavor, for it reflects the pursuit of truth—that will-o'-the-wisp which lies always just beyond the present state of knowledge in all sciences.

BUSINESS FIRMS DO NOT MAXIMIZE

In this section we shall try to recapitulate the arguments, presented largely by economists, that firms do not maximize profits. The emphasis herein is on the word maximize rather than on profits. As we shall see, these criticisms are for the most part destructive, and often the critics do not suggest substitutes for profit maximization.

The Failure to Maximize

For over two decades a number of economists have argued categorically that business firms simply do not maximize profits. Ordinarily they have based their objections upon their observations of the activities of businessmen. One of the earliest criticisms was advanced in a study by Oxford economists in 1939, and resulted from their examination of a number of British concerns.[28]

The marginal controversy. In 1946 Richard A. Lester's well-known article critical of marginal analysis began what has since been termed the "marginal controversy," which, like a ravenous bookworm, devoured huge parts of the economic journals in the late 1940's.[29] This article was followed in quick succession by rebuttals by Malchup,[30] and Stigler,[31] by a rejoinder by Lester,[32] and by the further involvement of still others in the controversy. This series set forth a pattern which was to be frequently followed in later years: the attack on the theory of the firm, no matter how apt or how inept, has always called forth a militant defense of traditional theory.

Although Lester's paper was based on woefully weak statistical foundations, it did represent an attempt to arrive at empirically derived conclusions. Like Hall and Hitch in 1939, Lester deduced from his survey that marginal analysis was not used in business decision making. For example, he tentatively concluded that: "In modern manufacturing, a firm's level of costs per unit of product is influenced considerably by the scale of output; the reverse as assumed by conventional marginalism, is not generally true."[33] He also, as a final illustration of his results, argued that his statistics indicated that businessmen considered marginal analysis impractical as an operating principle in the multi-process complexities of modern business enterprises.[34]

The least cost argument. A critique of traditional economic theory allied to that presented by Professor Lester has been offered by Wilford J. Eiteman of the University of Michigan.[35] It will be recalled from Chapter 3 that the least cost point in the theory of the firm is that level of output where average costs are at a minimum. At this quantity the U-shaped average cost curve is cut from below by the marginal cost curve. The AC curve declines until the least cost point is reached, and the MC function lies below the AC function at all levels of output less than this. It is Eiteman's surmise that the least cost point in traditional theory is assumed to be reached far to the left of capacity output, and the MC curve then (in almost any economic environment) cuts the MR curve at the most profitable output. This hypothesis is illustrated for a firm in an imperfect market structure by the AC_1, MC_1, AR, and MR curves in Figure 10. Under these cost and demand conditions the most profitable output will be OA, where $MC_1 = MR$. Now, continues Eiteman, engineers will customarily design plants so that the least cost point is attained at capacity output, as described by the AC_2 curve in Figure 10, where MC_2 comes up to intercept AC_2. Here the output, because it

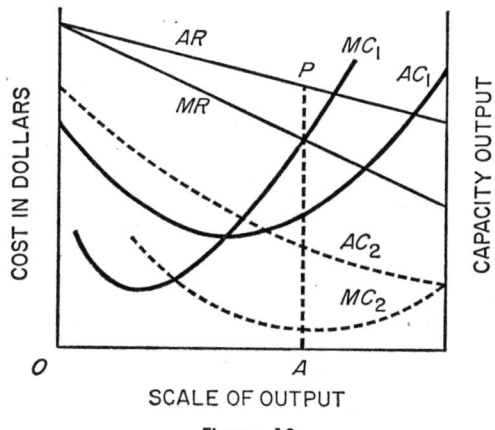

Figure 10

is at capacity, cannot be expanded further, and $MR > MC_2$. Eiteman then concludes:

> ... They may assume, what most businessmen believe to be a fact, that the efficiency of the variable factor is customarily greatest at or near the point of capacity output, in which event businessmen do not determine their scale of operations by reference to marginal cost and revenues at all: they simply produce all that they can sell.[36]

Thus, businessmen do not maximize in the manner (via marginal analysis) assumed in the traditional economic theory of the firm.[37]

Other attacks on the maximization principles. Many other students of business, for a variety of reasons, have also claimed that businessmen do not maximize profits. One of the most recent critics, Professor R. N. Anthony, has evidently based his remarks on his observations of business operations and a review of the literature.[38] Anthony points to several business practices which he feels are incompatible with profit maximization. The practices of cost accounting, separation payments to discharged employees, capital budgeting by businessmen, and even the lawns around plants are seen to be inconsistent with profit maximization.[39] He concludes that profit maximization is (1) too difficult, and (2) immoral.[40]

Henry Oliver notes several instances where business behavior is evidently at odds with marginal theory. He does not, for example, believe that businessmen have to calculate, even roughly, marginal costs or revenues to maximize profits. He does not feel that there is any positive evidence in favor of marginal theory. Finally, he does not think that marginal theory—regardless of how loosely it is interpreted—can account for the rarity of price changes among actual business firms.[41]

The rigidities of real life business organizations may also lead to a failure to maximize. For example, management may not wish to disturb the nonprofit maximizing routines of subordinates, for to do so will make them resentful. Even more important is the likelihood that subordinates may fear to suggest improvements which might disturb the routines of their superiors.[42]

R. A. Gordon has argued that conventional theory does not explain business behavior because it fails to encompass either a sufficient number of variables or to take account of the continuous changes which confront businessmen.[43] Executives must use short-cuts in real life situations, for the number of variables is so large that it is humanly impossible to use marginal analysis.[44] In the same way, changes occur so frequently and in so many different directions that businessmen cannot possibly adjust marginally for them.[45]

Other arguments by other authors could also be advanced to indicate the diversity of attacks on marginalism. However, a sufficient number of criticisms, we should imagine, have been noted to give the reader the impression that a segment of the economics profession does not approve of the principles of marginal analysis as an adequate explanation of business behavior.

Maximization and Uncertainty

The significant period for business executives is the future, for it is the only period about which anything worthwhile can be done. The past is changeless and, of course, the present—that brief fleeting moment between the past and the future—is already gone. Unfortunately, the future can never be known with certainty. One cannot, in making a typical business decision, know exactly what the outcome will be. It is true that, when the future becomes part of the past, only one outcome from a decision has occurred, but this is of little comfort to the executive who is trying to ascertain in the present this future outcome. Furthermore, it is generally assumed that the most important business decisions are undertaken in a fog of uncertainty, which means that business executives do not even know the probabilities that certain outcomes will occur. In a world in which uncertainty prevails the voice of the economist shouting maximize, or the desire of the businessman to maximize does not offer much in the way of a specific prescription which tells executives how to maximize.[46]

At the heart of most criticisms based on uncertainty, therefore, is the assumption that businessmen cannot maximize (except by chance) even if this is their motive. Firms do not maximize except in those rare instances when coincidence or luck intervenes. Even if the theory is interpreted more properly to be that businessmen try to—rather than necessarily do—maximize profits, uncertainty critics would state that this has little utility as a description, prescription, or predictive device for business behavior. Businessmen do not know, it is argued, which of the limited number of alternative courses of action which they perceive open to them will maximize profits, or what the probability of success of any decision will be. Under such conditions the notion of maximization becomes meaningless.

THE DEFENSE OF PROFIT MAXIMIZATION

Critics of conventional economic theory have met with heavy opposition from defenders of tradition. Setting forth the criticisms of theory in detailed fashion is somewhat like stepping onto a merry-go-round, for these criticisms have led to rebuttals by orthodox economists, then to replies by the critics, and to further rejoinders by defenders, and so on. Rather than go through this endless sequence of debate, we shall try to discuss the defense of orthodox theory in general terms.

The Methodological Defense

The first, and at this time the most important defense of the traditional economic theory of the firm concerns the methodology of theory construction and destruction, and is based upon Friedman's discussion on positive economics.[47] Briefly, it is Friedman's position that the purpose of a theory is to predict or explain the behavior of specific phenomena, and that the assumptions of a theory are necessarily unrealistic, and cannot be judged against reality.[48] The point is, therefore, that defenders of the traditional theory argue that its assumption of profit maximization cannot fruitfully be attacked as unrealistic, for it makes little difference whether profit maximization is realistic or descriptive, as long as the theory predicts or explains business behavior.[49] And traditional theory has been successful as a predictive device, claims Friedman.

The Traditional Assumptions Are Reasonable

As a part of the marginalist controversy in the late 1940's, Professor Fritz Machlup wrote an article in defense of marginal theory which has become a classic of sorts, although many economists today would probably disagree with Machlup's arguments.[50] Briefly, he took the then unique position that the relevant variables in marginal analysis are "subjective" rather than "objective." Costs, revenues, and profits are merely perceived or fancied by businessmen. "Marginal analysis of the firm should not be understood to imply anything but subjective estimates, guesses, and hunches."[51] In effect this approach treats the entrepreneur as a consumer who maximizes his satisfactions by doing what he wants to do. The defense of Machlup, therefore, is that the assumptions of traditional theory are reasonable. Unfortunately, the subjective approach to marginal analysis turns the theory of the firm into a tautology.

James Earley, on the other hand, has tried to demonstrate through empirical research that the assumptions of traditional economic theory are both reasonable and realistic.[52] Through a survey of 110 manufacturing companies rated as "excellently managed" by the American Institute of Management, Professor Earley inquired into accounting practices, organizational structures, and management operations. He found that these firms utilized what he terms "marginal" accounting methods which are informative for ascertaining incremental amounts and values. He concludes: ". . . Marginal accounting and costing principles have a strong hold among these companies, and the bulk of them also follow pricing, marketing, new product, and product investment policies that are in essential respects marginalist." [53] In other words, his investigations have convinced him that these selected enterprises use marginal analysis, and that "their influence is likely to be strongly in the direction of growing 'marginalism' in American enterprise." [54]

The survey by Earley, upon which his conclusion that respondent firms used marginal analysis is based, was conducted by mail, and contained questions that were only indirectly concerned with business behavior. The results of this study, therefore, are in the nature of inferences drawn from indirect evidence on what businessmen report that they do, rather than on direct observations of behavior. This inferential approach relies heavily upon the *interpretation* of data which seems to be tenuously related to the pertinent marginal variables of traditional economic theory.

Unlike Friedman's position, therefore, in which assumptions don't matter as long as the theory has utility as a predictive device, both Machlup and Earley attempt to defend marginal analysis by arguing the intrinsic merit and validity of the assumptions.

Other Defenses

It has been said that the best defense is attack, and economists have severely criticized publications by revisionists, stressing the weaknesses of these proposals. In fact, the replies attacking antitraditional arguments have perhaps been the strongest, and most frequently used line of defense.

One of the defenses often used is that which emphasizes the simplicity of the traditional model and the complexities and (sometimes) the vagueness of the alternative. It is claimed that, for example, the new proposals cannot be manipulated in an analytical fashion. Profit maximization offers the theorist a model which describes behavior in a quantitative and definite manner. Given the proper magnitudes of the pertinent variables an observer can predict exactly what the result should be, if it is assumed that businessmen use marginal analysis.[55] This sort of definiteness is of utility for theoretical purposes, even if it is unrealistic to assume that businessmen actually do behave in the fashion described by theory.

SUMMARY

In this chapter we have examined a wide variety of critiques of the traditional economic theory of business behavior. Despite the diversity and number of criticisms, one cannot but feel a sense of dissatisfaction with their scope and nature. Although it is true that the economic theory of the firm seems to describe a make believe world far removed from the everyday confusion of business, at least it is satisfying as an abstract model—a neat and simple theory which is internally consistent and logically cohesive. In comparison, the alternatives presented and the criticisms noted herein are neither elegant nor universal. Their very number, perhaps, is overwhelming, and causes each to be viewed with suspicion. Nevertheless, the fact that there exist so many alternatives and so many criticisms of orthodox theory leads one to believe that there is a good deal of discontent among economists with the latter. This discontent, we believe, is indicative of a widespread and general attitude which permeates below the superficial simplicity of the economic theory of the firm, and questions the validity of its usefulness as a description of business processes and a predictor of business behavior. Traditional theory, it would seem that most of the critics are saying, just does not coincide with what is observed in business situations, and neither helps to explain nor to foresee the alternative choices, the goals, or the outcomes of business decisions.

Notes and References

1. K. E. Boulding, "Implications for General Economics of More Realistic Theories of the Firm," *American Economic Review,* Vol. XLII, No. 2 (May, 1952), p. 35.

2. *Ibid.,* p. 36.

3. Tibor Scitovsky, "A Note of Profit Maximization and Its Implications," *The Review of Economic Studies,* Vol. XI (1943), pp. 57-60.

4. Actually, the argument that businessmen may not maximize profits because they desire leisure may be traced back through Benjamin Higgins' article, "Elements of Indeterminacy in the Theory of Non-Perfect Competition," *American Economic Review* (September, 1939), pp. 476-477, to the oft-quoted remark by J. R. Hicks in "Annual Survey of Economic Theory, The Theory of Monopoly," *Econometrica* (January, 1935), p. 8, "The best of all monopoly profits is a quiet life."

5. Scitovsky, *op. cit.,* p. 59.

6. *Ibid.,* p. 60.

7. J. P. Nettl, "A Note on Entrepreneurial Behavior," *The Review of Economic Studies,* Vol. XXIV (2), No. 64, February, 1957, p. 92.

8. *Ibid.,* p. 93.

9. *Ibid.,* p. 90.

10. George Katona, among others, would seem to agree with this analysis. He remarks: "As a rule, a salaried executive will strive for profits for his firm." *Psychological Analysis of Economic Behavior.* (New York: McGraw-Hill Book Company, 1951), p. 197.

11. This section is based largely upon M. W. Reder, "A Reconsideration of the Marginal Productivity Theory," *Journal of Political Economy* (October, 1947), pp. 450-458, copyright 1947 by The University of Chicago.

12. *Ibid.*, p. 455.

13. What we have here, of course, is a constrained maximum problem, analogous to Baumol's thesis, to be explored in Chapter 5. It can also be solved through the use of Lagrange multipliers.

14. Reder, *op. cit.*, p. 456.

15. It would be possible to use Reder's analysis with any one of a number of variables in place of "control." For example, line C could represent leisure, liquidity, efficiency in operations, or any other variable that might be a restraint on profit maximization.

16. K. W. Rothschild, "Price Theory and Oligopoly," *Economic Journal* (September, 1947), pp. 299-320.

17. William Fellner, "Average Cost Pricing and the Theory of Uncertainty," *Journal of Political Economy* (June, 1948), pp. 249-252.

18. Unless the price and cost changes are actually anticipated rather than merely feared, in which case the output level selected may well be that which maximizes profits.

19. This objective, and the others mentioned in this sentence, are discussed by a number of authors, and the citations given are merely intended to be illustrative. For example, "Share of the Market" is presented in Neil Chamberlain, *A General Theory of Economic Process* (New York: Harper & Row, Publishers, 1955), pp. 217-250.

20. A. Lester, "Equilibrium of the Firm," *American Economic Review* (March, 1949), p. 483.

21. George Katona, *op. cit.*, p. 203.

22. George Leland Bach, *Economics: An Introduction to Analysis and Policy* (Englewood Cliffs, N. J.: Prentice-Hall, Inc., 1954), p. 339.

23. P. J. D. Wiles, *Price, Cost and Output* (Oxford: Basil Blackwell & Mott, Ltd., 1956), pp. 180-181.

24. George L. Bach, *Economics*, 3rd ed. (Englewood Cliffs, N.J.: Prentice-Hall, Inc., 1960), p. 334.

25. John R. Meyer, "The Import of Some New Developments in Economic Theory: Exposition and Evaluation" (discussion), *American Economic Review* (May, 1957), p. 336.

26. Joel Dean, *Managerial Economics* (Englewood Cliffs, N. J.: Prentice-Hall, Inc., 1951), p. 33.

27. Richard Eels, *The Meaning of Modern Business* (New York: Columbia University Press, 1960), pp. 71-72.

28. R. L. Hall and C. J. Hitch, "Price Theory and Business Behavior," *Oxford Economic Papers*, No. 2 (May, 1939). The "full-cost" theory of pricing was an anti-marginalist doctrine, and perhaps was the most significant result of this article.

29. Richard A. Lester, "Shortcomings of Marginal Analysis for Wage-Employment Problems," *American Economic Review*, Vol. XXXVI, No. 1 (March, 1946), pp. 63-82.

30. F. Machlup, "Marginal Analysis and Empirical Research," *American Economic Review*, Vol. XXXVI, No. 4 (September, 1946), pp. 519-554.

31. George J. Stigler, "The Economics of Minimum Wage Legislation," *American Economic Review*, Vol. XXXVI, No. 3 (June, 1946), pp. 358-365.

32. Richard A. Lester, "Marginalism, Minimum Wages, and Labor Markets," *American Economic Review*, Vol. XXXVII, No. 1 (March, 1947), pp. 135-148.

33. *Ibid.*, p. 81.

34. *Ibid.*, p. 82.

35. Wilford J. Eiteman, "Factors Determining the Location of the Least Cost Point," *American Economic Review*, Vol. XXXVII, No. 5 (December, 1947), pp. 910-918.

36. *Ibid.*, p. 913.

37. This article by Eiteman is only one of many on the correct shape of cost curves. A few of the other articles on this matter are: A. H. Hansen, "Cost Functions and Full Employment," *American Economic Review*, Vol. XXXVII, No. 4 (September, 1947), pp. 552-565; Hans Apel, "Marginal Cost Constancy and Its Implications," *American Economic Review*, Vol. XXXVIII, No. 5 (December, 1948), pp. 870-885; G. J. Stigler, "Production and Distribution in the Short Run," *Journal of Political Economy*, Vol. 47 (June, 1939), pp. 312-322; and Hans Staehle, "Statistical Cost Functions: Appraisal of Recent Contributions," *American Economic Review*, Vol. XXXII, No. 2, Part 2 (June, 1942), pp. 321-332.

38. Robert N. Anthony, "The Trouble with Profit Maximization," *Harvard Business Review*, Vol. 38, No. 6 (November-December, 1960), pp. 126-134.

39. *Ibid.*, pp. 130-131.

40. *Ibid.*, p. 134.

41. This paragraph is based on H. M. Oliver, Jr., "Marginal Theory and Business Behavior," *American Economic Review,* Vol. XXXVII, No. 3 (June, 1947), pp. 375-383.

42. Reder, *op. cit.,* p. 452.

43. R. A. Gordon, "Short-Period Price Determination in Theory and Practice," *American Economic Review,* Vol. XXXVIII, No. 3 (June, 1948), pp. 265-288.

44. *Ibid.,* p. 267.

45. *Ibid.*

46. Stephen Enke, "On Maximizing Profits: A Distinction Between Chamberlain and Robinson," *American Economic Review,* Vol. XLI, No. 4 (September, 1951), pp. 566-578.

47. See the discussion in Chapter 1.

48. Friedman, *op. cit.,* p. 41.

49. Some of the publications pro and con Friedman's position are: T. C. Coopmans, *Three Essays on the State of Economic Science* (New York: McGraw-Hill Book Company, Inc., 1957); E. Rotwein, "In the Methodology of Positive Economics," *Quarterly Journal of Economics,* Vol. LXXIII (November, 1959), pp. 554-575; Diran Bodenhorn, "A Note on the Theory of the Firm," and Julius Margolis, "Traditionalist and Revisionist Theories of the Firm: A Comment," both in *The Journal of Business,* Vol. XXXII, No. 2 (April, 1959), pp. 164-174, and pp. 178-182 respectively; and Andreas G. Papandreou, *Economics as a Science* (Philadelphia: J. B. Lippincott Co., 1958).

50. Machlup, *op. cit.* Perhaps the statement that many economists would disagree with Machlup's approach is too strong. It may be that the subjective view is gaining ground. See, for example, J. de V. Graff, "Income Effects and the Theory of the Firm," *The Review of Economic Studies,* Vol. XVII, No. 2 (February, 1955).

51. *Ibid.,* p. 522.

52. James S. Earley, "Marginal Policies of 'Excellently Managed' Companies," *American Economic Review,* Vol. XLVI, No. 1 (March, 1956), pp. 44-70. See also his article: "Recent Developments in Cost Accounting and the 'Marginal Analysis,'" *Journal of Political Economics,* Vol. XLII (June, 1955), pp. 227-242.

53. *Ibid.,* p. 66.

54. *Ibid.,* p. 67.

55. See, for example, Andreas G. Papandreou, and John T. Wheeler, *Competition and Its Regulation* (Englewood Cliffs, N. J.: Prentice-Hall, Inc., 1954), p. 73.

5

ALTERNATIVE ECONOMIC THEORIES

In this chapter we shall explore a number of theories of business behavior proposed by economists disenchanted with the traditional economic theory of the firm. Disenchantment is the keynote to progress in all disciplines. However, the mere presence of dissatisfaction does not automatically produce improvement—especially in the social sciences.

Change in the behavioral sciences is rarely as dramatic as in the physical sciences, and revolutions occur infrequently. Major advances in the former disciplines depend not only upon the merit of the new concept, but often are also contingent upon the manner and place and time of its presentation, upon the obstinacy with which the old ideas refuse to yield to the new, and upon the reputation of the promoter of the innovation. Thus, even the so-called "revolutions" in, for example, economics, are more frequently evolutionary, with modifications occurring tortuously and gradually, much like water falling drop-by-drop upon the hard rock of conventional wisdom.

At present, then, the situation in the economics of business behavior is this: (1) Change is taking place. (2) Conventional theory remains strongly resistant to change. (3) Alternative theories have appeared, and some of these have gained support. (4) As yet, however, no alternative has proved to possess the attributes necessary to replace tradition. Nevertheless, there appears to be discontent with the conventional economic theory of the firm, and alternatives seem to be proposed today in greater numbers than in past years. In Chapter 4 we examined the reasons for dissatisfaction: here we shall examine a number of alternatives.

THE MAXIMIZATION OF VARIABLES OTHER THAN PROFIT

Profit, as distinguished from profit maximization, is considered by many business scholars to be too entrenched and too vital a variable to be omitted completely as a goal for business operations. Many alternative theories of business behavior, therefore, are constructed to include profits as one of the objectives of the firm; but the environment is ordinarily altered in these theories so that it is improbable or irrational to expect that profits will be maximized in the traditional sense. In this section we shall examine a few of the alternative theories of business which introduce new variables into the economic model, and by so doing change the framework of assumptions within which the more conventional theorist operates.

Sales Maximization

Professor William J. Baumol of Princeton University has recently advanced the thesis that oligopolistic enterprises seek to maximize their total revenues subject to a profit constraint.[1] Baumol arrives at this conclusion from his long-term observations of oligopolistic behavior in certain industries in the United States, and not from formal empirical research.

If businessmen do tend to maximize sales subject to a profit constraint, what sort of theoretical framework evolves? First, it should be stressed that sales in Baumol's theory do not refer to the physical volume of goods sold, but rather to the dollar volume of sales $[pq$ (= total revenue)]. Second, it is evident that the desired level of economic profits must equal or exceed zero ($\pi \geq 0$) and in the long-run, for should they be less than zero resources would leave the firm and it would have to go out of business. However, this last point is rather vague, for it says that profits must be zero or greater, but does not establish the exact level for profits, that is, it sets minimum acceptable limits rather than minimum desirable limits for profits. Baumol has tried to refine this concept by emphasizing that profits must be adequate to satisfy stockholders with acceptable earnings, and to permit management to retain those amounts they consider sufficient for investment for future expansion.[2]

Given these hypotheses, how does a profit maximizing firm's behavior differ from that of an enterprise in which the goal is sales maximization? The difference is illustrated in Figure 11.

If a firm were to maximize profits, it would produce at output OQ_p, for at this output $TR - TC$ is greatest. The sales maximization output, however, is OQ_s, where TR is largest. If sales maximization is to take place subject to a profit constraint—say, profit level O_{p2} is that required to satisfy stockholders and to retain a desired volume of profits for future expansion—then the output will be OQ_c.[3] This level of output will not ordinarily be the same as that at which either profits or sales are a maximum.[4]

It would be possible to go into greater detail in exploring the sales maximization model. However, the major features have been set forth above. For a number of reasons, Baumol concludes that businessmen will tend to increase output to the point where total revenues are maximized within the constraint of a minimum profit. He believes that this objective is more in accord with the actual goals and operations of business concerns than is the model of profit maximization.

One major weakness of the sales maximization hypothesis lies in the proper construction of the profit constraint. The forces sustaining minimum desired profits surely change over time, and probably are different for each enterprise.

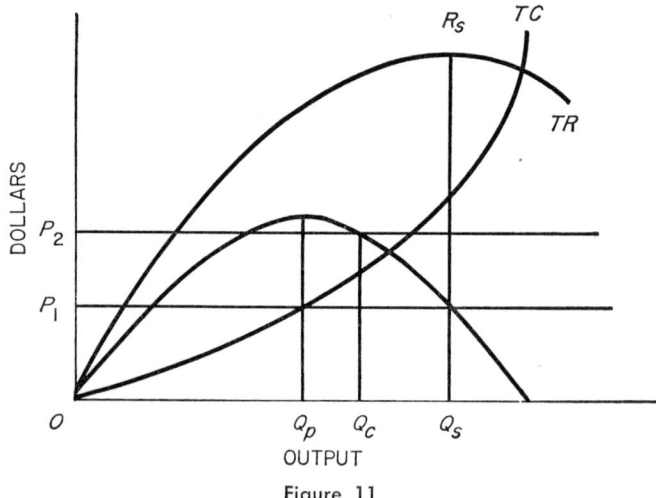

Figure 11

Liquidity and the Maintenance of Control

For several years economists have recognized that one type of business enterprise—the commercial bank—operates within a profit maximization framework limited by certain liquidity restraints. Thus, although the traditional analysis of the firm has been from the viewpoint of the profit and loss statement ($TR - TC = \pi$), the bank has been examined in theory in terms of the balance sheet (Assets − Liabilities = Net Worth). The banker is worried not only about his profits, he also is concerned with maintaining reserves (liquidity) adequate to fulfill requirements and to meet the demands of his depositors. It would seem, then, that a theory of the firm could be constructed which would contain both profit-and-loss and balance sheet considerations, and thus would depict and predict business operations more completely.

In order to analyze the operations of a firm with both liquidity and profit consciousness, we shall follow the model established by W. W. Cooper, with some small modifications.[5] First, it is assumed that a business enterprise has certain preferred combinations of liquid assets (let us limit these to cash positions, for simplicity) and profits for every level of output. We might combine these desires into the preference function:

$$q(t) = F[M(t), \pi(t)]$$

where M is the preferred cash position and π is the preferred profit position at time (t), given the output, q, at this time. It should be stressed that this formula indicates the desired or preferred cash and profit positions at a specific level of output.

Now, at any time certain *actual* outputs will be produced. This actual position may be different from, or the same as, that desired, depending upon the combination of M and π that actually exists at this output. However, because we assume that the preferred position of cash and profit will be the goal of production, we may write the following formula, which assumes that the actual level of output is a function of the desired cash and output positions, so that

$$q_{ta} = f[M(t), \pi(t)]$$

where q_{ta} is actual output during some time interval. If equilibrium exists q_{ta} will be equal to $q(t)$, as follows:

$$q = q_{ta} - q(t) = f - F = 0$$

It is basic to this model to assume that businessmen will attempt to move toward preferred cash and profit positions should they find that at an actual output in time they are not at these positions. Whether their movements toward this ideal will be oscillatory or nonoscillatory will depend upon whether their cash and profit positions move together when output varies. This point is illustrated by Figure 12.

In Figure 12 equilibrium exists at points AA and BB, and, for that matter, all along the 45° line F. This line is composed of equilibrium positions, where $q_{ta} = q(t)$, or where $F = f$. This line also represents the desired balance between π and M at any output position. The two curves, f_1 and f_2, are the paths which a firm *must* follow as it tries to adjust to equilibrium. f_1 describes a nonoscillating path toward equilibrium, whereas f_2 produces oscillations.

If, for example, output is at q_{ta}, along f_1, the actual level of cash (M) and π is not that desired. The tendency, then, would be to return to the F line. However, this can be accomplished only along line f_1. If the firm gives up profits in order to obtain a more satisfactory cash position by moving to q_{tn}, it is still on the f_1 path, at "b," and its M and π positions will still not be satisfactory, although they will have improved. Movement will continue, therefore, until AA is attained.

On the other hand, if the output is at q_{ta} along the f_2 line, adjustments to the desired position (BB) will be oscillatory. Thus, an effort to improve cash position will bring the firm to the other side of BB on f_2, at "c," where profits and cash are unsatisfactory at q_{tn}, and lead to movements to the right to obtain an equilibrium point ultimately at BB. The feature of this description to remember is that movements must take place along the f lines, for these represent the paths of actual positions, in accord with our formula

$$q_{ta} = f[M(t), \pi(t)]$$

Thus, on f_2 a movement from q_{ta} to q_{tn} to obtain a more desirable balance between M and π actually ends up at c, and the following change toward equilibrium results in point d being attained.

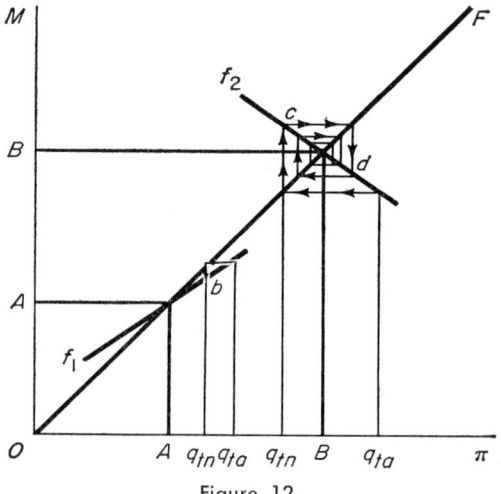

Figure 12

In more economic terms, the f_1 path describes a situation where cash position is decreased relative to profits, but increased absolutely to the right of the equilibrium line F; whereas the f_2 line shows both a relative and absolute decrease in cash. Thus, if output is increased from A to q_{ta} along line f_1 the absolute amount of cash is increased, although its ratio to profits is lowered. On the other hand, if output rises from B to q_{ta} along f_2, cash position is reduced both absolutely and relatively. This latter case may be too strong for a general explanation of what occurs in the typical business firm. When the typical enterprise expands output it is likely that its cash position will be improved at least relatively, for it will sell this output, and will receive at least part of the payment for these additional goods in cash. The case of oscillatory movements, explained above by the f_2 function, may thus overstate reality, because it is more likely that cash does not normally decrease absolutely with an increase in output. But, it is possible that π and M move inversely, one with the other, so that oscillations are produced, but so that M is not reduced absolutely. This more general case is illustrated by Figure 13.

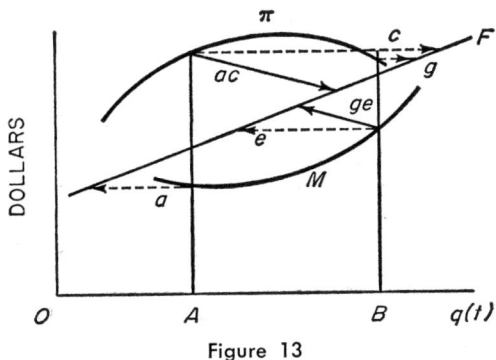

Figure 13

The conflict between π and M is indicated in Figure 13, wherein profits are more than satisfactory for any given output, and cash position is less than satisfactory for these same outputs. If the firm were interested only in maximizing profits, with no thought to liquidity, output would be expanded; whereas if cash position were all important, output would be contracted. Thus, at output A, cash position would be satisfactory at the output indicated by the arrow "a," whereas profit would be satisfactory at the output given by the arrow "c." The strength of the π and M forces is given by the length of the arrows, and a compromise position in this case is given by the arrow "ac," which is simply $c - a = ac$. This arrow indicates that the profit force is greater than the desire for liquidity (although modified by the latter), and that expansion will take place despite the risks that are involved. At output B much the same phenomena are exhibited, but here the M vector (e) is longer than the profit vector (g), and the result will be a compromise contraction of output to the level indicated by the arrow "ge."

Through this model, then, Cooper is theorizing that liquidity considerations are important for many business enterprises, and that the case of maximization of profits may not be as simple as assumed in economic theory. Profit maximization is not precluded in Cooper's model, although it would appear to be but one possible result of the firm's behavior.[6] Whether or not a firm maximizes profits, however, is not the point of this theory. The point is that, if it is assumed that liquidity (and thus control retention) is commonly an important force, it may alter the way in which the business concern moves toward maximum or less than maximum profits, and in this manner the firm will behave differently from the description contained in the traditional model. Furthermore, as we may observe from this argument, it would appear to be unlikely that firms which are affected by liquidity and control considerations move toward maximum profits as a normal goal, for the need to attain desired cash positions would seem usually to bring output down below those levels at which profits are greatest.

There is, unquestionably, a good deal of merit in Cooper's arguments that items other than profit considerations intrude upon the decision-making processes in the business enterprise, and lead to results which may consist of a balancing of conflicts rather than to the simple maximization of one variable at the expense of others. Liquidity and control retention are undoubtedly important influences in many enterprises on the decisions which are made on output. The proper ratios between π and M, which are desired by entrepreneurs at any level of output, are established subjectively, and may be (for all we know) continually changing over time, so that the F function may be discontinuous, may shift, may curve, or may kink. Under such conditions these models become rationalizations of the process of what is, rather than explanations and theories with utility for establishing the dynamics of business behavior. The preference function becomes a subject in the realm of personality theory rather than economics unless—and this is important—it can be hypothesized through empirical research that certain established and conventional significant ratios can be found to exist in business. Actually, it is possible that such ratios do exist, and that, for concerns in specific occupations, there are desired cash and profit positions for each level of output.

A Deliberative Model of Business Behavior

It is evident, even in the economic theory of business behavior, that the business enterprise is a creature of its environment. In the deliberative model of the firm, this environment consists of a state of nature about which entrepreneurs have imperfect information, yet about which they have enough information so that they structure their internal organization in specific directions. In addition, it is evident that firms influence the environment in which they operate, as well as being affected by it. One of the chief elements in the environment is uncertainty. Because of uncertainty, claims Professor Julius Margolis of the University of California, business concerns cannot maximize profits in the manner described by the traditional firm in economic theory.[7] Instead, because of the inaccuracy of, and limited amount of, information, the firm is "deliberative" in its actions, rather than "maximizing."

The entrepreneur in a business enterprise does not have all the information necessary for maximization, for he does not know all the alternative courses of action open to the firm. Instead, he is aware only of the present state of certain pertinent variables, and has a faulty memory of business history. Given these assumptions, the entrepreneur of the deliberative firm, according to Margolis, will attempt only to "satisfice"—to make satisfactory profits. Satisfactory levels of profit, of course, are satisfactory introspectively to the firm, and are contingent upon the firm's aspiration level. Thus, "a level of profits will be satisfactory if it earns the firm a return at least equal to its aspiration level."[8] Only three aspects of aspiration levels may be known to an outside observer: (1) Aspiration levels are defined relative to some time period. Thus, a businessman has desires or aspirations (which are "feasible desires") for profits which relate to the future, but which extend into the future only so far as his planning period extends. The period of a year, for example, might very well encompass his planning period. (2) Needless to add, the profit level which is desired must be sufficient to keep the firm viable. (3) Finally, the aspiration level must always be set at a point higher than, or at least equal to, current normal profits. It is this last feature of aspiration levels which is most important, for it implicitly assumes that the profits that will satisfy the entrepreneur's aspirations during any discrete time period will tend to move upward as actual profits increase.

Here then, is the picture of the deliberative business firm: it operates in an uncertain environment with incomplete information, and aspires to earn a level of profits which is just as great as, and probably greater than, the level which it is now earning. When faced with alternative courses of action in this environment, it draws upon its past and present experiences and upon business conventions, which limit the range of alternatives that it perceives, and bases its decision to undertake one course of action rather than another by assuming that this act will result in satisfactory profits. Now, given these assumptions, it is evident that the deliberate firm may (but not necessarily) ultimately end at a position where profits are maximized. If in each period the aspiration levels of the firm for profits are greater than the current level of profits, then, in a series of discrete steps over time profits would tend to advance incrementally toward a maximum. However, although maximization *might* result, it is not necessary that this be the end of the firm's actions; nor is it necessary that the firm strive toward maximization within any one period. For example, aspiration levels might set the desired profit level merely equal to those prevailing; or economic fluctuations may lead to a drop in actual profits and in aspiration levels (which must be attainable).

Given the goal of satisfactory profits, established in a planning period by aspiration levels, and assuming that the firm operates in a state of uncertainty which it reduces through its imperfect knowledge of business history and experience, what pattern of behavior might be expected? In order to analyze the decision-making processes of the management, we can examine how adjustments might be made in price-output decisions through the use of breakeven charts.

A breakeven chart, such as that presented in Figure 14, is used

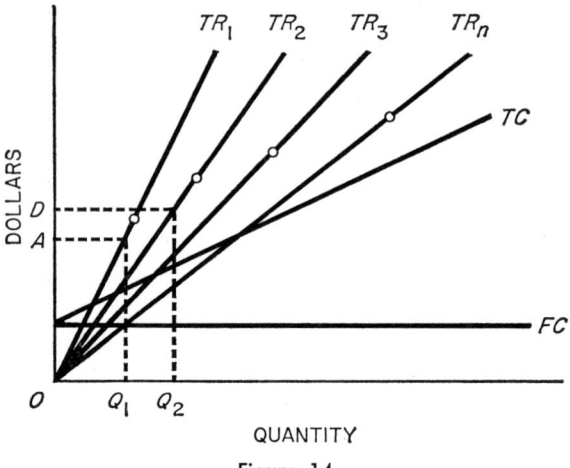

Figure 14

frequently by business managers. There are several types of these charts, and the one illustrated here is used primarily because it enables us to present the data relevant to price-output decisions by the deliberative firm, and because it does so in a highly simplified manner. In Figure 14, the line FC is fixed costs, whereas TC represents total costs (the sum of fixed and variable costs). The TR lines are, of course, simply total revenue lines, made up of pq, and because these are linear, it is presumed that the price of the product remains the same anywhere along one of these lines. In the family of lines TR_1 to TR_n, each line represents a different revenue for the commodity Q, dependent upon the price which prevails.

In the short-run planning period illustrated in Figure 14, therefore, although output may vary, fixed costs and variable costs per unit of output are assumed to remain constant. The TR lines illustrate the revenues which would result at any level of output given the price established for this planning period. The dots on the TR lines represent the locus of the economists' TR curve, and represent the maximum volume of commodities which might be sold at given prices. The deliberative firm, of course, does not possess knowledge of all these points of maximum revenues at a variety of prices. It knows only about those points where it has experienced maximum sales at a given price.

Suppose that this deliberative firm is currently selling an output equal to OQ_1 for a total revenue OA, so that the price per unit of output is OA/OQ_1, and that profits at this level of output are satisfactory. We know, then, that in the coming planning period, the firm will have aspirations of attaining profits greater than, or at least equal to, those attained at output OQ_1. How will it try to attain these higher profits? Margolis believes that the deliberative firm always finds that price changes are hazardous, because it has insufficient information about its competitive and customer environment. Thus, it will probably at first try to increase profits by producing a greater output at the same price, and eventually adjust its output to the dot on TR_1, which indicates the maximum it can sell at this price OA/OQ_1. However, once it arrives at this level of output it has no more excess demand, but its aspirations demand profits greater than or equal to those attained at this point. It is probable now, therefore, that the firm will be forced to change its price. The new price should be such that there exists an opportunity of earning greater profits than at the present price, and yet be one which will assure the firm that it will at least earn current profits. Such a price might be OD/OQ_2, where the level of satisfactory profits ($TR_1 - TC = TR_2 - TC$) would be maintained. This sort of analysis would at least inform management of the volume of sales needed to maintain profits at the same level, given the new price. Whether the decision to change price to OD/OQ_2 will be made will probably be based upon managerial expectations and experience.[9] The point is, once again, that price changes are not undertaken lightly in the real world, and that deliberative firms undertake such changes with reluctance.

For example, Margolis claims that it would be less risky to develop multiple products than it would be to change prices, and it would also be more profitable, because new segments of demand can be exploited. Given the existing maximum output at price OA/OQ_1 (which is that output marked by the dot on TR_1) for instance, management is aware of the following: (1) Its aspirations demand profits at least equal to, and probably more than, those attainable at this output and this price. (2) There is uncertainty about the firm's ability to sell output OQ_2 if price is changed to OD/OQ_2, and yet this is the output needed if the firm is to receive profits at least equal to its present profits. (3) Once it changes its output to OQ_2 it cannot fully exploit all of the information it now possesses, and which it has painfully obtained through experience and experimentation, about the price OA/OQ_1. In this sort of situation Margolis believes that businessmen are more likely to introduce a new type of the same commodity, which would be differentiated in some fashion from that originally produced. By so doing the firm sells its original model at the price OA/OQ_1, and sells the new model at a different price. In this fashion the firm reduces its uncertainty. This situation is illustrated in Figure 15. The lines TR_1 and TR_2 are identical with those

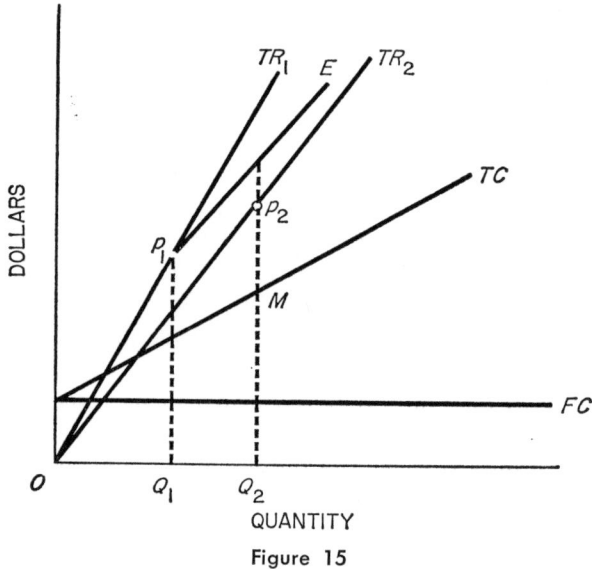

Figure 15

given in Figure 14, as are the TC and FC lines. The firm is selling all of its original product at p_1 ($= OA/OQ_1$). In addition, however, it is selling its differentiated product, OQ_2, at the lower price, p_2. The firm's TR curve now becomes the kinked line Op_1E, and the total revenue received by the firm should it sell Q_1 of its original product at p_1, plus Q_2 of its secondary product at p_2, would be equal to Q_2D. Generally, managers should continue to produce differentiated products so long as the slope of the resulting kinked revenue function is greater than the slope of the TC line.

In summary, then, the deliberative firm of Margolis is quite different from the traditional firm of economic theory. The deliberative firm attempts to "satisfice" and the desired profit goal is established by its aspirations. The behavior of such a concern may result in maximum profits, but this is only one of the possible ends of its actions. Furthermore, because it operates within the confines of history and business customs, and uses these to reduce uncertainty, it is likely that it will always tend to act first in areas where uncertainty is reduced. For example, it will introduce multiple products wherever possible to avoid price changes.

The model of the deliberative concern is in reality almost as closely structured as the traditional model of the firm. It presumes a more limited amount of information to be possessed by entrepreneurs, but assumes that within this framework entrepreneurs act rationally. There is a certain appeal about the argument that business firms act deliberatively —that they adopt rules or conventions to enhance their profit positions. However, is this model adequate to explain unconventional operations? Does it not omit the substantial history of uniqueness and experimentation which has been exhibited by many business enterprises? Even if it could be assumed that the firm does not have the information to seek to maximize its profits, does this necessarily mean that firms do not *in fact* try to do so—even with imperfect information? There are other questions which also could be raised about the deliberative model of the firm. These, however, should suffice to illustrate that it is not without difficulties.

BIOLOGICAL MODELS OF BUSINESS BEHAVIOR

The evident preciseness of the physical sciences has long fascinated the social scientist, who in turn has tried to emulate the methodology employed in the former (for example *ceteris paribus,* which is used frequently, often necessarily, and always presumptuously in the social sciences, is borrowed from the method of the physical scientist), and has often based his theories upon analogies borrowed from the physical sciences. Analogical reasoning is a useful explanatory device wherein the nature of more obscure phenomena may be clarified in terms of other, perhaps more familiar, events or conditions, or processes. Thus, in one of the most famous passages in economics, Alfred Marshall compared the life of the firm to the rise and fall of trees in the forest.[10]

In establishing alternative theories of business behavior, different in some manner from the traditional economic theory of the firm, it does not appear to be unnatural or without precedent, therefore, that several economists have drawn heavily upon analogies from the physical sciences. Two of these alternatives, in particular, have attracted attention in recent years, and shall be discussed in detail here: the theories of homeostasis and viability.

Homeostasis

Homeostasis is a coined word introduced by the physiologist Walter B. Cannon to mean a condition of stability in the bodies of highly evolved animals.[11] It was Cannon's thesis, based upon thorough studies of body fluids and their chemical elements, body temperatures, and other physiological observations, that living beings tend to maintain their own physiological constancy or stability, and that certain adaptive responses to stimuli occur which tend to bring the homeostasic state into being when the body is disturbed. Thus, the body establishes homeostasic equilibria, and certain changes take place when homeostasis is disturbed which tend to bring about its return. Cannon has further argued that nonphysiological states, such as social, political, and industrial organizations, have evolved means for preserving their homeostasic condition.[12]

Homeostasis has been applied to the theory of the business enterprise principally in the work of Kenneth Boulding.[13] In his theory Boulding incorporates as a central feature the concept of the "homeostasis of the balance sheet." The balance sheet is a formal accounting document which indicates the firm's *ex post* position at a point in time. Through an observation of sequential balance sheets it is possible to ascertain the changes in assets (for example, transformations, purchases, sales, and revaluations) and liabilities (the creation or destruction of debt) which have occurred during the intervening period. The operations of the enterprise bring about alterations in its asset and liability accounts. If balance sheets were drawn up at very frequent intervals they would indicate all the financial and physical changes which occurred within the concern, and present a "dynamic" picture of the firm. Boulding compares the dynamic balance sheet to the "state" of a living body, wherein the homeostasic condition is a preferred asset structure which the firm attempts to maintain. The asset preference structure may be measured roughly by the preferred asset ratio, which is that proportion of the value of his total assets which an individual (firm) wishes to hold in a specific form.[14] These asset ratios may be altered with time, and especially with price changes,[15] but given the conditions that exist at any moment of time, there is some preferred position of assets for the enterprise. Should the assets of the firm at that time differ from those desired, the concern reacts to bring assets into preferred positions.

It would seem that the concept of homeostasis of the balance sheet might lead ultimately to profit maximization, for expectations, and thus asset preferences, are based upon values, and are biased in favor of value increases. However, Boulding emphasizes that this is not the case. Maximization is at best only a special case of the more general theory of homeostasis, which may be established at levels other than optimum.[16]

Boulding's homeostasis concept produces an unusual picture of the business enterprise as primarily a reactive, rather than an active unit. The alterations in assets, where these move the value of specific asset items away from their desired relationships with total assets, bring about reactions by the firm. The reactions appear always to be deliberative and positive. The movements away from equilibrium, on the other hand, seem to be stimulated initially by forces external to the entrepreneurial function.

Other writers have also employed the notions of homeostasis, or at least of equilibrium, at the center of their theories of business behavior. Oswald Knauth, for example, has a theory that somewhat resembles Boulding's.[17] Knauth argues that it is trade position and its maintenance which are all important to the firm. By trade position he means ". . . the maintenance or increase of a proportionate share of the market of the industry." [18] The trade position of the enterprise, Knauth implies, is a tangible expression of its relative role in the industry, and by analyzing this position management can tell objectively whether the firm is, or is not, performing satisfactorily. Furthermore, trade position is the result of a balance of variables such as costs, research, volume, prices, and other items, and thus is a satisfactory and concrete indicator of business performance. If the firm has the maintenance or enhancement of its trade position as its objective, as Knauth believes it does, management can judge its actions during a period by the results at the end of this period. On the other hand, Knauth does not believe that businessmen can maximize profits, or know that they have maximized profits *ex-post*, so that the goal of maximum profits is of little utility to businessmen as a guide to future actions. As he states:

> Management concentrates on the maintenance of an equilibrium in motion among all its elements—not on profits alone. The dominant motive in setting prices is to induce a continuous and increasing flow of demand on the part of the customers. If this equilibrium can be obtained—especially an expanding equilibrium—profits result as part of the flow. Profits cannot be planned in advance, for they depend on the equilibrium of all the parts that go into the unit. . . . In a permanent flow there is no way of maximizing profits, or even of knowing whether they are maximized.[19]

Neil W. Chamberlain has set forth a bargaining theory of the firm which has homeostasic overtones.[20] The business enterprise is observed primarily as a budgeting entity which establishes a "projected balance," which is the balance of *ex-ante* inflows and outlays at a level of activity which conforms to the aspiration level of the firm.[21] The environment in Chamberlain's theory is given a much more prominent and complex position than in traditional economic theory; and the entrepreneur is pictured as adapting to or altering this environment through marketing, pricing, and other processes—that is, through bargaining procedures.[22] In this way firms strive to balance cost and revenue flows to attain the satisfaction of a given level of aspirations. Chamberlain suggests three proximate objectives as being important to American management: satisfactory profit, satisfactory market position, and satisfactory growth.[23] Given these objectives, he believes that the firm will most likely attempt to balance these goals rather than to try to maximize any one of them, for to attempt to do the latter would often mean that the other ends could not be achieved. The balance of goals is set by aspirations, which produce satisfactory objectives rather than maximums.

Once the multiple goals of the firm are established the entrepreneurial effort is directed toward their attainment through a complex of decisions and bargains, which, in large part, are concerned with revenues and budgets. Management attempts to equate *ex-ante* income (revenue) and outgo (budget) flows at a level and composition determined by the strength of groups competing for these funds and by its own aspirations.[24] Thus, for example, management may set prices with consumers (as the result of real or impersonal bargains) at relatively high levels because its bargaining power is more powerful than that possessed by this group; or it may have to establish wages higher than it desires because its bargaining power is weaker than that of unions. As Chamberlain points out: "Whatever discretion and income remain unallocated after all bargains have been coordinated accrue to management as a basis for managerial initiative and achievement. To maintain the balance at a preferred level management must continually manipulate and renegotiate bargains." [25]

All homeostasic theories of the firm stress the importance of the stability of the business enterprise as a system related to either (or both) internal or external forces. Boulding emphasizes the equilibria relationships of balance sheet assets. Knauth is concerned with the maintenance of trade positions *vis-à-vis* other business units in an industry. Chamberlain's theory rests upon the notion of the balances which result from bargains between conflicting interests. Furthermore, implied in all homeostasic theories is the notion that there exists some sort of desideratum apart from or inclusive of, profit maximization, which is either internally conceived by the entrepreneur, or which is foisted upon the firm by environmental forces. The behavior of the firm consists almost exclusively, in homeostasic theories, of the efforts of management to obtain, or, in most cases, to return to, the equilibrium positions desired. Finally, theories of business behavior based upon homeostasis are usually considered to be short-run, because it is evident that the equilibria points to be obtained must be altered as fixed assets are changed, or as environmental conditions (including time itself) change.

Viability Analysis

Viability analysis is based upon, or at least is analogous to, the Darwinian concept of natural selection and evolution. Its primary purpose is to explain how business firms can survive in a world in which uncertainty prevails. Under uncertainty, as we shall observe more fully in the next chapter, the outcome of actions cannot be foreseen. All that the decision maker can expect is that one of a distribution of potential outcomes might materialize if he undertakes one particular course of action; and that other distributions of potential outcomes are connected with each alternative course of action. Furthermore, these distributions overlap one another, so that it is possible that the same outcome might be forthcoming regardless of the course of action selected.[26] Suppose, for example, that the entrepreneur is faced with two possible courses of action. The first of these may produce a distribution of outcomes which contains a higher "mean" value, but which also contains the possibility of substantial deviations from this mean, so that one of the outcomes might possibly produce large profits, but other outcomes might result in substantial losses, should the entrepreneur select this course. The second alternative course of action has a smaller mean, with smaller deviations from it, which would mean that the best outcome would result in smaller profits than the first potential distribution, but also in smaller losses. Given this sort of situation, how does the entrepreneur select that course of action which will maximize profits? According to Armen Alchian, profit maximization under conditions of uncertainty, with potential outcomes describable only as distributions and not as unique amounts, is not a meaningful guide to action. As Stephen Enke has stated:

> The fundamental difficulty is that a desire to maximize profits does not provide the entrepreneur with an action prescription. He does not know how he should act just because he knows he wishes to secure maximum profits. When the future outcomes of present decisions are uncertain, motivation does not constitute a criterion for each entrepreneur.[27]

Because of uncertainty, then, viability advocates believe that the traditional theory of the firm is not a useful device for directing the entrepreneurial choice of alternatives. Nevertheless, it is evident that firms which survive must at least avoid long-term losses, and probably make long-term positive profits. The viability analysts begin with this fact: Some firms do survive for long time periods. From this point they move backward to examine the variety of causal chains which might bring about this result. In general, there are two ways in which an enterprise, operating in an environment of uncertainty, can remain viable: First, the firm might be "adopted" by the environment; and, second, the firm might "adapt" itself to the environment. Of course, it is also possible to survive through a mixture of "adoption" and "adaption."

The viable firm is one that is successful. This statement says nothing about the motives of the concern, but it does indicate that those firms which survive must be "successful" in the sense that they have not suffered losses and disappeared. It is possible that, through no effort on the part of the entrepreneur, the enterprise might be adopted by the environment. Thus, firms may flourish just as plants do, when they by chance locate at the right place and at the right time, or when they fortunately adjust to a situation which they do not even "know" exists. It is not necessary that the entrepreneur be properly motivated, and have an excellent predictive sense, in order for his concern to survive. All that is needed is for the firm to "happen" to act properly, and thus be selected by the environment. If the outside observer knows what the conditions of viability are he can predict what the effects of change in the environment will be upon existing enterprises. Success, then, is based upon continued existence, not upon motivation.[28]

Alchian has expanded his argument by stating that firms may survive through their "adaption" to the environment, as well as through their "adoption" by it. Business concerns adapt to the environment largely through imitation of what seems to them to be the successful behavior of other firms. Thus, most enterprises follow certain conventional behavior patterns, such as the use of ". . . 'conventional' markup, price 'followships,' 'orthodox' accounting and operating ratios, 'proper' advertising, etc." [29] Even innovation (mutation), says Alchian, results from the imperfect attempts of firms to imitate successful business procedures and operations. Finally, an enterprise may purposively try to adapt to the environment through the use of a "trial and error" method. Through experimentation the concern may "hit upon" an action which is compatible with the surrounding economic system, and thus survive. It cannot, however, deliberately maximize its profits through trial and error, for this presumes that one knows how to improve his business position through a sequence of acts—an assumption which Alchian asserts cannot hold true in uncertainty.[30]

Stephen Enke has carried Alchian's arguments further by pointing to the special case wherein competition is so intense that in the long-run zero profits would result, so that, therefore, economists would be able to predict that surviving firms must have acted as if they knew how to secure profits.[31] Even in this case, however, economists must supplement traditional marginal analysis with viability analysis, or false conclusions may be obtained.[32]

The Critique of Biological Theories

The chief criticism of the biological theories of business behavior has been that they omit the impact on the environment of the deliberate and purposeful actions of human beings. Biological theories of homeostasis and viability stress the effects of the environment upon the activities of the business firm; but they leave out completely or partially the notion of the entrepreneur as a planning, motivated, acting entity.

The concept of homeostasis, for example, demands that an ideal state be established physiologically, to which the body attempts to return if disturbances to this state occur. In Boulding's theory there exists a similar "ideal of the balance sheet" toward which certain forces within the enterprise seek to move. Knauth assumes that there is a "trade position" which each firm possesses, and which it will strive to maintain should external factors attempt to alter this position. Chamberlain likewise advances the theory that management tries to balance its operations along the line of an expanding equilibrium, and seeks to regain its balance should forces push it away from this line. In all these theories it is never explained how the "ideal" is established, or why it is as it is rather than something else. As Edith Penrose has pointed out:

> The theory of homeostasis provides a formal framework of explanation into which many routine responses can be fitted, but it throws no light at all—nor does it claim to—on why and how the "ideal" relationships between the relevant variables which the firm is now attempting to maintain were originally established or on the conditions under which decisions may be made to alter them.[33]

The concept of viability has likewise been criticized because it omits from consideration the human aspects of business behavior. For example, the very presence of competition, it has been argued, is indicative of the role of purposive action in the firm, which is overlooked by the viability analysts. If the environment is altered through, let us say, the evolution of new products which do not affect conditions in existing industries, firms do respond by entering this new field. Under viability conditions, however, if existing firms were making positive profits in their current occupations, they could not be enticed into the new endeavors, for they would not be interested in making "more" profits—only positive profits. If human motivation, therefore, is omitted from viability analysis, the latter is weakened.

Furthermore, the assumption, inherent in both the work of Alchian and Enke, that economists can "predict" business behavior seems to be inconsistent with their assumption that businessmen cannot have reasonably accurate ideas on how profits can be made.[34] If in uncertainty economists can predict things about survival conditions, it would seem reasonable to expect that businessmen could do the same things, and, therefore, know generally what sort of behavior would make their firms viable in the long run.

SUMMARY

In this chapter we have discussed several alternative theories of business behavior. All these have been introduced by economists, and all have argued that either because of the complexities of the environment or of the personalities of decision makers, the traditional economic theory of the firm is inadequate as an expository or predictive device. These theorists, however, have not simply limited themselves to criticisms of tradition. They have also tried to construct new theories which they believe more fully, or more appropriately, describe business behavior, or at least to construct theories which have greater utility for students of business. These theories, as we shall see later, are closely allied with those drawn from the other behavioral sciences. They are, especially, very similar to some, and almost identical with others, of the hypotheses introduced in Chapter 8 on organization theory, and in Chapter 9 on psychological theories. The alternative economic theories presented in this chapter are not entirely unique, therefore. Nor do they stand separate and apart from one of the major streams of thought about business behavior. These theories not only resemble one another, but they are also closely connected with many other theories from other social disciplines. The seeming multiplicity of theories is somewhat of an illusion, for in many instances the differences between them consist largely of superficial details, and not of essentials.

All the theories presented in this chapter, for example, have a great deal in common. First, they share the general premise that the objective function that enters into the firm's decisions is typically something less simple than profit. Second, because of the complex nature of the environment, the lack of information, uncertainty, or the inadequacy of the decision maker, these theories recognize explicitly or implicitly that maximizing is an unattainable procedure, and in its place substitute other guidelines or various rules of thumb to determine what is "satisfactory." Other similarities, less significant than these, also tend to draw these alternative theories together, and to place them in close relationship with theories that are discussed in later chapters.

It is patently evident that we shall never be able to choose between these theories and the classical theory of profit maximization by ascertaining whether or not profits are, in fact, maximized or satisficed through empirical research. Nevertheless, it is very likely that empirical research can, over time, establish what the decision-making processes of the business firm actually are. In other words, as one step toward the selection of a theory we could study empirically decision-making phenomena at the micro-level of the individual firm, thus pursuing a course diametrically opposed to that advocated by Milton Friedman. The newer "alternative" theories can also be tested to some extent by examining the decision-making mechanisms they propose, and by comparing these with the theories of choice that have been set forth in other behavioral science disciplines. For example, there is a considerable amount of laboratory evidence which tends to support mechanisms of the satisficing or "aspiration-level" type.

We shall not, of course, be able to "prove" in this book that one theory is "the" theory of business behavior, superior to all others. We can, however, emphasize that through research it may be possible to construct a theory which realistically portrays the decision-making process, which contains pertinent and significant variables, and which is useful for the prediction of behavior. We can also, as we have done here, continue to stress the similarities as well as the differences between individual theories of business.

Notes and References

1. William J. Baumol, "On the Theory of Oligopoly," *Economica,* New Series, Vol. XXIV, No. 99 (August, 1958), pp. 187-198; and *Business Behavior, Value and Growth* (New York: The Macmillan Company, 1959).

2. Baumol, *op. cit.,* 53.

3. Baumol also illustrates cases wherein the profit constraint is proportional to sales rather than a fixed level, and where it is a return on investment or proportional to costs. The fixed level constraint, however, is the simplest to understand, and is illustrative for our purposes herein.

4. Because it is likely that where sales are maximized subject to a profit constraint $(TR - TC = K)$, $dr/dx > 0$ and $d\pi/dx < 0$, it would be most unusual for this output position to be the same as that where TR is at a maximum $(dr/dx = 0)$ or where π are maximized $(d\pi/dx = 0)$.

5. W. W. Cooper, "Theory of the Firm: Some Suggestions for Revision," *The American Economic Review,* Vol. XXXIX, No. 6 (December, 1949), pp. 1204-1222.

6. *Ibid.,* especially pp. 1219-1221.

7. J. Margolis, "The Analysis of the Firm: Rationalism, Conventionalism, and Behaviorism," *The Journal of Business,* Vol. XXXI, No. 3 (July, 1958), pp. 187-199.

8. *Ibid.,* p. 190.

9. All the pertinent information which the firm may have at this stage is that derived from its breakeven chart. Thus, it may know only that the price being considered will produce the same revenue as present prices and output, given output OQ_2. However, there is no assurance that the firm will be able to attain OQ_2 at the new price. It would, therefore, attempt to obtain as much information about the possible quantities it would be able to sell at the new price as it could. Even with its new information it is likely that there would be considerable risk to the firm in altering prices, for it could never "know" that, given the new price, it would be able to sell an output which would bring it a profit at least equal to that it was currently earning.

10. Alfred Marshall, *Principles of Economics,* 8th Edition (London: Macmillan & Co., Ltd., 1920), pp. 315-316.

11. Walter B. Cannon, *The Wisdom of the Body,* Revised and Enlarged Edition (New York: W. W. Norton & Company, Inc., 1939), p. 24.

12. *Ibid.,* Chapter XVIII, Epilogue.

13. Kenneth E. Boulding, *A Reconstruction of Economics* (New York: John Wiley & Sons, Inc., 1950), in particular.

14. *Ibid.,* pp. 48-49.

15. *Ibid.,* pp. 88-91.

16. *Ibid.,* pp. 35-38.

17. Oswald Knauth, *Business Practices, Trade Position, and Competition* (New York: Columbia University Press, 1956).

18. *Ibid.,* p. 163.

19. *Ibid.,* p. 169.

20. Neil W. Chamberlain, *A General Theory of Economic Process* (New York: Harper & Row, Publishers, 1955). He further elaborates upon certain parts of his theory in *The Firm: Micro Economic Planning and Action* (New York: McGraw-Hill Book Company, Inc., 1962).

21. *Ibid.,* p. 198.

22. See comments by Lee S. Burns, "Recent Theories of the Behavior of Business Firms," *University of Washington Business Review,* Vol. XIX, No. 1 (October, 1959), pp. 30-40.

23. Chamberlain, *op. cit., A General Theory,* Chapter 12.

24. *Ibid.,* pp. 358-359.

25. *Ibid.*, p. 359.

26. Armen A. Alchian, "Uncertainty, Evolution and Economic Theory," *Journal of Political Economy*, Vol. LVII (June, 1950), p. 212.

27. Stephen Enke, "On Maximizing Profits: A Distinction Between Chamberlain and Robinson," *The American Economic Review*, Vol. XLI, No. 4 (September, 1951), p. 568.

28. Alchian, *op. cit.*, p. 213.

29. *Ibid.*, p. 218.

30. *Ibid.*, p. 219.

31. Enke, *op. cit.*, p. 567.

32. *Ibid.*, p. 572.

33. Edith Tilton Penrose, "Biological Analogies in the Theory of the Firm," *The American Economic Review*, Vol. XLII, No. 5 (December, 1952), p. 818.

34. Edith T. Penrose, "Biological Analogies in the Theory of the Firm: Rejoinder," *The American Economic Review*, Vol. XLIII, No. 4, Part I (September, 1953), p. 608.

6

DECISION THEORY IN CERTAINTY, RISK, AND UNCERTAINTY

The behavior of businessmen may be thought of as a function of the amount of information they possess about the potential future outcomes of their decisions. The state of information (or its obverse—ignorance) possessed by a decision maker may range along a continuum from certainty to uncertainty. For convenience, this continuum has been divided into three separate analytical stages: (1) certainty, (2) risk, and (3) uncertainty.

The traditional economic theory of the firm is essentially an explanation of business behavior under conditions of certainty. This theory assumes that the entrepreneur has several choices among costs, outputs, and prices in a given environment, and that only one choice among these alternatives will maximize profits. Most of the alternative theories of business behavior examined in Chapter 5 also depict the enterprise operating in an environment of certainty, because they typically have assumed a goal or goals which could be attained through the choice of a maximizing strategy.

Probability and decision theory utilize a convenient device known as the payoff matrix, which will help us to distinguish between certainty, risk, and uncertainty. A matrix is a two-dimensional array of numbers, each of which is termed an element of the matrix. These numbers are arranged in rows and columns called vectors. The row vectors of a payoff matrix represent the strategies available to the businessman, whereas the column vectors are the states of nature, that is, environmental conditions over which the executive has no control. Each element of the matrix, therefore, is called a payoff: it is the joint outcome of a particular strategy and a given state of nature. Figure 16 depicts a generalized payoff matrix. The N's are states of nature; S's are alternative strategies; and the P's are payoffs.

STATES OF NATURE

	N_1	N_2	...	N_j
S_1	P_{11}	P_{12}	...	P_{1j}
S_2	P_{21}	P_{22}	...	P_{2j}
...	...	...	...	...
S_i	P_{i1}	P_{i2}	...	P_{ij}

STRATEGIES

A GENERALIZED PAYOFF MATRIX

Figure 16

Under certainty there exists only one state of nature, although there may be a vast number of strategies under some circumstances. Thus, in Figure 16, a decision would have to be made among strategies S_1, S_2, ..., S_i, given, say the state of nature N_1. For example, N_1 might consist of certain labor and union demands which the entrepreneur assumes with certainty to exist. Given this information one type of labor costs, P_{11}, might be $2 per hour, and P_{21} $1, with no other P's lower than P_{21}. Under these conditions an executive, acting rationally to minimize costs, would select strategy 2. In theory, therefore, the decision to undertake a particular course of action in a certain environment is reached by selecting that valued result or payoff which is most satisfactory for the attainment of desired goals. We shall note later in this chapter that the number and complexity of strategies can at times be dealt with best through programming procedures and activity analysis.

The realms of risk and uncertainty have intrigued statisticians and social scientists alike, and have produced the analytical concepts of probability and decision theory. The interest of economists in uncertainty is rooted in the work of Frank Knight.[1] Specific applications to business problems did not occur until the 1930's.[2] However, it has been the confluence of diverse strands from both mathematics and the social sciences which, in the 1950's, truly gave impetus to the study of risk and uncertainty. Now, in the analysis of business behavior, as Mary Jean Bowman has observed:

> It is quite impossible to discuss dynamic micro-economics without anticipating the contributions of mathematical probability theory and statistical decision theory to the analysis of business behavior under conditions of uncertainty.[3]

Mathematical probability theory and decision theory are both concerned primarily with rational behavior in an environment in which the decision maker's knowledge of the future is limited. The decision maker is assumed to possess a goal or goals toward which he desires to move. In order to attain this end (or ends) a selection must be made from alternative strategies which will tend to bring about the desired outcome.[4]

Risk was termed "measurable uncertainty" by Professor Knight. Others, including Jacob Marschak and A. G. Hart, have amplified this definition by specifying that the parameters of the frequency distributions in a risk situation are known to the decision maker.[5] What this means, more simply, is that the executive is assumed to know with what mathematical probabilities each of two or more states of nature will occur.

Suppose, for example, that the decision maker is confronted with a problem where he has to select that size of a perishable goods inventory which should be disposed of within one day at fixed prices and costs. In other words, he must decide on an inventory size that will maximize his net revenues. However, he does not know with certainty what the demand for these goods will be, that is, he does not know exactly which state of nature will prevail. He does, however, know their probability distributions from, let us say, many prior days' demands. Through this knowledge he may decide on a particular inventory strategy in view of the probabilities of various states of demand, and thus take a course of action which he believes will maximize his net revenues. Note that risk analysis is not interested primarily in what does happen; but in the mechanism used by a rational person to arrive at a decision or strategy given two or more states of nature about which the decision maker has established probability judgments. We shall discuss decisions under risk conditions more fully in a later section of this chapter.

Under conditions of uncertainty the decision maker finds it impossible to assign objective mathematical probabilities to the states of nature which affect the payoffs of his strategies. Under uncertainty, therefore, many scholars assume that the entrepreneur establishes his own individual or personal probabilities subjectively, and constructs a payoff table which may be unique in the sense that other observers might enter completely different payoff probabilities in it. In order to draw up such a payoff matrix the decision maker must base his probabilities upon some criterion, such as the Laplace criterion, wherein, because the probabilities of future states of nature are unknown, they are assumed to be equal. Once the criterion is selected, however, the matter of deciding on strategy resembles that described above for risk.

Let us examine decision-making processes under conditions of certainty, risk, and uncertainty in greater detail.

DECISION MAKING UNDER CERTAINTY

Business behavior problems frequently involve the determination of maxima. The economic theory of the firm, for example, utilizes marginal analysis to arrive at that price-output-cost point at which profit is maximized. In recent years a different sort of analysis—mathematical programming—has been widely used to arrive at maximum values. As in the case of conventional economic analysis, mathematical programming is usually presented as though certainty conditions prevail.

Programming is a mathematical technique designed to find "optimal levels of productive processes in given circumstances."[6] It can, therefore, be used much like a marginal analysis to solve certain business problems. Like the calculus, programming is an inherently mathematical rather than business or economic technique. Nevertheless, programming techniques are sometimes less cumbersome than marginal analysis, and in certain instances may be employed when the latter technique cannot be used.[7] Marginal analysis for example, does not operate satisfactorily when constraints prevent the attainment of a maximum. Thus, if output is at a level where $d\pi/dq = 0$ cannot be reached, it is difficult to discover through marginal analysis just what the maximizing output should be, given the assumption that there exist "side-conditions" which must be met.[8] One advantage of programming is that the side conditions or constraints can be inequalities as well as equalities.

Let us examine a simple linear programming problem. Suppose there exists a profit maximizing firm that can produce two products, X and Y. Product X requires 1 minute of work performed on machine group A and 10 minutes on machine group B. Product Y requires 2 minutes' work on machines of group A and 5 minutes on B. In a given interval of time, 50 minutes are available on machines of group A, and 300 minutes on machines of group B. Each unit of X has a profit margin of $1.00, and each unit of Y a profit margin of 70 cents. With these assumptions, how can this firm find the mix of X and Y that will maximize profits?

From this information, how can we approach the problem? First, we know that neither X nor Y can be less than zero, for the firm cannot produce minus products. Thus, $X \geq 0$ and $Y \geq 0$. These are sometimes called implicit restrictions. We can also establish two inequalities expressing the capacity restrictions given. These would be:

$$X + 2Y \leq 50 \quad \text{(constraint on machines of group A)}$$
$$10X + 5Y \leq 300 \quad \text{(constraint on machines of group B)}$$

We now have four inequalities (counting our two implicit restrictions), and it is evident that there are a number of "feasible" solutions to this problem. The multiplicity of feasible solutions can be observed in Figure 17, where the four inequalities are graphed. The shaded area, including

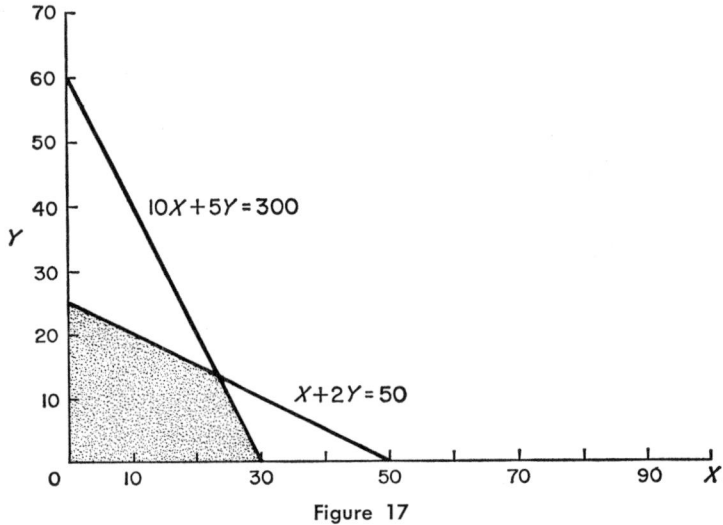

Figure 17

the lines which contain it, satisfies all four restrictions, and indicates the combinations of products X and Y which this firm could manufacture in the stated period without exceeding capacity.

The firm, however, is not interested only in the possible or feasible production combinations of X and Y. It desires to produce that combination which will maximize its profits. From the information given we know that each unit of X has a profit margin of $1.00 and each unit of Y a profit margin of 70 cents so that we can set forth a profit formula

$$\pi = 1.00X + .70Y$$

By using various values for π we can construct a series of iso-profit lines, which are overlaid on Figure 17 in Figure 18 below:

The problem, as may be observed in Figure 18, now becomes quite simply that of selecting the point on the boundary APC which will maximize π. This occurs at P in Figure 18. The value of X and Y can be found algebraically as the intersection, P, of the two lines by solving these equations simultaneously.

$$X + 2Y = 50$$
$$10X + 5Y = 300$$

The amount of X to produce, then, is $23\frac{1}{3}$ and of Y, $13\frac{1}{3}$. These amounts will satisfy all four constraints and will maximize profits at $32.66 ($1.00 [$23\frac{1}{3}$] + $.70 [$13\frac{1}{3}$] = $32.66).

The procedure described above is called linear programming because the constraints are defined by straight-line relations. The iso-profit lines

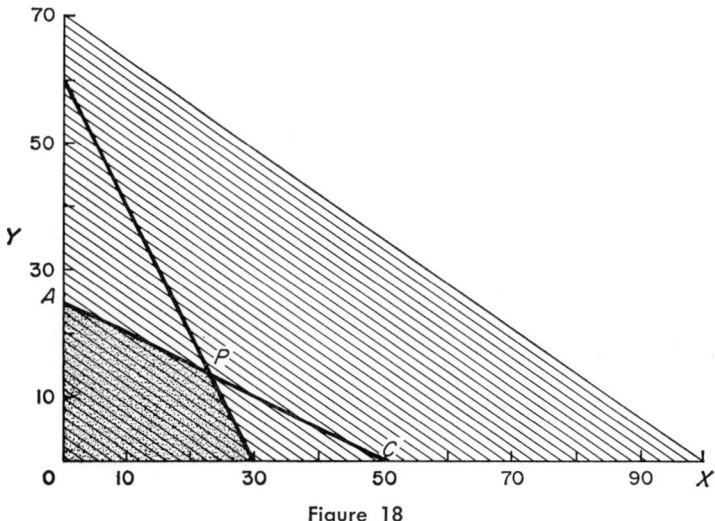

Figure 18

are also straight, because it is assumed that prices are constant. These lines are also always parallel, and in this case the further they are from the origin, the greater the profit. Thus, it is evident that profits will always be maximized at the boundary of the feasible region. In fact, we can say that maximization will always occur at a corner of the feasible region.[9]

The above illustration is an extremely simple example of programming procedures. Linear programming techniques can become most complex.[10] In addition, situations in which there exist diminishing or increasing returns to scale, which approximate more closely the conditions of conventional economic analysis, have been described through nonlinear programming methods.[11] Integer programming has also been useful for certain business problems where indivisibilities occur.[12]

Although it would be most interesting to explore such areas of operations research as mathematical programming, it is more important that we attempt to examine the significance of this sort of analysis for theories of business behavior.

Professor Almarin Phillips has pointed out that the relations between operations research and the theory of the firm may be thought of in any one of three ways: (1) That operations research methods can be used to extend the theory of business behavior in a variety of areas. (2) That operations research can be the means whereby firms can attain more completely the maximization of profits. (3) That the results of operations research can be used to construct a completely new theory of business behavior.[13]

It is apparent, even from our brief excursion into linear programming, that this can be used in a methodological fashion to extend and amplify the notion of profit maximization. However, although programming techniques can, and have, helped in the treatment of complex business problems, their additions to the literature have been primarily mathematical. They have not contributed yet, in any significant manner, to the body of business or economic theory. Operations research has customarily been applied to the operations of a single firm in a unique environment, but this work has not been extended or generalized as an addition to the theory of business behavior.

The evidence is clear that operations research methods, such as mathematical programming, can be of substantial assistance in helping firms to increase their profits. However, these techniques do not help much to determine the over-all profit maximum for the firm. Most investigators have found the firm to be such a complex entity that they have been discouraged from pursuing optimization procedures for the entire organization, and have had to be satisfied instead with the development of suboptimal techniques for parts of the firm.[14] Other difficulties, such as control, communication, and similar constraints (among which are such basic questions as: "Do firms maximize profits?") would seem to constitute almost insurmountable obstacles to the use of operations research methods in moving business firms very far toward the goal of maximum profits.

Finally, operations research techniques, *per se*, have not yet been used (nor were they intended, in general, to be used) in any organized fashion to construct a new theory of business behavior. In combination with other disciplines, however, such as certain behavioral sciences, these techniques might be of assistance in the development of new theories. Through combinations of bargaining and game theories (discussed in Chapter 7), which may be considered to be part of operations research, and economic, small group, and organization theories, it might be possible that new theories of business behavior will be forthcoming. These lie in the future, perhaps, but at present operations research is a normative approach to decision making that is not designed to provide a base for a descriptive theory of business behavior.

To return to the main theme of this section, mathematical programming, as our linear programming example illustrates, is generally presented as though certainty exists. The assumptions of constant costs and prices are symptomatic of a certainty environment. Given a state of nature, the type of question typically asked is: How can firms undertake optimal operations? In the next section we shall examine situations in which risk prevails.

DECISION MAKING UNDER RISK

We started this chapter with the statement that business behavior may be examined as a function of the information possessed by decision makers. The amount of information about outcomes may be thought of as a continuum ranging from certainty to uncertainty, and this range has been divided into the separate stages of certainty, risk, and uncertainty. Each of these stages may be defined in terms of amount of information. However, even within these stages it is evident that the continuum exists. There may, for example, exist many alternative optimizing strategies within the environment termed certainty, so that maximization could be attained through following any one of a number of paths. It would be possible, in this context, to define risk as that part of the continuum in which the information possessed is less than is possessed under certainty, but more than is possessed by the decision maker in uncertainty. However, although this definition may be accurate, it is not sufficiently precise.

The Expected Value Criterion

The definition of risk can be refined by stating, as we did earlier, that the decision maker knows the probability with which each of two or more states of nature will occur. We can illustrate the decision-making process under risk by working a very simple problem. Suppose that an investor wants to invest $100 in either stocks or bonds. From an observation of the past movements in certain industries in which he will invest, he has ascertained that the probability of an increased rate of growth in stock prices during the coming year is .50, of the same rate of growth, .25, and of a decreased rate .25. The appreciation expected as a result of these investments in either stocks or bonds is known. We could summarize this information in the following payoff matrix.

Alternative strategies \ Probability of the existence of a given state of nature	0.25 Reduced Growth N_1	0.25 Same Growth N_2	0.50 Increased Growth N_3
Invest in Stocks, S_1	$ 90.	$ 101	$ 110
Invest in Bonds, S_2	$ 102	$ 103	$ 104

Figure 19

If the investor is to maximize his returns, he must select either strategy S_1, to purchase $100 of stocks, or S_2, to purchase a similar dollar volume of bonds. We can see which strategy would be a maximum by the following computations

$$S_1 = 90(.25) + 101(.25) + 110(.50) = 102.75$$
$$S_2 = 102(.25) + 103(.25) + 104(.50) = 103.25$$

Given the assumptions of this problem, the purchase of bonds would most likely bring a return higher than the purchase of an equivalent value of stocks.

One of the assumptions inherent in the above problem is that the decision maker will select that alternative course of action which maximizes his expected returns. In order to ascertain the alternative which will bring about this desired result, it is necessary to compute the expected value (EV) of each possible outcome by adding the products of the numerical outcomes ($W_1, W_2, \ldots W_n$) and their associated probabilities ($p_1, p_2, \ldots p_n$). Thus,

$$EV = W_1 p_1 + W_2 p_2 + \ldots + W_n p_n$$

Because the outcomes are mutually exclusive, if one occurs the others cannot occur, and it is evident that the sum of the probabilities must equal one

$$(p_1 + p_2 + \ldots + p_n = 1)$$

The expected value basis for choices under conditions of risk is used most frequently. It does, however, have its flaws. The primary objection to basing decisions on the maximization of expected value is that this average has empirical content only if it is founded upon a very large number of similar sorts of past decisions. The expected value that is obtained is an average based upon past experience, and as the number of decisions increases toward infinity, the probability that the expected outcome will differ from the actual outcome by any given amount approaches zero. This result is termed the weak law of large numbers:

$$\text{Probability} \left\{ \left| \frac{W_1 + W_2 + \ldots + W_n}{n} - E(W) \right| > X \right\} \to 0$$

This formula indicates simply that the probability that the average outcome, observed successively

$$\frac{(W_1 + W_2 + \ldots + W_n)}{n}$$

differs from the expected outcome $E(W)$ by any amount (X), approaches zero as the number of outcomes observed increases without limit. Thus, as we toss an unbiased coin over and over a countless number of times, we know that we can expect that tails will turn up roughly one half of the time. Note that the weak law of large numbers does not inform the decision maker what the outcome of his next decision will be; it only indicates that, given an extremely large number of identical and independent decisions, the average outcome will most probably be very close to the expected outcome. On the other hand, if the decision maker bases his actions upon only a few *a priori* experiences, the weak law of large numbers does not apply, and the expected value basis for decision making becomes somewhat meaningless. However, these remarks should not be taken as a criticism of the expected value techniques, but of decisions based only upon limited observations of the distributions of probability. If the decision maker *knows* the parameters of these distributions, then even this criticism is not valid.

Utility and Money

Daniel Bernoulli, in 1730, was the first to doubt the applicability of the expected value criterion, because of the St. Petersburg Paradox. This involves the determination of the fair value of a certain type of coin-tossing proposition under which the expected value of the gamble is infinite. However, because most persons will only play for a finite and relatively small amount, a paradox exists. Bernoulli solved this paradox by assuming that the marginal utility of an additional increment of money is inversely proportional to the amount of money already possessed. More specifically, by assuming that the utility of money could be measured by the use of the logarithmic function, Bernoulli was able to assign a finite value to this game. The applicability of the logarithm to the measurement of utility is not important for our purposes. However, what is significant from this discussion of Bernoulli and the St. Petersburg Paradox is: (1) That the way in which people do react to a risk environment may be contingent upon goals and variables which are nonmonetary; (2) That utility is a broader guide for behavior than money gain, and that the two are not always identical. There may be circumstances when a gamble with a substantial monetary reward and a relatively trivial loss will not be taken because the loss might mean a loss in utility far greater than the utility gain obtained by winning.

Von Neumann and Morgenstern, in their famous work on game theory, devised a method known as the standard-gamble to measure the utility of alternative payoffs.[15] Assume there are three payoffs, X, Y, and Z. The decision maker ranks these (let us say, in the order listed) in order of preference as though they were certain outcomes, so that a utility of 1 unit is assigned to X and 0 units to Z. One arbitrarily assigns a probability, p, to the utility of X and to the utility of Z a probability of $(1-p)$. Suppose the choice between the expected gain $pX + (1-p)Z$ and the certain payoff of Y is a matter of indifference to the decision maker. What utility should be assigned to Y? It can be seen that if we use the following formula, where $u(Y)$ represents the utility of Y, then:

$$u(Y) = pu(X) + (1-p)\,u(Z)$$
$$= p(1) + (1-p)(0)$$
$$= p$$

The utility of the certain outcome Y, therefore, will be equal to the utility of the expected value of the highest ranked outcome (X) of the gamble. The use of the von Neumann-Morgenstern standard gamble technique permits an outside observer to establish a cardinal utility index for a decision maker merely by finding the preference order of some of the potential outcomes of his decisions under very risky circumstances.

Perhaps it would be easier to grasp the standard gamble technique by reintroducing our stock-bond illustration once again, in slightly modified form. The possible outcomes, as illustrated by Figure 20, are five: $110, $104, $103, $101, and $90. Given his choice, we ask the decision maker if he would prefer a certain payoff of $104 to a lottery between $110 with a probability of 3/5 and $90 with a probability of 2/5. Let us say he is indifferent between these payoffs. Further assume we can follow the same procedure, finding the point where the decision maker is indifferent between the certainty of a payoff of $103 and subsequently $101, and the lottery with varying probabilities assigned to $110 and $90, so that we obtain the following utilities for the possible payoffs:

Payoff	Utility
$110	1
$104	3/5 = .6
$103	2/5 = .4
$101	1/5 = .2
$90	0

Figure 20

Now, by using the expected value formula, the decision maker may select a strategy based upon his evaluation of utilities rather than money, as below:

$$S_1 = 0(.25) + .2(.25) + 1(.50) = .550$$
$$S_2 = .4(.25) + .4(.25) + .6(.50) = .500$$

In this case, given the utilities shown, the decision maker would select strategy one, and invest in stocks rather than bonds, as opposed to the selection of bonds if money rather than utility was the goal of the investment.

Professors Mosteller and Nogee, through empirical experiments, have attempted to determine the utility of money prizes in a manner analogous to the von Neumann-Morgenstern method.[16] They found that certain subjects had increasing marginal utility, and others decreasing, as the values of the prizes increased.

The connection between utility and money is extremely important for the theory of the firm. The expected value rule presumes that money gain has a constant marginal utility to the firm, so that the two may be equated. Thus, underlying the assumption of the quest for higher profits is the further assumption that this quest will be pursued strongly because this activity will just as strongly increase the satisfactions of the decision maker. However, if the marginal utility of money to individuals diminishes, or if, as in the Mosteller-Nogee experiments, the issue is confused, it would appear that the drive toward higher profits could decrease as realized profits increase.

A Return to Risk Analysis

We have defined risk as that situation in which the decision maker knows the probability with which two or more states of nature will occur. Is there anything in the above discussion of decision criteria which might lead us to believe that decision makers act in risky situations differently from how they are supposed to act under certainty?

First, under conditions of risk the decision maker appears implicitly to be a person or persons. In other words, theories of decision making in a risk environment seem to be more personalized than is the traditional theory of business behavior. The firm, as such, is ordinarily discarded as the unit for investigation, and the discussion of risky choices assumes that decisions are made by a person or persons within the firm.

Second, the criterion of expected value based upon knowledge of the stochastic process is designed to maximize expected gains. This criterion presupposes that a rational decision maker, acting on the basis of substantial *a priori* evidence, will select that alternative which maximizes expected gains. However, expected value analysis is of little assistance in maximization processes where there exist only a few prior decisions.[17] There may be many of the latter sorts of decisions upon which not only the maximization of profits, but even the viability of the firm may hinge.

Third, the discussion of the relation between money and utility is indicative of some of the difficulties surrounding profit maximization. If additional increments of profit always have a constant marginal utility to the firm decision makers will behave differently than if profit gains possess a diminishing marginal utility, or if the marginal utility of profit increments proceeds at an increasing rate. Furthermore, if a person desires to maximize utilities rather than profits, and if by these we mean separate (and perhaps even conflicting) objectives we may find his actions in risky situations differing considerably from what might be (under other assumptions) considered the appropriate actions to maximize profits.

Fourth, there are other criteria for choices in risk environments which would seem to point to the difficulties inherent in the too simple assumption of profit maximization. To give but two illustrations, a choice might be made on the basis of the variance of the probability distributions rather than their means. If one outcome promises a higher expected value (mean) but a wider distribution (chance of a wide range of gains and losses), as compared to a second outcome with a slightly lower mean but with a smaller variance the decision maker might well select the latter. This implicitly assumes utility analysis. Second, there is some evidence that some decision makers simply focus on the most probable outcome in a risky choice situation, and assume tacitly that this is certain. This disregard of realities is hardly in accord with the rationality assumptions of conventional theory.

DECISION MAKING UNDER UNCERTAINTY

Situations in which the probabilities associated with potential outcomes are not known involve the making of decisions under uncertainty. As with risk and certainty, the state of uncertainty is part of the information continuum. The mark of uncertainty is that the decision maker does not know with what probabilities future states of nature will exist.

The payoff matrix under conditions of uncertainty, then, might appear quite similar to that described under risk, but it would not include a statement of objective probabilities. Thus, in Figure 21 below, the payoff matrix is identical with that presented in Figure 20, but the probabilities of alternative states of nature are omitted.

Decision Theory in Certainty, Risk, and Uncertainty

Alternative strategies \ Alternative states of nature	Reduced Growth N_1	Same Growth N_2	Increased Growth N_3
Invest in Stocks, S_1	$90	$101	$110
Invest in Bonds, S_2	$102	$103	$104

Figure 21

Many uncertainty situations arise because decisions must be made in unique business situations. Under such circumstances, for example, a new product, an investment in a new firm, the decision maker may have to make his decisions even though he is ignorant of their future outcomes. How can he logically make such decisions? What criteria can he use to undertake one course of action rather than another?

Unfortunately, although the decision maker may justify his decision, and rationalize the basis for selecting a strategy, there does not appear to be any one criterion which is most satisfactory for making decisions in an uncertain environment. There are, however, a number of criteria which have been evolved, any one of which might be used to justify uncertainty decisions. If the decision maker bases his behavior on one of these he may find that the strategy he selects would be different than that selected if he used another criterion. Let us examine some of the better-known criteria for decision making under uncertainty.

The Laplace Criterion

The Laplace principle bases decisions under uncertainty upon the assumption that, because the probabilities of future states of nature are unknown, they should be considered to be equal. In Figure 21 three states of nature are shown, each of which, through the use of the Laplace criterion is equally probable, so that we assign a probability of 1/3 to each, and select strategy 2 rather than invest in stocks:

$$EV = W_1 \frac{1}{n} + W_2 \frac{1}{n} + \ldots + W_n \frac{1}{n}$$

so that:

Invest in Stocks, S_1

$$EV = (\$90)\tfrac{1}{3} + (\$101)\tfrac{1}{3} + (\$110)\tfrac{1}{3} = \$100.33$$

Invest in Bonds, S_2

$$EV = (\$102)\tfrac{1}{3} + (\$103)\tfrac{1}{3} + (\$104)\tfrac{1}{3} = \$103.00$$

EV is the expected value, the W's are numerical outcomes in the payoff matrix, and $1/n$ is simply the reciprocal of the number of states of nature.

The Laplace criterion is sometimes called the "Principle of Insufficient Reason." Because it is assumed that all possible states of nature are of equal probability, there is no likelihood that any one will actually occur. Thus, this principle is sometimes interpreted to mean that if there is no reason for one course of action rather than another to be taken, no action at all will occur. Because the lack of action in itself is a course of action (based on insufficient reason), this explanation hardly appears to be rational.

Nevertheless, if a decision is based upon the Laplace principle equal probabilities are assigned to each possible state of nature, and the alternative which maximizes expected value is selected.

The Maximin Criterion

The maximin criterion, first suggested by Abraham Wald, is based upon the conservative hypothesis that the alternative which produces the maximum of the minimum returns should be selected. Thus, in the matrix presented in Figure 21, the minimum payoff through strategy one is $90, whereas the minimum given by strategy two is $102. If we were to make a decision based upon Wald's maximin criterion, then, in this case we would invest in bonds rather that stocks, for the maximin is $102.

The maximin criterion can also be employed (as can the Laplace and other principles) to form the basis for decisions in minimizing rather than maximizing problems. Thus, to find that strategy which should be selected from a cost viewpoint, examine the maximum costs of all alternatives, and then select the alternative which gives the minimum of all maxima. The maximin criterion in this circumstance thus becomes a minimax.

Decision makers using the maximin criterion are inherently prepared for the worst rather than the best. They seek to hedge against the poorest payoff by looking primarily at the most satisfactory of the generally unsatisfactory states of nature which may materialize. They look at the dark side of things; they are basically pessimistic.

Maximax Criterion

Just as the maximin criterion is pessimistic and conservative, so is the maximax criterion optimistic—perhaps overly so. The concept is that the decision maker should select that strategy which produces the maximum of the maxima. Through the use of our Figure 21 it may be observed that the maximum that can be obtained through strategy one is

$110, whereas the best that can be obtained through strategy two is $104. The maximax is therefore $110, and strategy one, to invest in stocks, will be chosen.

A somewhat similar criterion is the dominance principle which, although it does not always yield a unique strategy, may help the decision maker to reduce the number of alternatives from among which he has to choose. An alternative course of action is said to be dominated when a second alternative is preferred to it, regardless of the state of nature that occurs. All dominated strategies, therefore, should be eliminated from the payoff matrix. This is a perfectly rational procedure, and is often carried out unconsciously by the decision maker. Because those strategies which are eliminated are inferior to those which remain in the payoff matrix, the dominance process is a maximizing type of procedure.

The Hurwicz Criterion

Leonid Hurwicz has attempted to provide a criterion for decisions which lies between the extremities of the conservative maximin and the optimistic maximax principles. Decision makers vary in their optimism, not only in their personalities, but also in their views of particular decisions. For example, a generally pessimistic decision maker may feel "lucky" about the outcome of a specific decision. Hurwicz assumed that rationality could be introduced into this sort of decision as well as in all other decisions through the use of a device termed the coefficient of optimism. This concept, in effect, measures the optimism of the decision maker on a scale from 1 to 0. An optimistic decision maker would have a position, α, near 1, while the α of a pessimist would be nearer 0. Hurwicz then advocated the multiplication of the maximum payoff for each strategy by α, and the minimum payoff for each strategy by $1 - \alpha$. The so-called "Hurwicz criterion" consists of the sum of these products, and the strategy with the maximum sum should be selected.

Suppose the decision maker is extremely optimistic in our Figure 21, so that $\alpha = 1$. The maximum payoff in S_1 is $110, and in S_2 $104. $1 - \alpha = 0$, and the minimum payoff in S_1 is $90, and under S_2 $102. The Hurwicz criterion for such an optimistic individual would, therefore, be applied as follows:

Invest in Stocks, S_1

$$EV = \$110(1) + \$90(0) = \$110$$

Invest in Bonds, S_2

$$EV = \$104(1) + \$102(0) = \$104$$

An extremely optimistic decision maker would select strategy one. In fact, when the decision maker is this optimistic, the Hurwicz criterion is actually the maximax principle.

On the other hand, if the decision maker is extremely pessimistic, he will minimax, as advocated by Abraham Wald. This is illustrated by the example below, wherein all the α's have been assigned a value of zero, and $1 - \alpha$ becomes equal to 1.

Invest in Stocks, S_1
$$EV = \$110(0) + \$ 90(1) = \$ 90$$
Invest in Bonds, S_2
$$EV = \$104(0) + \$102(1) = \$102$$

Strategy two would be selected in this case.

Figure 22 plots the payoffs for strategies one and two under varying values of the coefficient of optimism. If $\alpha > .6666$, S_1, the purchase of

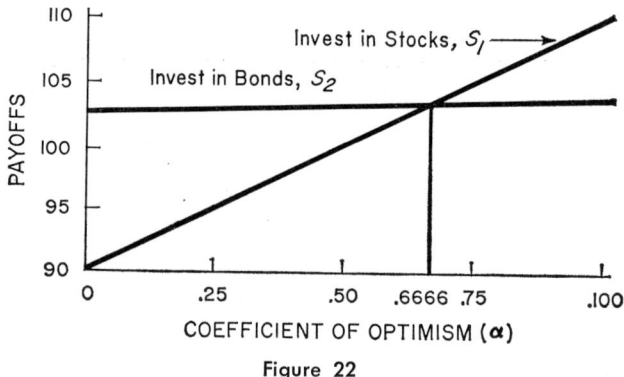

Figure 22

stocks will be preferred, whereas if the decision maker is more pessimistic, and has a coefficient of optimism less than .6666, he will invest in bonds. When $\alpha = .6666$ the decision maker is indifferent between S_1 and S_2.[18] Furthermore, .6666 must be the decision maker's coefficient of optimism obtained through the use of the Hurwicz criterion when the decision maker is indifferent between S_1 and S_2.

The Regret Criterion

L. J. Savage has advanced the concept of regret as a suitable criterion for decision making.[19] The idea is that a decision maker attempts to evaluate the alternatives available in the light of what might occur *ex post* should certain states of nature prevail and, because all payoffs but one will be less than satisfactory, he will experience regret should any but this one materialize. Savage believes that the decision maker should compute the difference between the payoffs realized should various states of nature occur, and the maximum payoff possible, and act to minimize this difference, which he calls regret. Because this regret is a difference in payoffs, it may be expressed in a matrix form called a regret matrix, derived from Figure 21.

As may be observed in Figure 23, the regret figure placed in any ele-

Alternative states of nature / Alternative strategies	Reduced Growth N_1	Same Growth N_2	Increased Growth N_3
Invest in Stocks, S_1	12	2	0
Invest in Bonds, S_2	0	0	6

Figure 23

ment of the matrix is simply the difference between the payoff which might occur should the wrong strategy combine with a given state of nature, and the maximum possible payoff for the same state of nature. Thus, should S_1 be selected and N_1 occur, the payoff would be $90, as compared with the $102 payoff that would have materialized had S_2 been chosen. The regret figure in the element formed by S_1 and N_2 is computed by subtracting $101 from $103, and the number 2 indicates the degree of regret that the decision maker would experience should N_2 occur. The figure 6 in element S_2 N_3 is simply the result of $110 − $104.

Savage proposes that the information obtained from the regret matrix should be used to calculate a minimax, much as suggested by Abraham Wald. Thus, the maximum regret that could be obtained through strategy one in Figure 23 is 12, whereas the maximum in strategy two is only 6. In order to minimax his regret then, the decision maker following Savage's criterion would select strategy two, and invest in bonds, for S_2 contains the minimum maximum.

The Shackle Criterion

G. L. S. Shackle has suggested, in a number of books and articles, that subjective probability considerations do not adequately portray the traumatic processes involved in many kinds of major decisions.[20] He has constructed a "potential surprise function," which he feels is a more representative depiction of how somewhat unique, important, and uncertain decisions are actually made.

Shackle's potential surprise function purports to be a measure of the consequences of a decision under uncertainty. A decision may have many alternative outcomes, some of which seem to the decision maker to be so improbable that he would be most surprised should they occur. The outcomes with a potential surprise of zero, on the other hand, are those which the decision maker believes are perfectly possible. In Figure 24 below is presented a Shackle potential surprise function, where (X)

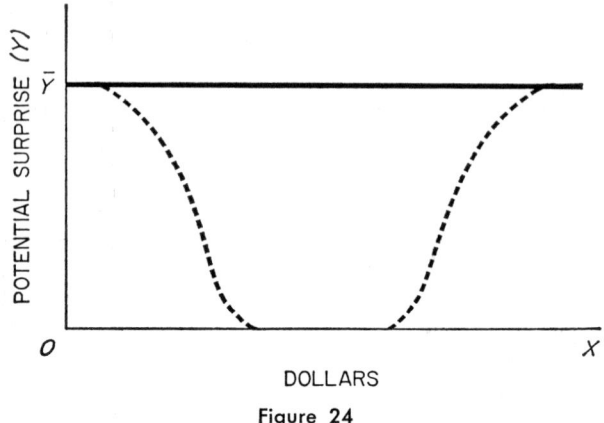

Figure 24

equals the values resulting from various payoffs which might occur, and (Y) measures the potential surprise associated with these payoffs. The continuous function, $Y = Y(X)$, is saucer shaped between zero Y and $\overline{Y}$, which is total disbelief. Between zero Y and $\overline{Y}$ are possible outcomes which the decision maker feels might occur, but which, by degrees, he does not feel are perfectly possible (as are those which touch the X axis), but which are not totally improbable.

Now, in making his decision, the decision maker will not focus upon all possible outcomes. Certain of these outcomes, termed "focus outcomes" by Shackle, will attract and hold the decision maker's interest. In order to pinpoint these specific focus outcomes, Shackle has devised a stimulation function, $\phi = \phi\{X, Y\}$, which is a measure of the attention arresting power of each pair of potential payoff values to the decision maker. ϕ is associated with both X and Y; it appears reasonable to assume that it is an increasing function of the values of payoffs (X), and a decreasing function of the potential surprise (Y). Furthermore, Shackle argues that ϕ will be zero for all totally improbable outcomes $\overline{Y}$. One would not expect that the decision maker would be attentive to payoffs which he considered impossible, nor would perfectly possible outcomes necessarily possess that attention arresting quality essential for his serious concern. What he is interested in, primarily, are certain extreme consequences of his decision, which he believes might occur, and which will determine whether he makes the decision or not. Finally, as indicated in Figure 25, Shackle regards ϕ as a surface, like an indifference map, because it is a

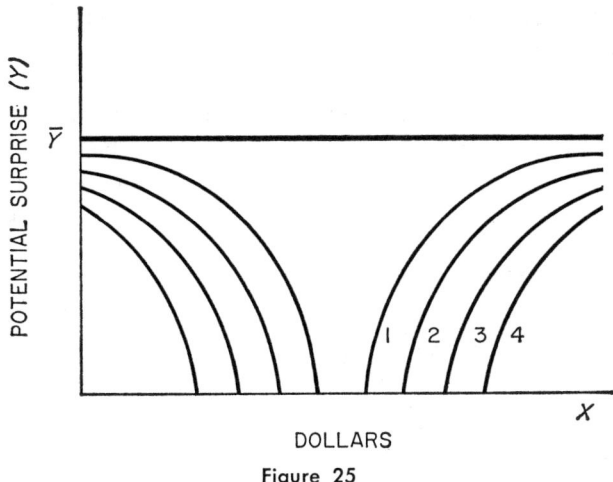

Figure 25

function of two variables $\{X, Y\}$, and curves 1, 2, 3, and 4 are contours with ϕ a constant along each curve.

There are two sets of ϕ functions in order to indicate the pairs of potential payoffs, one of which is the "best" and the other the "worst" which can be produced by the decision. The "best" outcome is that which, in the mind of the decision maker, is the payoff which is considered possible, and which produces the largest gain within the range of possibility. The "worst" outcome is the poorest possible payoff value which the decision maker believes can occur. The potential surprise function $Y = Y(X)$ is combined with ϕ surface in Figure 26. By so combining these two functions, Y and ϕ, it may be observed that the two are tangent at points a and b. These points are called by Shackle "primary focus outcomes," representing the "best hope" and "worst fear" of the

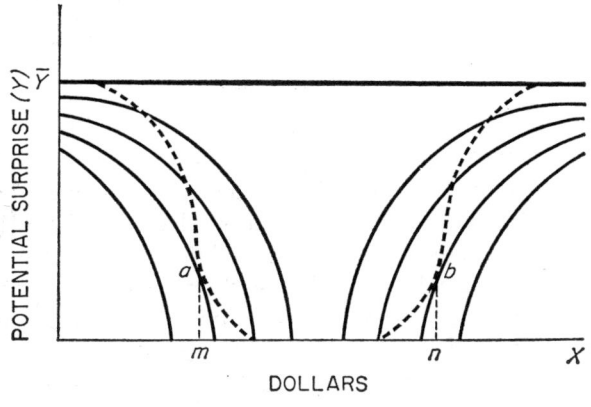

Figure 26

decision maker. By dropping a perpendicular vector from a to m, and from b to n, it is possible to connote these outcomes in terms of the values of X (payoffs) only, and to eliminate Y. Points m and n are, in Shackle's terminology, called "standardized focus outcomes." It is upon these "standardized focus outcomes" that a decision will be based.

C. F. Carter has proposed a modification of Shackle's potential surprise thesis.[21] He argues that the potential surprise function Y should move up from the X axis in a series of steps, rather than rising continuously and smoothly as Shackle suggests. Each step would contain "typical" outcomes, representative of similar outcomes with about the same degree of surprise. Carter believes that decision making is a simplification process, and that human minds tend to concentrate on only typical outcomes, rather than compare the successive increments of values depicted by a continuous Y function. Carter claims that his modification recognizes the existence of an irreducible element of doubt in the appraisal of marginal changes in the Y function.

Conclusions on Criteria

All the criteria presented herein, with the possible exception of that given by Shackle, assume that the decision maker, even when confronted with uncertainty, attempts to optimize. Just what optimization means under these conditions, however, is not clear, for the choice among alternatives will produce varying results depending upon the criterion employed. For example, our illustration presented first in Figure 21 has indicated that the decision maker should choose between S_1 and S_2 as noted below:

Laplace criterion:	Choose S_2, invest in bonds
Maximin (Wald) criterion:	Choose S_2, invest in bonds
Maximax criterion:	Choose S_1, invest in stocks
Hurwicz criterion:	Choose S_1 or S_2, depending on decision maker's coefficient of optimism
Regret (Savage) criterion:	Choose S_2, invest in bonds

Although S_2 comes out well, because it would be selected surely in three of the five cases illustrated, the evidence is not overwhelmingly in favor of a specific criterion. One criterion is selected rather than another, it seems, in an intuitive way. If one is basically an adventurous or optimistic sort of person he will choose a criterion different from that selected by a conservative or cautious individual. Furthermore, none of the criteria is foolproof, nor does there seem to be any generally accepted criterion for decision making under uncertainty.

What, then, does all this mean for business behavior? It is evident, first, that the notion of maximizing behavior loses a great deal of its uniqueness in uncertainty environments. The statement that profit maximization is no prescription for business behavior, and that the mechanics of maximization are not constant, becomes clear when one understands the uncertainty decision-making process. Second, this examination of decision theories under uncertainty tends to confirm the conclusions reached in our analysis of risk decisions, that behavior is personal rather than institutional, that is, that persons, not firms, make decisions.

Subjective Probability

The above discussion of decision criteria under uncertainty does not quite complete our treatment of all the problems involved in decision making. One vital question concerns the meaning and significance of subjective probabilities. The frequency concept of probability, which was discussed in connection with risk decisions, involved the weak law of large numbers, so that it was related to the limit of the outcomes of a large series of repeated experiments or experiences. Decisions made on a frequency basis may be said to have a mathematical foundation. This foundation, termed mathematical or objective probability, differs from subjective probability, which Edwards has defined as ". . . a name for a transformation on the scale of mathematical probabilities which is somehow related to behavior." [22] Subjective probability, then, is sometimes defined as a measure of the decision maker's degree of belief in the outcomes of his decision. The decision criteria discussed previously attempt to give the decision maker an automatic prescription for assigning subjective probability values to potential states of nature. There is no reason to assume, however, that the probabilities assigned are the same as those that might be assigned objectively.[23] It is likely that different decision makers will not hold the same subjective probabilities.[24] On some decisions, especially where they are unique, subjective probabilities do not seem to coincide with those ascertained through relative frequency analyses. Despite these flaws, some observers still argue that subjective probability is a perfectly sound basis for decision making under uncertainty.[25]

Of more importance, perhaps, to our interest in behavior under conditions of uncertainty have been the experiments conducted in the area of subjective probabilities. Ellsberg, for example, has argued that businessmen tend to pursue current behavior strategies to minimize uncertainties, even though a change in behavior might contain outcomes with higher expected values.[26] Feather has advanced the hypothesis that the greatest payoffs might be assigned smaller subjective probabilities than would be expected, simply because the decision maker feels these to be less attainable.[27] Littig suggests that fear of failure, and a subsequent reduction in prestige might have significant influence on subjective probabilities.[28] Hermann and Stewart have observed that individuals seem to have a greater tendency toward speculative behavior when they are losing than when they are winning.[29] Irwin has proposed that favorable events are assigned a higher subjective probability than unfavorable ones.[30]

Now, what does all this mean? First, many of these experiments reinforce previous comments on the complexity and meaningless nature of generalizations about simple decision structures for profit maximization. Second, some of these findings suggest that perhaps individuals can realistically assess value and probability, but that they deliberately operate with a decision rule which is *not* the maximization of expected values. Third, the results of many of these experiments indicate that personality factors and the attitudes and perceptions of decision makers are of vital importance in the selection of alternative strategies. Finally, even within the spectrum of uncertainty, decision situations seem to vary considerably, and are affected by such variables as information, peer groups, skills, chance, and the bases for evaluating performance.

SUMMARY

In this chapter we have examined decision theory within the context of certainty, risk, and uncertainty. Decision theory, it may be observed, is primarily a methodological theory; its interests are principally in the *way* decisions are made. rather than *why* they are made. It emphasizes *how* decisions are made, but has little to say about objectives or the reasons for decisions. Goals, of course, are implicit within decision theory, but are not emphasized.

To illustrate decision theory under certainty a simple example of linear programming was presented. It was noted that, although programming techniques—in nonlinear as well as linear form—may be useful for many purposes, and although they may have wider applications in business than the more conventional marginal analysis, they as yet have not made unique contributions to the *theory* of business behavior.

Decision making techniques under risk and uncertainty are similar in that the future is assumed to be unknown. The hallmark of both kinds of decisions is that the payoffs from alternative strategies cannot be known. In risk, however, the decision maker can know with what probability certain outcomes will flow from his behavior, whereas he does not know these probabilities under uncertainty. Risk, as defined in this chapter, is associated with mathematical or objective probabilities. Coin tossing, dice games, and some types of business operations involve decisions under risk. Outcomes of any one decision may not be those desired, but relative frequency is indicative of the long-run probabilities of given outcomes.

Criteria to assist the decision maker to select his strategies under uncertainty are available, and may be useful in specific situations where courses of action must be undertaken in uncertain environments. Probability weights used in uncertainty are subjective rather than mathematical, and as such are affected by a host of personal and environmental variables.

Decision theory offers considerable promise for the analysis of business behavior. Its emphasis upon methodology makes it amenable and flexible to a variety of theories, and does not bind it rigidly to any one theory. More work, however, remains to be done in this relatively new area before it can fulfill its promise.

Notes and References

1. Frank H. Knight, *Risk, Uncertainty and Profit* (Boston: Houghton Mifflin Company, 1921).

2. See especially I. Svennilson, *Ekonomiske Planering* (Uppsala: Almquist and Wiksells, 1938).

3. Mary Jean Bowman, ed., *Expectations, Uncertainty, and Business Behavior* (New York: Social Science Research Council, 1958), p. 2.

4. See, Irwin D. J. Bross, *Design for Decision* (New York: The Macmillan Company, 1953), especially Chapter 2.

5. J. Marschak, "Money and the Theory of Assets," *Econometrica*, Vol. 6, No. 3 (October, 1938), pp. 311-325; and A. G. Hart, "Risk, Uncertainty and the Unprofitability of Compounding Probabilities," *Studies in Mathematical Economics and Econometrics* (Chicago: University of Chicago Press, 1942), pp. 110-118. Reprinted in American Economic Association, *Readings in the Theory of Income Distribution* (New York: McGraw-Hill Book Company, Inc., 1949).

6. Robert Dorfman, "Mathematical or 'Linear' Programming: A Nonmathematical Exposition," *The American Economic Review*, Vol. XLIII, No. 5, Part I (December, 1953), p. 798.

7. See Yuan-Li Wu and Ching-Wen Kwang, "An Analytical and Graphical Comparison of Marginal Analysis and Mathematical Programming in the Theory of the Firm," in Kenneth E. Boulding and W. Allen Spivey, *Linear Programming and the Theory of the Firm* (New York: The Macmillan Company, 1950).

8. William J. Baumol, "Activity Analysis in One Lesson," *The American Economic Review*, Vol. XLVIII, No. 5 (December, 1958), p. 840.

9. If the iso-profit lines happen to parallel a portion of the boundary, then the entire portion, *including the corners*, will produce maximum profits. Even in this case, however, the "corner" rule holds true.

10. See, for example, Robert Dorfman, Paul A. Samuelson and Robert M. Solow, *Linear Programming and Economic Analysis* (New York: McGraw-Hill Book Company, Inc., 1958).

11. See *Ibid*. Also K. J. Arrow, Leonid Hurwicz, and H. Uzawa, *Studies in Linear and Non-Linear Programming* (Stanford: Stanford University Press, 1958).

12. See, for example, George B. Dantzig, "On the Significance of Solving Linear Programming Problems with Some Integer Variables," *Econometrica*, Vol. 28 (January, 1960).

13. Almarin Phillips, "Operations Research and the Theory of the Firm," *The Southern Economic Journal*, Vol. XXVIII, No. 4 (April, 1962), pp. 357-364.

14. See, on this point, the comments in Stafford Beer, *Cybernetics and Management* (New York: John Wiley & Sons, Inc., 1959), pp. 16-17, Russell L. Ackoff, *Progress in Operations Research* (New York: John Wiley & Sons, Inc., 1961), pp. 28-30; and C. Hitch, "Suboptimization in Operations Problems," *Operations Research*, Vol. I, No. 3 (May, 1953), pp. 87-99.

15. John von Neumann and Oskar Morgenstern, *Theory of Games and Economic Behavior* (Princeton: Princeton University Press, 1947).

16. Frederick Mosteller and Phillip Nogee, "An Experimental Measurement of Utility," *Journal of Political Economy*, Vol. 59 (October, 1951), pp. 371-404.

17. Some scholars would disagree with this statement, arguing that it is best to approach a unique decision as though it were part of a repetitive series.

18. α can be found in this case as follows: We know that at the point where both lines intersect,

$$104(\alpha) + 102(1-\alpha) = 110(\alpha) + 90(1-\alpha)$$

so that:

$$104\alpha + 102 - 102\alpha = 110\alpha + 90 - 90\alpha$$

and by clearing both sides of the equation, $12 = 18\alpha$, or $\alpha = .6666$.

19. L. J. Savage, "The Theory of Statistical Decision," *Journal of the American Statistical Association*, Vol. 46 (1951), pp. 55-67.

20. Most notable among his writings, perhaps, is *Uncertainty in Economics and Other Reflections* (Cambridge: Cambridge University Press, 1955).

21. C. F. Carter, "A Revised Theory of Expectations," *The Economic Journal*, Vol. LXIII, No. 252 (December, 1953).

22. Ward Edwards, "The Theory of Decision-Making," *Psychological Bulletin*, Vol. 51, No. 4 (July, 1954), p. 397.

23. F. Attneave, "Psychological Probability as a Function of Experienced Frequency," *Journal of Experimental Psychology*, Vol. 46 (1953), pp. 81-86; M. G. Preston and P. Baratta, "An Experimental Study of the Auction-Value of an Uncertain Outcome," *American Journal of Psychology*, Vol. 61 (1948), pp. 183-193; and several others have experimentally confirmed this result.

24. See, for example, F. W. Irwin, "Stated Expectations as Functions of Probability and Desirability of Outcomes," *Journal of Personality*, Vol. 21 (1953), pp. 329-335.

25. For example, L. J. Savage, *The Foundations of Statistics* (New York: John Wiley & Sons, Inc., 1954).

26. Daniel Ellsberg, "Risk, Ambiguity, and the Savage Axioms," *Quarterly Journal of Economics*, Vol. 75, No. 4 (November, 1961), pp. 643-669.

27. N. T. Feather, "Success Probability and Choice Behavior," *Journal of Experimental Psychology*, Vol. 58, No. 4 (October, 1959), pp. 257-266.

28. L. W. Littig, "Motivation, Probability Preferences, and Subjective Probability." Paper read before the *Annual Meeting of the American Psychological Association*, Chicago, 1960.

29. Cyril Hermann and John B. Stewart, "The Experimental Game," *Journal of Marketing*, Vol. 22, No. 1 (July, 1957), pp. 12-20.

30. Francis W. Irwin, "Relation Between Value and Expectation as Mediated by Belief in Ability to Control Uncertain Events." Paper read before the *Annual Meeting of the American Psychological Association*, Chicago, 1960.

7

THE THEORY OF GAMES

Modern business behavior can be thought of as a product of internal and external forces that impinge upon the enterprise. These forces present the firm with its aspirations and goals, tend to direct its course of action and the alternatives that are perceived, and determine its payoffs. In economic theory the emphasis in models of pure competition is upon the environment. It is necessary only to know that the entrepreneur has a goal and that he is rational, for the number and nature of enterprise is such that the actions of any one firm cannot have an effect upon market forces. The market mechanism is the dominating force in pure competition, and only if the firm behaves most efficiently will it survive.

Economic theory, however, has not been able to provide an adequate or universally acceptable explanation of the policies and actions of an individual firm interacting with other firms, and affecting the market. Because, as was observed in Chapter 2, the firm in economic theory has no personality, it is most difficult for it to "affect" anything, for the theory is not amenable to explanations which involve behavioral assumptions other than the simple and single assumption of rationality. It is not possible to establish what "rational economic behavior" is when such rationality is contingent upon the behavior of other enterprises or persons. As Hurwicz has pointed out:

> ... the individual's "rational behavior" is determinate if the patterns of behavior of "others" can be assumed *a priori* known. But the behavior of "others" cannot be known *a priori* if the "others," too, are to behave rationally! Thus, a logical impasse is reached.[1]

To many economists, and to others, a framework for exploring business behavior in situations of imperfect competition, and for solving some of the complex problems in oligopoly theory was provided by the theory of games.

> The basic feature of this theory is to show that in economics one is not confronted with maximum problems but with a conceptually different and, *a fortiori*, more difficult situation. This stems from the fact that the outcome of the behavior of firms and individuals does not depend on their own actions alone, nor on those combined with chance, but also on the action of others who sometimes oppose, sometimes fortify, those of the former. Stating it differently: firms and individuals are not in control of all variables on which the result or "payoff" depends.[2]

It has been two decades since von Neumann and Morgenstern claimed that game theory ". . . is the proper instrument with which to develop a theory of economic behavior." [3] Some success has been achieved in utilizing game theory during this period. For example, it has been used to explain such heterogeneous aspects of business behavior as advertising policies,[4] capital budgeting,[5] investment decisions,[6] management-union bargaining,[7] and purchasing parts.[8] However, the great promise of game theory, foreseen so clearly in 1944, has not yet materialized. Perhaps, as the authors anticipated, the theory is still, after a full twenty years, in the "first stage" of development, and more time must pass before it is successfully used for predictive purposes.[9] Nevertheless, whether one believes that the theory of games has been applied usefully or will be, it is of interest for the light that it throws upon the theory of business behavior within an environment in which the number of firms is small.

DEVELOPMENT OF GAME THEORY

The theory of games was evidently initiated by the French psychologist, Emil Borel, in a series of long neglected papers written between 1921 and 1927.[10] Borel observed the parallels which exist between games, war, and economic behavior.[11] He introduced analytical techniques for examining two-person games, and the concepts of pure and mixed strategies. He did not, however, ". . . prove the decisive 'minimax theorem' or even to surmise its correctness." [12] The central feature of the theory of games was not derived until John von Neumann published a paper in 1928 in which he proved the minimax theorem—the *sine qua non* of game theory.[13] In subsequent investigations von Neumann enlarged the theory of games to include more than two players.

Despite the fact that the theory of games was originated in the early 1920's, it was not until the appearance of von Neumann's and Morgenstern's book in 1944 and its subsequent revision in 1947 that a considerable interest in the subject was created.

THE TERMINOLOGY OF GAME THEORY

As noted in Chapter 2, one of the chief advantages of game theory is that it introduces a unique set of terms which can be utilized by all social scientists without traditional confusion. Von Neumann and Morgenstern defined a game as ". . . simply the totality of the rules which describe it." [14] The rules of a game rigidly specify the conditions under which the game is played, the choices persons should (or may) make, the resulting outcomes, and in some cases the collusion or communication which may take place among the players when they attempt to improve their outcomes.

Players are decision makers who make the moves of a game. Individuals, groups, or firms may be single players in a game. Thus, in the game of bridge, partners are considered as a single player. In a duopoly situation there are two players, each of which is a firm. As in decision theory, a player must select one of the alternatives available to him. The exercise of his choice is termed a move. The summation of all moves in a game is called a play. The word "move" does not necessarily imply a physical act nor does the word "play" mean the act of participation. Luce and Raiffa define move as ". . . a point of decision for a given player from among a set of alternatives" and a play as ". . . a detailed statement of the actual decisions made." [15] These may be more satisfactory definitions because they connote the specific meaning of the terms without being too closely linked to the more conventional use of these words.

A strategy is a plan which sets forth all the moves the player would make in a game under all possible contingencies. This plan is ". . . so complete that it cannot be upset by enemy action or nature; for everything that the enemy or nature may choose to do, together with a set of possible actions for yourself, is just part of the description of the strategy." [16] A strategy may be either pure or mixed. A pure strategy is one which assigns a particular choice of alternatives for each move. Thus, a play would consist of the summation of all the particular choices which have determined each move. A mixed strategy, on the other hand, is composed of pure strategies and a probability distribution designed to conceal the choice of a specific pure strategy for a given play. For example, if a player decides to use one pure strategy two-thirds of the time and a second pure strategy one-third of the time, the particular employment of either pure strategy in a play may be determined at random, perhaps by the draw of a card or the roll of a die. Even the player does not know which pure strategy will be used for a given play. All he knows is that one strategy will tend to be employed two-thirds of the time whereas the other strategy will be used one-third of the time.

A payoff function assigns the winnings (or losses) to each player for all possible combinations of strategies that may be used. Payoffs are arranged in a matrix, similar to that discussed in Chapter 6, and each player has a separate payoff matrix. The size of the matrix is determined by the number of strategies available to each of the players.

A payoff matrix for player A in a two-player game, in which each player has three available strategies, assumes the following form.

B'S CHOICE OF STRATEGIES

	B_1	B_2	B_3
A_1	a_{11}	a_{12}	a_{13}
A_2	a_{21}	a_{22}	a_{23}
A_3	a_{31}	a_{32}	a_{33}

A'S CHOICE OF STRATEGIES

Figure 27

The row vectors indicate the strategies available to player A; the column vectors show the strategies available to his opponent, player B. The elements in the matrix are the payoffs which result (profits, in this case) to player A. If player A chose to employ pure strategy A_2, for instance, and B selected his pure strategy B_3, the resulting payoff would be a_{23}.

The value of the game is the amount paid to player A by his opponent, B. If the sum of all the payoffs for each possible combination of strategies is the same the game is said to be a constant sum game. The special case of a constant sum game, wherein the sum of one player's gains offsets exactly the second player's losses, is called a zero sum game. If the payoff totals differ within the matrix the game is designated a variable sum game.

Games are not only categorized by type of payment, but also by the number of players participating. The theory of games may deal with two players, three players, or any finite number of players (n-person game). As the game acquires more players the solutions, of course, become increasingly complex. In the following sections of this chapter we shall examine: (1) two person constant-sum games; (2) a description of games with more than four strategies; (3) nonconstant sum games; (4) n-person games; (5) and finally, we shall attempt to relate the theory of games specifically to the theory of business behavior.

Before we move to these matters, one more comment on definitions should be made. There are two "forms" used in game theory. A game is in normal form if the players formulate their plays before any moves are made. In a game of checkers, for instance, each player would construct a list of his moves, covering all possible circumstances. The players then might present their lists to an umpire. After deciding which player should make the first move, the umpire could compare each player's list of moves and determine the winner of the game. Although the reduction of most games to the normalized form may seem tedious, this form represents a comparatively simple model for mathematically analyzing any game. The normal form is better suited to the derivation of general theorems and the establishment of properties common to all games than is the extensive form. A game takes the extensive form if each player plans or considers each move as he encounters it. If an individual is interested only in the analysis of a specific case, for example, advertising policy in a particular oligopoly, the extensive form of a game will prove to be a better tool. Von Neumann and Morgenstern observe that both forms of games are "strictly equivalent," and that ". . . it is entirely within our province to use each particular case whichever is technically more convenient at that moment." [17]

TWO-PERSON GAMES

Zero-Sum
Two-Person Games

The zero-sum two-person game is strictly competitive: each player gains what the other loses. Each player is the direct adversary of the other. In such a game each player knows the values of all elements in the matrix, that is, he knows the available alternatives and their consequences. Each player has a preference ordering for certain outcomes, and he knows his opponent's preferences.[18]

Suppose that two firms, A and B, are duopolists attempting to select the proper advertising strategy to follow. Assume that each firm has only two alternative strategies and that the matrix in Figure 28 describes the numerical outcomes of these strategies.[19]

Which strategy should firm A use in order to maximize its gains? If each firm knew its opponent's strategy, it could easily decide on the

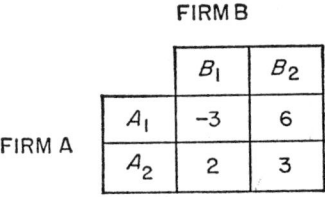

Figure 28

proper strategy. If firm B employs strategy B_1, firm A would obviously use strategy A_2; whereas if B selects B_2, A should choose A_1, because in this way A's gains would be maximized. On the other hand, B should select strategy B_1 if A picks A_1, and B_1 if A chooses A_2. The fact remains, however, that neither A nor B knows which strategy the other will employ. Under these circumstances, what strategies should the two firms use?

Game theory provides a criterion for the firms to use. It suggests that ". . . the sensible objective of the player is to gain as much from the game as he can, safely, in the face of a skillful opponent who is pursuing an antithetical goal." [20] If firm A values security it will act to maximin, that is, regardless of what B does, A will try to guard against receiving less than the largest minimum outcome he possibly can. B, on the other hand, wants to surrender the least to A as possible—to minimax. Thus, if firm A employs a maximin strategy, B should use a minimax strategy. Both players assume that they should make the best of the situation, and attempt to obtain the highest of the minimum payoffs. These strategies are logical in a two-person game, for it is assumed that each player believes the other is "out to get him," and each, therefore, believes that he must protect himself in a dangerous situation.

Given the matrix in Figure 28, then, firm A should select the maximin strategy A_2, for the smallest gain it could receive is 2. Firm B, following similar reasoning, will select its minimax strategy B_1, for the most it could lose is 2, whereas its loss through the choice of strategy B_2 might be as great as 6.

The element in the payoff matrix where the pure strategies of the two firms intersect, A_2B_1, indicates that the value of the game is 2— that is, firm B must make a payment of 2 to firm A. An element in a matrix (such as 2) which is both the maximin of the row vectors and minimax of the column vectors is defined as a saddle point. When a saddle point exists the game is strictly determined. It will pay both players to utilize the strategy which corresponds to the saddle point.[21] If one of the players deviates from this strategy, his opponent will benefit. Thus, if in our illustration firm A employs its maximin strategy A_2, but firm B uses B_2, A's gains rise from 2 to 3. Similarly, if B plays its minimax strategy B_1, and firm A selects A_1 rather than A_2, firm A will lose 3 rather than gain 2.[22] If both players deviate from their optimal strategies the situation becomes indeterminate, and one of the firms will suffer needlessly.

Not all two-person games using pure strategies possess a saddle point. Assume that the matrix facing the two firms were as follows.

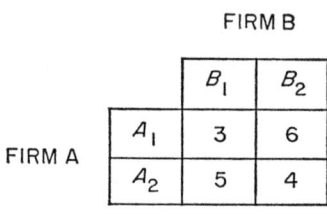

Figure 29

Firm A, following the maximin rationale described above, should choose strategy two, which will guarantee it a gain of at least four. Firm B, similarly motivated to minimax, will select strategy one, which will ensure that its largest loss could be five.

In this illustration no saddle point exists, that is, no one element in the payoff matrix is both the maximin in a row and the minimax in a column, because either A or B could improve its payoff by deviating from a minimax strategy if the other adhered to it.

Because no saddle point exists, each firm (acting rationally) would want to protect itself by obscuring its strategy from its opponent. If firm B knew that firm A intended to use strategy A_2, B would select B_2 to restrict its loss to 4. If A knew that B_2 was to be employed, it would use A_1, and gain 6.

This sort of game, which is not strictly determined, was solved first by von Neumann, who proved that there is a single rational course of action which is representative of the best strategy and of a saddle point, even in games which are not strictly determined.

Von Neumann's method uses mixed strategies. The firms may conceal their decisions by using a "chance" device to select the pure strategy which will be employed on each play. A zero-sum two-person game with a finite number of strategies always has a saddle point if mixed strategies are used. A set of probabilities can always be found which will ensure

THE THEORY OF GAMES   145

that there is a determinate solution to such a game. As Stone has written: "The introduction of probabilities is seen to be no arbitrary device, but an obvious means by which a player may protect himself from having his strategy in any particular play discovered by his opponent." [23]

From Figure 29 we can see how the firms might select a mixed strategy in order to make the game determinate. Suppose that firm A selected a mixed strategy which combines pure strategy A_1 with a probability of $\frac{1}{2}$ and pure strategy A_2, also with a probability of $\frac{1}{2}$. Now, if player B uses his pure strategy B_1, we can calculate A's expected return

$$\tfrac{1}{2}(3) + \tfrac{1}{2}(5) = 4$$

On the other hand, if firm B employs its pure strategy B_2, A's expected value is

$$\tfrac{1}{2}(6) + \tfrac{1}{2}(4) = 5$$

At the very worst, if A were to use either of its pure strategies, it would gain at least a value of 3, the minimum of the row minima. By employing a mixed strategy with probabilities of $\frac{1}{2}$, $\frac{1}{2}$, the least firm A can obtain is a payoff value of 4. It is evident that this mixed strategy would produce a more satisfactory outcome (that is, a higher valued payoff) than either pure strategy A_1 or A_2.

However, it may also be assumed that both firm A and firm B will want to use not only a mixed strategy that is better than their pure strategies, but rather will try to obtain the best payoff under the rules of the game. Thus, player A will choose that strategy, called an optimum strategy, that will maximize its minimum expected value. The optimal strategies for both A and B may be found through a modification of the expected value formula introduced in Chapter 6. For A,

$$\begin{aligned} p(3) + (1-p)(5) &= 5 - 2p \\ p(6) + (1-p)(4) &= 4 + 2p \\ \hline 4 + 2p &= 5 - 2p \\ 4p &= 1 \\ p &= \tfrac{1}{4} \\ 1 - p &= \tfrac{3}{4} \end{aligned}$$

where p denotes probability, and the sum of the probabilities must equal 1. Through this formula, then, firm A arrives at its optimal mixed strategy of using strategy A_1 one-fourth of the time. The firm should employ a chance device which will produce these odds—perhaps a four card deck, from which, if card one is drawn at random, strategy one would be used; whereas if cards two, three, or four are drawn, strategy two would be employed.

Firm B, in similar fashion, can select its own optimal mixed strategy

$$p(3) + (1-p)(6) = 6 - 3p$$
$$p(5) + (1-p)(4) = 4 + p$$

$$4 + p = 6 - 3p$$
$$4p = 2$$
$$p = \tfrac{1}{2}$$
$$1 - p = \tfrac{1}{2}$$

and employ its pure strategies in a 1:1 ratio. The pure strategy to be used in any given play could be determined by the toss of a coin.

The value of this game is the expected value based on the probability-determined employment of strategies. In Figure 29 the value of the game would be:

Firm A

$$\tfrac{1}{4}\{(p)(3) + (1-p)(6)\} + \tfrac{3}{4}\{(p)(5) + (1-p)(4)\} = 4.5$$

Firm B

$$\tfrac{1}{2}\{(p)(3) + (1-p)(5)\} + \tfrac{1}{2}\{(p)(6) + (1-p)(4)\} = 4.5$$

Firm B would, therefore, make a payment of 4.5 to Firm A.

This sort of "two-by-two" game is the simplest illustration of the use of optimal mixed strategies. The result, 4.5, is the highest possible minimum payoff (maximin) that A can hope to obtain in this game. In the same way, 4.5 is the lowest possible payoff (minimax) which firm B can hope to lose to firm A.[24]

Two-by-n Zero-Sum Games

In two-by-n or rectangular games there are still two players involved, but at least one of the players has more than two strategies. There are several methods of analyzing two-by-n games, one of which is graphical. Through the graphic method such a game can be solved, and the players provided with optimum strategies. Let us examine a game in which one player has two pure strategies, and the other has three, as in Figure 30. Suppose firm A directs its attention to strategy A_1. With what proba-

FIRM B

	B_1	B_2	B_3
A_1	2	5	6
A_2	5	4	1

FIRM A

Figure 30

bility (p) should it play this strategy? The abscissa of the graph in Figure 31 is the probability of A_1 ranging from 0 to 1. The ordinate plots the payoffs to A. The straight lines labeled B_1, B_2, and B_3 are the pure strategies from which B may choose. Now the payoffs to A may be computed, assuming that A employs A_1 with a probability p, and B uses either B_1, B_2, or B_3.

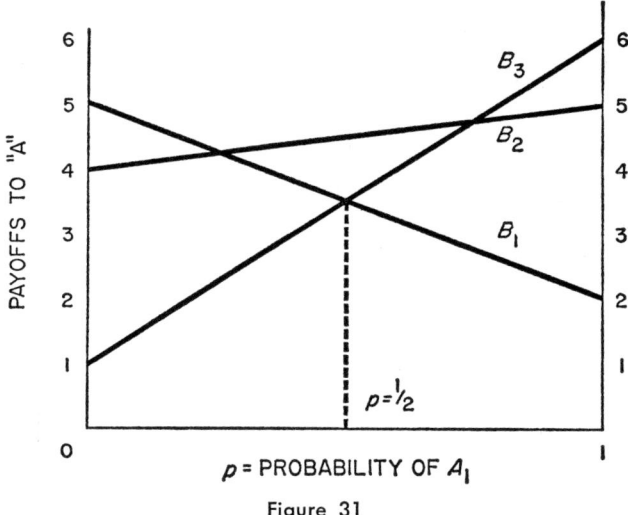

Figure 31

Thus, if A uses A_1 and B uses B_1, the payoff to A is:

$$p(2) + (1 - p)(5) = 5 - 3p$$

If B uses B_2, the payoff to A is:

$$p(5) + (1 - p)(4) = 4 + p$$

And if B employs B_3, the payoff to A is:

$$p(6) + (1 - p)(1) = 1 + 5p$$

Obviously, from Figure 31, B can minimax by using a combination of B_1 and B_3, because one or the other of these strategies gives the lowest payoff possible to A for any given p. This combination of B_1 and B_3 can be found through discovering the value of p which will satisfy the equation

$$5 - 3p = 1 + 5p$$

which, in this case, is 1/2. Firm A, therefore, should use A_1 with a probability of 1/2, employing a chance device such as a coin toss to determine when A_1 or A_2 should be used.

Because strategy B_2 obviously will not produce a minimax solution through the mixed strategy technique previously discussed, and because the game is now represented by a 2 × 2 matrix: B's optimal strategy is

$$\begin{array}{cc} 2 & 6 \\ -5 & 1 \\ \hline -3 & \overline{5} \end{array}$$

(5/8, 0, 3/8), and the value of the game may be found to be:

Firm B

$$\tfrac{5}{8}\{(p)(2) + (1-p)(5)\} + 0\{(p)(3) + (1-p)(4)\} \\ + \tfrac{3}{8}\{(p)(6) + (1-p)\} = 3.5$$

Firm A

$$\tfrac{1}{2}\{(p)(2) + (1-p)(6)\} + \tfrac{1}{2}\{(p)(5) + (1-p)(1)\} = 3.5$$

Two-by-n games do not necessarily have to have a unique optimal solution. Some games may present a range of optimal mixed strategies. The solution to any two-by-n game, however, may be found through the graphical method. Figure 32, below, illustrates a somewhat generalized solution to such games:

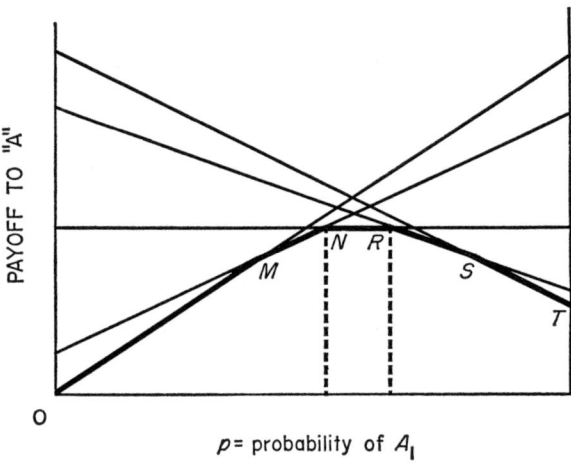

Figure 32

There are n straight lines in Figure 32, each of which represents a choice of a pure strategy by player B. The minimum expectation of A varies with p according to the locus OMNRST, made up of the lowest line segments in the diagram. The highest point or points on the locus represents the optimal value or values of p according to the minimax principle. In general there is either a range of optimal p's (on a horizontal line, such as NR in Figure 32), or a single optimum p at the apex of the minimal line segments. A special case of this general solution

The Theory of Games

occurs when the apex is at the point where $p = 0$ or $p = 1$, in which case A will play a pure strategy with a stable outcome.[25]

NONCONSTANT-SUM GAMES

The games examined thus far have been constant sum or strictly competitive, and have clear-cut solutions if the players behave in a fashion defined by von Neumann and Morgenstern (and generally accepted) as rational. Once one leaves the realm of strictly competitive games, however, there is no generally accepted concept of "rational" behavior. Furthermore, because most games which are of interest in business situations are not constant sum, this is a most regrettable state of affairs.

Nonconstant-sum games are of two types: (1) cooperative, where there is collusion among players, and where preplay activities are permitted; or (2) noncooperative, where there is no collusion and no preplay communication between players prior to the selection of their strategies.[26]

Noncooperative Games

We may illustrate some of the difficulties involved in noncooperative games by using payoff matrices similar to those constructed earlier.[27] In Figure 33 there exist two equilibrium strategies (A_1, B_1) and (A_2, B_2). These are equilibria because there would be no incentive to change either player's strategy, even should each player be informed of the other's choice. However, A prefers A_1, B_1, and B would rather settle at A_2, B_2.

	B_1	B_2
A_1	3	0
A_2	0	2

PAYOFF MATRIX FOR "A"

	B_1	B_2
A_1	2	0
A_2	0	3

PAYOFF MATRIX FOR "B"

Figure 33

Player A has a maximin strategy of $(2/5, 3/5)$, while B's minimax strategy is $(3/5, 2/5)$, so that the value of such strategies for either player is only 1.2.

Firm A
$$\tfrac{2}{5}\{(p)(3) + (1 - p)(0)\} + \tfrac{3}{5}\{(p)(0) + (1 - p)(2)\} = 1.2$$

Firm B
$$\tfrac{3}{5}\{(p)(2) + (1 - p)(0)\} + \tfrac{2}{5}\{(p)(0) + (1 - p)(3)\} = 1.2$$

Obviously both A and B would obtain a more satisfactory payoff from either A_1, B_1 or A_2, B_2 than they would from following their maximin and minimax strategies. Furthermore, if player A chooses its maximin, B will select B_2, whereas A will pick A_1 if B decides to minimax.

This sort of noncooperative game can be discussed in less formal language. Firm A is not permitted to communicate with firm B. Thus, player A knows that (A_1, B_1), which produces a payoff of 3 is his highest gain, but he also knows that B would prefer (A_2, B_2). A might reason, then, that if he selects strategy A_1 and B takes B_2, the final payoff to both will be zero (A_1, B_2). A could do better than this by compromising on A_2, so that his payoff at (A_2, B_2) would be at least 2. But, then, A might recall, B is also thinking about his moves, and may decide to capitulate to A by selecting B_1, in which case the game would end up at (A_2, B_1). In fact, it would soon become clear to A that, as long as he could not communicate with B, he could not be sure which of his pure strategies would be best.

Firm A, therefore, might decide to turn to a mixed strategy, and play A_1 two-fifths and A_2 three-fifths of the time, as determined at random by some sort of chance device. However, if A does this B might realize it, and play B_2 continuously. On the other hand, if B minimaxes, A should play A_1. In this type of noncooperative game, then, there is no satisfactory solution.

Similarly unsatisfactory is the solution to the noncooperative game known as "the prisoner's dilemma."[28] This is illustrated in Figure 34.

	B_1	B_2
A_1	9	0
A_2	10	1

PAYOFF MATRIX FOR "A"

	B_1	B_2
A_1	9	10
A_2	0	1

PAYOFF MATRIX FOR "B"

Figure 34

In this noncooperative game A should select his maximin strategy A_2, whereas B should minimax by choosing B_2. These choices will result in a joint payoff of one to each player at A_2, B_2. It would be to the advantage of both A and B to select their first strategies, and end at A_1, B_1, where the payoff to each would be nine. If, however, A selects A_1, B might "doublecross" A by choosing B_2, whereby B would obtain a payoff of 10, and A would receive zero. If B chooses B_1, A might try a "doublecross" by selecting A_2, thus receiving a payoff of 10 and leaving B with zero. Thus, A_1, B_1 is the best outcome only if both A and B are guaranteed that there will not be a doublecross. By the very nature of noncooperative games, such a guarantee is of course impossible.

Although the games illustrated above do not produce satisfactory solutions, they do contain several interesting features which cast some light upon certain aspects of business behavior.[29] Both A and B, in the games presented, would benefit if either could disclose the strategy that was going to be selected, and if each has a reputation for stubbornness and inflexibility. Thus, if A in the game illustrated in Figure 34 publicized that he intended to select A_1 so long as B picked B_1, and if A had a reputation which justified B's belief in the honesty of this announcement, both firms would benefit. Preplay communication and a knowledge of the opponent's character and personality traits, therefore, might lead to satisfactory payoffs for both players. If A, given the matrices in Figure 33, knew that firm B was directed by a spiteful person, it might be better to let B select its strategy first. Also, if B was a large firm, with vast resources, it might prefer to settle on A_1, B_2 or A_2, B_1, simply to drive A out of business. In both games illustrated, however, only some sort of cooperation (which of course is strictly verboten) can help the players reach solutions which will be to their advantage.

Cooperative Games

In cooperative games preplay messages are permitted between players. If any agreements are reached between the players they are binding, and are enforceable by the rules of the game. It is further assumed (and this assumption often seems unpalatable) that these preplay discussions and agreements do not affect either players' opinions concerning the payoff values of the game.

> Most authors feel that, if such economic problems as duopoly, labor-management disputes, trade regulations between two countries, etc., can be treated as games at all, then it will have to be in the cooperative context . . . Given the present state of game theory, we are indeed skeptical that many such problems can be given a realistic formal analysis; rather, we would contend that a case can be made for studying simplified models which are suggested by and related to the problem of interest. The hope is that, by analogy, their analysis will shed light —however dim and unreliable—on the strategic and communication aspects of the real problem.[30]

There are several types of solutions to cooperative games. We shall examine one of these here.

Von Neumann and Morgenstern have prepared a generalized (non-unique) solution for cooperative games. In Figure 35 below the matrices of the noncooperative game presented earlier in Figure 33 are reproduced.

In a cooperative version of this game communications between the players can provide a solution much more satisfactory than could be

	B_1	B_2
A_1	3	0
A_2	0	2

PAYOFF MATRIX FOR "A"

	B_1	B_2
A_1	2	0
A_2	0	3

PAYOFF MATRIX FOR "B"

Figure 35

obtained when both players were involved in a strictly competitive situation. Thus, if the game in Figure 35 is to be repeated over and over again, both players can agree to alternate payoffs between A_1, B_1 and A_2, B_2, with an average payoff to each of 2.5. If the game is to consist of only a single play the players could decide, through the toss of a coin perhaps, whether to play A_1, B_1 or A_2, B_2.

By plotting the points formed through the combination of common elements in both matrices in Figure 35, for example (3,2), (0,0), (2,3) a region R can be obtained. R is the smallest convex body containing these points.[31] In this instance, as is shown in Figure 36, R includes all the correlated pure and mixed strategies included in this game.

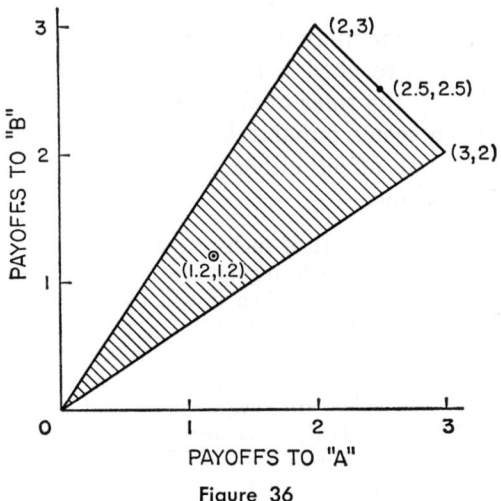

Figure 36

Suppose we examine a game, the convex body R of which is that described in Figure 37. It is assumed that neither A nor B is interested in payoffs which are less satisfactory than others, that is, which are jointly dominated by higher payoffs or points. The undominated outcomes in Figure 37 are those on the boundary of the convex body R, described by the dark line a, b, c, d. These undominated outcomes are called the *Pareto optimal set* of R.

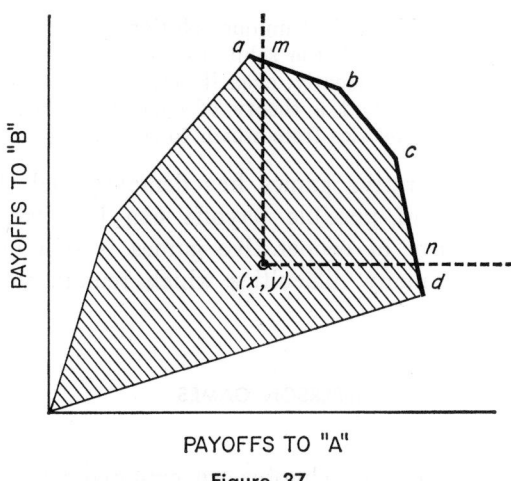

Figure 37

In Figure 37 it is evident that player A would most desire outcome d, whereas B would most prefer a. These points, however, are clearly unattainable, for the opposing player, by using a mixed strategy and acting noncooperatively, can obtain guaranteed amounts equal to (x,y), so that he would never accept less than his maximin payoffs. Through cooperation, then, the satisfactory solution to A and B must be along the boundary m, b, c, n, which is termed the *negotiation set* of the game.

This is as far as von Neumann and Morgenstern go in the direction of solving cooperative two-person games. When the players have discarded all jointly dominated payoffs, and all undominated payoffs which are less than that which could be obtained by acting in a noncooperative fashion, the actual solution lies on the negotiation set, but just where the outcome will be depends upon a number of variables of a psychological rather than a mathematical nature.

Actually, not all game theorists would agree that the outcome of a cooperative game must lie on the negotiation set. Through threats, for example, a player may force his opponent to accept a solution which is less desirable than the maximin payoff.[32] However, most of the "advances" in the solution of cooperative games in the past decade have suggested a single point on the Pareto locus, which is reached through arbitration, bluffing, threats, or compromise.[33] Modern game theorists, therefore, have extended the Pareto optimum technique beyond the solution of von Neumann and Morgenstern to settle on unique points within the Pareto optimum.

> The various treatments purport either to characterize how people react dynamically in conflict situations, or to suggest a system of fair and reasonable principles by which the conflict should be arbitrated. With a sufficient number of additional axioms or behavioral postulates,

the authors are able to find unique solutions to any conflict problems. As might be anticipated, the solutions themselves differ from theorist to theorist, and consequently, even if one is wedded to the notion that economists should adopt a theory of conflict resolution, there is still a wide variety of theories from which to select.[34]

The work on cooperative games has demonstrated that situations with a large number of possible payoffs can be "solved" uniquely. Nevertheless, the theory of cooperative games is still quite unsophisticated, and contains many difficulties which remain to be overcome.

n-PERSON GAMES

In the above sections of this chapter we explored noncooperative and cooperative nonconstant-sum games, and concluded that these portions of game theory require further study. N-person games contain many of the same difficulties found in nonconstant-sum games, and in addition introduce a host of new problems.

In n-person games the number of players is three or larger. Potentially, n-person games should have the greatest application in business, for most business problems involve more than two buyers, or sellers, or competitors . . . or other business players.

If there are three players in a game, two players may form a coalition against the third. Or it is possible that all three might get together to divide maximum rewards among themselves. If coalitions do form, furthermore, there are the additional problems of how to allocate payoffs among the coalition members.

Before we illustrate n-person games, a few terms should be defined. An assignment of payoffs to players in a coalition is termed an *imputation* if each player obtains an amount equal to or greater than that which he can obtain independently and if the total payoffs equal at least the amount all players would receive if they were all members of a coalition. An imputation possesses the characteristic of domination when members of a coalition prefer it to at least one other coalition. A *solution* of an n-person game is reached (in von Neumann's and Morgenstern's terms) when the undominated imputations are known. This concept is similar to the "negotiation set" definition used in our discussion of cooperative games. It also possesses the same difficulties, because a solution to an n-person game does not ordinarily result in a unique outcome to the game.

The above concepts, and some of the difficulties involved in n-person games may be illustrated through an example of a simple three-person game.[35] Suppose that there are three firms, A, B, and C, engaged in the production and sale of a specific commodity. If they each act independently, their profits (perhaps because of the intensity of competition) will be zero, as described by (I) below.

(I) $\quad\quad\quad\quad\quad\quad \pi(A) = \pi(B) = \pi(C) = 0$

On the other hand, if any pair of these firms form a coalition it will receive the maximum profits of 100, and the player which is not a coalition member will receive zero, as in (II).

(II) $\quad\quad\quad\quad\quad\quad \pi(A, B) = \pi(A, C) = \pi(B, C) = 100$

If all three firms form a coalition it will receive the maximum profits of 100.

(III) $\quad\quad\quad\quad\quad\quad\quad \pi(A, B, C) = 100$

Suppose that A and B form a coalition (thus excluding C) which receives the entire profits, 100, from the game. It would appear most likely, given this situation, that A and B would each receive 50. Actually there is no reason to assume that this specific coalition will form, and any of the imputations in (II) appear equally likely, as below.

(IV) $\quad\quad\quad\quad (50, 50, 0), \quad (50, 0, 50), \quad (0, 50, 50)$

If, however, as we assumed, A and B do form a coalition with an imputation (50, 50, 0) player C would have to act to obtain a share of the profits. C might, then, approach B, to form the coalition C, B with a total payoff of 100. However, it is evident that B will not be attracted to this new coalition unless C promises a division of the 100 profits so that B will receive more than 50, the amount B could obtain in the A, B coalition. Assume that C promises B a payoff of 75 in the new coalition, so that the imputation would be

(V) $\quad\quad\quad\quad\quad\quad\quad (0, 75, 25) = 100$

Both B and C would benefit more from (V) than from (IV), so that (V) dominates (IV), and the change should occur.

However, imputation (V) is far from stable. Firm A could now approach C and propose the following:

(VI) $\quad\quad\quad\quad\quad\quad\quad (50, 0, 50)$

in which case a coalition would be formed between A and C, and B would be left out, and the whole process could begin over again.

Even the possibility of all three players forming a coalition with equal shares in the outcome

(VII) $\quad\quad\quad\quad\quad\quad (33\tfrac{1}{3}, 33\tfrac{1}{3}, 33\tfrac{1}{3}) = 100$

does not produce stability.

In von Neumann's and Morgenstern's terms, however, the solution to this game is reached, because it may be observed that none of the imputations in (IV) dominates the others, and at least one of the imputations in (IV) dominates all imputations external to (IV) (for example, 50, 0, 50 in VI dominates 0, 75, 25 in V). As may be noted, however, this sort of "solution" is far from satisfactory, because the game does not produce one unique outcome which results from the pre-play discussions or plays by A, B, and C.

There has been a great deal of further work in the area of n-person games. Therefore, the above remarks are incomplete, and the illustration relatively superficial. Nevertheless, the example presented is representative of the grave analytical problems inherent in n-person games, and the unsatisfactory nature of the results which have been forthcoming.

SUMMARY

From the discussion of game theory presented in this chapter it is clear that the zero-sum two-person game has been most carefully analyzed. Noncooperative and cooperative nonconstant-sum and n-person games, on the other hand, still contain many difficulties which appear most untractable to investigators. Despite the unsatisfactory state of current game theory, it has made certain contributions which could be of utility for the study of business behavior.

Williams, for example, has argued that the greatest contribution of game theory

> . . . has been an intangible one: the general orientation given to people who are faced with overcomplex problems. Even though these problems are not directly solvable—certainly at the moment and probably for the indefinite future—it helps to have a framework in which to work on them.[36]

Shubik has used a game theoretical framework in examining certain aspects of the automobile and tobacco industries.[37] It is possible—in fact it is probable—that the structure of game theory will become even more useful for analyses of oligopolistic behavior.[38] At the same time, however, game theory does not appear today to promise the convenient route for the analysis of oligopoly that it seemed to offer in the 1940's.

Another contribution of game theory is that each player is provided (at least in the zero-sum two-person game) with a principle by which he can behave rationally in a conflict situation. The theory casts doubt upon the wisdom of adhering to the conventional principle of maximization. Even if individual firms desired to maximize a potential game, they could not possibly do so unless they had complete knowledge of the actions and reactions of their competitors. As Hurwicz has written:

Not that maximization (of utility or profits) would not be desirable if it were feasible, but there can be no true maximization when only one of the several factors which decide the outcome (of say, oligopolistic competition) is controlled by the given individual.[39]

Von Neumann and Morgenstern's theory suggests that the maximization principle should be replaced by the concept of maximin-minimax. The latter concept recognizes that prudent players will adopt strategies which will guarantee them the largest minimum gain or the smallest maximum loss. No matter how clever an opponent may be, a player can be guaranteed that he will at least attain a certain gain or that he will not lose more than a certain amount.

Furthermore, the theory of games focuses attention upon the behavior of other business players, as well as upon the firm itself. Opponents are vitally concerned not only with their own strategies but also with those of their competitors. As H. L. McCracken has stated:

> Regardless of how professors of economic theory write their books or draw their demand and cost curves, the chief concern of the successful businessman is that of watching daily the moves of his competitors and the possible or prospective changes in mood or habit of prospective customers. Every new move made by competitor or customer makes imperative some new move or considered adjustment in his own business to meet the new contingency.[40]

However, game theory always presumes perfectly rational behavior on the part of the players. If McCracken, in the above passage, wanted to make his concern with business behavior even more "realistic" he would have to assume that businessmen do not always act or react rationally, an assumption which further complicates the analysis of behavior, and separates game theory from the real world of business.

Inasmuch as the discussion has turned toward realism, it should be noted here that it would be most difficult, because of the volume and complexity of the mathematical calculations, to construct even a two-person game based upon real business situations. Morgenstern, for example, has estimated "that the calculations for a game in which one manufacturer had 100 possible strategies and his competitor had 200 (a not uncommon situation) would take about a year on an electronic computer.[41]

Not only the mathematical complexities, but even more significantly the costs of obtaining and processing the information necessary to construct a game are overwhelming. Shubik claims that "by attaching even slight costs to the acts of storing, gathering, and processing information, any firm can compute that the cost of getting anything like complete information will be astronomical.[42]

The theory of games, then, has enhanced the study of business behavior by providing an improved framework for the examination of conflict situations and by establishing a criterion for rational behavior in such situations. Nevertheless, it has not been as useful for business theory as it promised to be in the 1940's. It is not surprising, therefore, that we can, almost twenty years after von Neumann's and Morgenstern's work, conclude this chapter with Hurwicz's still pertinent comment:

> The potentialities of von Neumann's and Morgenstern's new approach seem tremendous and may, one hopes, lead to revamping, and enriching in realism, a good deal of economic theory. But to a large extent they are only potentialities: results are still largely a matter of future development.[43]

Notes and References

1. Leonid Hurwicz, "The Theory of Economic Behavior," in G. J. Stigler and K. E. Boulding, editors, American Economic Association, *Readings in Price Theory* (Homewood, Ill: Richard D. Irwin, Inc., 1952), p. 506.

2. Oskar Morgenstern, foreword to Martin Shubik, *Strategy and Market Structure* (New York: John Wiley & Sons, Inc., 1959), p. viii.

3. John Von Neumann and Oskar Morgenstern, *Theory of Games and Economic Behavior* (Princeton, N. J.: Princeton University Press, 1944), pp. 1-2.

4. Martin Shubik, "The Use of Game Theory in Management Science," *Management Science*, Vol. II (October, 1955), pp. 40-48.

5. E. G. Bennion, "Capital Budgeting and Game Theory," *Harvard Business Review*, Vol. XXXIV (November-December, 1956), pp. 115-123.

6. E. L. Kropa, "Game Theory in Development," *Industrial and Engineering Chemistry*, Vol. XLVIII (March, 1956), pp. 388-392.

7. H. Bierman, Jr., L. E. Fouraker, and R. K. Jaedicke, *Quantitative Analysis for Business Decisions* (Homewood, Ill.: Richard D. Irwin, Inc., 1961), pp. 94-106.

8. S. B. Smith, "Game Theory: New Tool for P. A.'s," *Purchasing*, Vol. L. (February 13, 1961), pp. 86-89.

9. Von Neumann and Morgenstern, *op. cit.*, pp. 7-8.

10. See, for example, Emil Borel, "The Theory of Play and Integral Equations with Skew Symmetrical Kernels;" "On Games that Involve Chance and the Skill of the Players;" and "On Systems of Linear Forms of Skew Symmetrical Determinants and the General Theory of Play," translated by L. J. Savage, *Econometrica*, Vol. XXI (January, 1953), pp. 97-117. Apparently the concept of the matrix game and its solution by means of mixed strategies goes back at least to 1713. See: Martin Shubik,

"Game Theory as an Approach to the Firm," *The American Economic Review,* Vol. L, Supplement (May, 1960), pp. 556-557.

11. Maurice Frechet, "Commentary on the Borel Notes," *Econometrica,* Vol. XXI (January, 1953), p. 118.

12. John Von Neumann, "Communication on the Borel Notes," *Econometrica,* Vol. XXI (January, 1953), pp. 295-320.

13. John Von Neumann, "Zur Theorie der Gesellschaftsspiele," *Mathematische Annalen,* Vol. C (1928), pp. 295-320.

14. John Von Neumann and Oskar Morgenstern, *op. cit.,* p. 49.

15. R. Duncan Luce and Howard Raiffa, *Games and Decisions* (New York: John Wiley & Sons, Inc., 1954), pp. 39-40.

16. J. D. Williams, *The Compleat Strategyst* (New York: McGraw-Hill Book Company, Inc., 1954), p. 16.

17. Von Neumann and Morgenstern, *op. cit.,* p. 85.

18. See Luce and Raiffa, *op. cit.,* p. 58 for a fuller account of the assumptions necessary to a two-person zero-sum game.

19. Although each firm has a separate payoff matrix, two-person zero-sum games can be portrayed by utilizing only one matrix because what one player gains, the other player loses. By convention, the payoffs in the matrix represent the payments of firm B to firm A. Positive payoffs signify a payment from firm B to firm A; negative payoffs indicate a payment from firm A to firm B. Payments in this case may represent a percentage share of the market.

20. Williams, *op. cit.,* p. 23.

21. Von Neumann and Morgenstern observe that a game may possess several saddle points. However, each of these saddle points renders a determinate solution to the game.

22. This result does not necessarily hold in all instances. If one of the players is irrational or ignorant, or for some reason does not wish to minimax, the firm which uses a maximin strategy may find that this course of action is unprofitable. As Baumol has written ". . . the prudent maximin strategy is only guaranteed to be good when playing against another prudent man!" Baumol, *Economic Theory and Operations Analysis* (Englewood Cliffs, N.J.: Prentice-Hall, Inc., 1961), p. 352.

23. Richard Stone, "The Theory of Games," *Economic Journal,* Vol. LVIII (June, 1948), p. 191.

24. This chapter, to this point, is based almost entirely upon an unpublished paper written by Mr. Walter Hill of Syracuse University.

25. We can use the same graphical method to solve payoff matrices of the order $m \times 2$. In this case player B uses mixed strategies. It would also be possible (but not very practical) to use the graphical method to solve $3 \times n$ or $m \times 3$ games. Such games, however, would involve the use of three dimensional planes, which would be difficult to construct. The horizontal plane or line, or an apex, would still indicate the optimal mixed strategies for the player with three strategies.

26. Harvey M. Wagner, "Advances in Game Theory," *The American Economic Review*, Vol. XLVIII, No. 3 (June, 1958), p. 382.

27. These are similar to those presented in Luce and Raiffa, *op. cit.*, p. 90ff.

28. *Ibid.*, pp. 94-97.

29. Not all noncooperative games are unsolvable. Those with finite sets of pure strategies have at least one mixed strategy pair so that, for example, the prisoner's dilemma in Figure 35 is solvable, *in the sense* that the equilibrium pairs are equivalent and interchangeable. See: *Ibid.*, pp. 106-109 and J. F. Nash, "Non-cooperative Games," *Annals of Mathematics*, Vol. 54 (1951), pp. 286-295.

30. Luce and Raiffa, *op. cit.*, p. 115.

31. A convex body is simply a half-space (as illustrated in our linear programming examples in Chapter 5) which also includes its boundaries.

32. See the illustration in *Ibid.*, pp. 119-120.

33. See, among others: J. F. Nash, "The Bargaining Problem," *Econometrica*, Vol. 18 (1950), pp. 155-162; J. C. Harsanyi, "Approaches to the Bargaining Problem Before and After the Theory of Games: a Critical Discussion of Zeuthen's, Hicks, and Nash's Theories," *Econometrica*, Vol. 24 (1956), pp. 144-157; J. F. Nash, "Two-Person Cooperative Games," *Econometrica*, Vol. 21 (1953), pp. 128-140.

34. Wagner, *op. cit.*, p. 384.

35. Based upon an example in Luce and Raiffa, *op. cit.*, pp. 199-203.

36. Williams, *op. cit.*, p. 217.

37. Martin Shubik, *Strategy and Market Structure* (New York: John Wiley & Sons, Inc., 1959), pp. 296-321.

38. See the interesting experiments in bilateral monopoly in Sidney Siegal and Lawrence E. Fouraker, *Bargaining and Group Decision Making* (New York: McGraw-Hill Book Company, Inc., 1960).

39. Hurwicz, *op. cit.*, pp. 506-507.

40. H. L. McCracken, "Discussion of Morgenstern's Article, Oligopoly, Monopolistic Competition, and the Theory of Games," *The American Economic Review*, XXXVIII (May, 1948), p. 28.

41. Oskar Morgenstern, "The Theory of Games," *Scientific American,* Vol. CLXXX (May, 1949), p. 24.

42. Martin Shubik, "Information, Theories of Competition, and the Theory of Games," *Journal of Political Economy,* Vol. LX (April, 1952), p. 148. Copyright 1952 by The University of Chicago.

43. Hurwicz, *op. cit.*, p. 523.

8

ORGANIZATIONAL
THEORIES
AND
BUSINESS BEHAVIOR

In this chapter we shall examine several of the concepts and problems which appear to occupy a central position in organization theory. The field of organization theory is somewhat special in the social sciences, for it has evolved through the efforts of a large number of scholars with a wide variety of backgrounds. As a result, although research on organizations has produced several persons who write with authority, it has not created a ". . . single, well-defined community of scholars with responsibility for research in organization theory, as there is for physics, psychology, or economics." [1] Contributions to an understanding of organizational behavior currently originate in diverse disciplines, and consequently have been somewhat diffuse. A theoretical mosaic has been constructed with a myriad of ideas and concepts, many of which are held together only by the most tenuous, unsystematic, and noncumulative ties. Nevertheless, despite the nebulous character of much of the area of organization theory, there have emerged certain fundamental notions upon which the skeleton of a theoretical structure may be built.

Much of the more significant recent work in organization theory has tended to focus on two broad areas: (1) The viability of organizations and the inducement-contributions balance which maintains viability; and (2) The questions of rationality and decision-making behavior. These two categories encompass a wide band of more specific topics which have been singled out in the recent literature for considerable attention. We shall, in this chapter, examine a number of these subjects, such as theories which stress the tendencies toward or away from organizational equilibrium, roles, motivational constraints, goals, and the constraints upon rational action, in addition to other variables which enter into or impinge upon the decision-making process.

One final comment of a general nature appears to be in order before we embark on our exploration of the subjects listed above. Organization theory has as its objective the study of all types of human organizations. In this book, of course, our primary concern is the behavior of the firm and its members but, because the business firm is one of our most prominent organizations, the parallels between theories of organization and of business behavior are obvious.

FRAMEWORKS FOR ORGANIZATIONAL VIABILITY

Classical Structures

Every discipline is built to some extent upon the work of innovators which, whether later accepted or discarded, forms the foundation for the accumulation of knowledge in the field. It is this basic work in organization theory to which we have given the title "classical structures." The scientific management school, led by Frederick W. Taylor, the human relations movement pioneered by Elton Mayo, and the classic theory of bureaucracy created by Max Weber form a large part of this foundation. Scientific management, because of its empirical, engineering, and mechanistic emphasis, has been focused primarily upon that combination of procedures which surrounds the efficient conduct of a specific task.[2] As a result it has remained somewhat outside the mainstream of organization theory and, because it does not contain those elements from which theoretical organizational generalizations have been drawn, it will not be discussed in this section. Instead, we shall examine briefly the frameworks for organizational viability contained in the theories of Mayo and Weber.

Human relations. Elton Mayo, the founder of the human relations movement, was distrustful of what he termed "grand theory" in the social sciences, and of the theorists who created such theory. For example, he complained:

> Their standard of intellectual achievement is high; their knowledge-of-acquaintance of actual human situations is exceedingly low. They dwell apart from humanity in certain cities of the mind—remote, intellectual, preoccupied with highly articulate thinking. They have developed capacity for dealing with complex logic, they have not acquired any skill in handling facts.[3]

Despite his feelings about "grand theory," a theoretical structure did emerge from the research of Mayo and his colleagues at the Hawthorne plant of the Western Electric Company.[4] Mayo, like Taylor and his followers, found that adaptation was a significant characteristic of men in business. However, whereas Taylor observed only the physiological process of human adjustment toward the most efficient attainment of goals, Mayo noted an adaptation which was primarily psychological and social.

Mayo conceived the business concern to be an integrated and self-contained social system.[5] He viewed the firm apart from its external environment, and closely scrutinized the internal mechanisms which tend to create a stable and harmonic social equilibrium. Thus, Roethlisburger and Dickson, Mayo's colleagues, emphasize that the chief characteristic of a social organization is: ". . . an interaction of sentiments and interests in a relation of mutual dependence, resulting in a state of equilibrium such that if that state is altered, forces tending to re-establish it come into play."[6]

Mayo and his colleagues thought of the formal organization of the business enterprise as the goal setting, administrative, and policy making framework within which social and economic activity takes place. Such activity, moreover, is affected by the informal groups which spring up spontaneously within this framework, as well as by the formal organization itself. Conflict, or disequilibrating movement, occurs when the informal structure is not in accord with the objectives of the formal organization, and ordinarily is caused by a lack of communication between management and workers, by human tensions, lack of proper orientation, and similar difficulties.[7]

Advocates of the human relations approach to industry, therefore, view the business firm as a social microcosm which needs a harmony of interests between the society and its members in order to maintain its viability. The social values possessed by the informal society of a firm must be recognized and "handled" by the administrator in order to align these values with those essential for the maintenance of the viability of the organization. Viability and the attainment of formal goals is perceived by the human relations school as the result of internal equilibria, which in turn are dependent upon employee satisfactions with the work environment. These satisfactions are the outcomes of variables which are primarily social, and include such factors as stability, cohesion, integration, cooperation, productivity, teamwork, harmony, and morale. Management works upon these factors to tailor a social equilibrium designed to further organizational goals through the emphasis upon cooperation and the removal of conflict.[8]

Because Mayo and his followers stress the societal and cooperative nature of the organization their definition of the inducement-contributions balance is not precise. Inducements are couched in general terms, for example, the members of the organization continue their membership because of the satisfying lives they are enabled to develop therein.[9] The definition of contributions is equally vague. Nevertheless, it is evident in Mayo's system that (1) organizational members are disposed to contribute and (2) that (at least up to some level) inducements and contributions are related linearly. These two features of the human relations theory of organization permit inducements frequently to consist of positive activities by management whereby measures are undertaken to alleviate conflict which has occurred, as well as those positive actions designed to prevent future conflict, such as the molding of an *esprit de corps*.

Mayo's organizational contributions have been criticized on a variety of grounds. The organizational system created by the human relationists is noteworthy for the fact that its component parts are composed principally of those variables which tend to maintain a viable equilibrium, and for its neglect of those which tend to produce conflict.[10] Sherman Krupp, in particular, has objected to the "harmony of interest" theme which he feels Mayo introduced into the stream of modern organization theory and which he believes is analogous to ". . . a description of a jungle using a theory of a farm." [11] The failure of Mayo to consider external or environmental forces also, to some critics, weakens his explanation of organizational behavior. Although all theories are abstractions, and although consequently some variables must be deleted from every theory, these critics claim that the variables omitted by Mayo are in fact too significant to be left out of any theory of business behavior. Finally, the concept of equilibrium in human relations theory is essentially an artificial norm to which individual and group contributions are adjusted through inducements offered by management. It is artificial because it is designed to forward management values alone, and is maintained largely through management efforts.[12]

Bureaucratic structure. The bureaucratic model designed by Max Weber is of interest to our study of business behavior for three reasons: (1) It forms the point of departure for several modern bureaucratic theories. (2) It stresses the design rather than the behavior of organizations, and in this way is typical of a type of theoretical studies. (3) Finally, it serves as an introduction to the terminology and concepts utilized frequently by organization theorists.

The structure of Weber's bureaucracy resembles Taylor's scientific management framework because both are "design" theories, that is, they portray the organization in a mechanistic, legalistic, and pragmatic fashion, with an emphasis upon the attributes of the formal structure rather than the behavior of the persons who inhabit it.[13]

Weber was particularly concerned with what he termed an "ideal type" of bureaucracy. This is a pure or perfect construct evolved in order to isolate the characteristics of bureaucracy from other organizational features. Weber's ideal type establishes the definition of bureaucratic concepts and also generalizes upon the interactions between those characteristics which tend to enhance organizational efficiency.

The principal features of Weber's ideal bureaucratic structure are: (1) An administrative hierarchy of offices, with each lower tier of offices being accountable to a higher office.[14] (2) Each office is staffed by specialists.[15] (3) "Within this structure of hierarchically arranged authority, the activities of 'trained and salaried experts' are governed by general, abstract, clearly defined rules which preclude the necessity for the issuance of specific instructions for each specific case."[16] (4) An atmosphere of impersonality, which is equated with a lack of human emotions and an emphasis on rationality, prevails.[17] (5) The rules of bureaucracy are written, are stable, and are capable of being learned.

The formal rationally constituted organizational structure perceived by Weber involves patterns of behavior in which every series of actions is functionally related to the organization's purposes.[18] Weber envisaged a bureaucracy of the ideal type as possessing attributes which permit the attainment of maximum organizational efficiency. The hierarchy of offices, the rules and regulations, and the other paraphernalia of Weber's bureaucratic system are designed as constraints upon individual decisions and actions, and to serve as stringent guidelines, forcing personnel to behave in a manner which is directed rationally toward organizational rather than personal goals.

Weber's bureaucratic structure, like the organization which evolves from Mayo's human relations approach, possesses a functional bias. Both scholars are primarily engaged in producing a model wherein each part contributes to the viability and efficiency of the entire organizational entity. Weber, like Mayo, became so engrossed in this endeavor that he failed to examine (except in a very cursory manner) those contradictory tendencies—those disturbances—which might, or do, tend to disrupt the smooth adjustment of the structure toward organizational objectives. It is the omission of the problem-causing elements in Weber's bureaucratic model upon which his critics have focused their attention, and the introduction of these elements into Weber's system has led to more modern theories of bureaucracy.

Both Weber's and Mayo's theories, therefore, have elements in common. Both are functional, both stress the forces within organization which contribute to viability. However, Mayo was more concerned with the attainment of equilibrium as a viable resultant, whereas Weber emphasized rationality enforced by structure as the key to reaching organizational goals. Mayo and Weber both based their theories upon the adaptability of man, and both noted the need for discipline (although Weber built this into his formal structure, Mayo assumed it would emerge through administration) in organizations. Mayo paid more attention to inducements and contributions, whereas Weber was more concerned with decision-making centers and their limits.

Dysfunctional Elements in Organization

Modern extensions of the classical theories of organization have tended to stress those dysfunctional elements which reduce the adaptability of organizations. As we have noted, neither Mayo nor Weber examined those forces which are tangential to the established goals and rationally ordered structures of organizations.[19] More recent theorists have not neglected the importance of functional forces which contribute to organizational viability; but they have recognized dysfunctional factors, such as the elements producing conflict, and in so doing have constructed theories which appear to conform more closely to reality, and to be capable of treating a greater variety of organizational problems, than traditional structures. In Chapter 2 we examined briefly the bureaucratic theories of Robert K. Merton, Philip Selznick, and Alvin W. Gouldner. Although there are many important differences between these theories, even more important are their similarities, and especially their common interest in dysfunctional elements. We shall look only at Selznick's theory here, as illustrative of the features of the other two theories.

Selznick's theory of organization. Selznick perceives the organization as a dynamic totality, constantly changing under pressures from within and without, and continually in a process of evolution.[20] As a general rule there is a tendency toward increasing rationality in bureaucratic systems,[21] but individuals resist being treated as a means to organizational goals. Thus, Selznick has written:

> From the standpoint of organization as a formal system, persons are viewed functionally, in respect to their *roles*, as participants in assigned segments of the cooperative system. But in fact individuals have a propensity to resist depersonalization, to spill over the boundaries of their segmentary roles, to participate as *wholes*.[22]

Within the organization, then, individuals constitute fresh problems for the administration, largely because of their individuality. Selznick illustrates these problems, and their effects upon the organization, by examining the delegation of authority, an act which requires the enlargement and elaboration of the structure of control and coordination.[23] Through delegation, assignments are made to organizational offices. These assignments must, of course, involve specific individuals with unique personalities, and consequently their interests and goals may differ from those of the organization. As a result, especially in large organizations, these personality differences tend to become institutionalized into informal rules for cooperation, and built into informal structures. These informal patterns are eventually absorbed into the formal organization. From this new formal structure deviations again take place, fresh informal rules and combinations are established, and these are subsequently transformed into the formal organization on a new level.

Thus, through a "structural-functional analysis" Selznick views the organization as an adaptive, cooperative system. The organization contains self-defensive mechanisms whereby it remains viable, and is enabled to respond through alterations in goals, structure, or other organizational attributes, to internal and external pressures. One mechanism of organizational adjustment stressed by Selznick (in accord with his illustration of the delegation process) is cooptation. "Cooptation is the process of absorbing new elements into the leadership or policy-determining structure of an organization as a means of averting threats to its stability or existence." [24]

The theory of organization produced by Selznick is, therefore, one of adjustment and adaptation. Goals, other than the goal of viability, are of secondary importance in the theory. Pressures, responses, changes, conflict, . . . these are the significant variables in the system. The rigidity of Weber's bureaucracy is gone, and the easy manipulability of Mayo's variables has disappeared.

Small Group Theory

In the years following World War II there occurred a great upsurge of interest in the study of a subject closely allied to organization theory —small group analysis.[25] As Golembiewski has pointed out:

> . . . The "small group" concept has been found to be a useful and a relevant one in behavioral study; the concept implies a social unit, a content-filled system, and systems can be rigorously studied; and the small group is amenable to experimentation, largely because of modest size.[26]

Because the vast majority of business firms are extremely small, it is evident that small group analysis, in itself, may be most useful to theories of business behavior. More than this, however, the small group may be examined as a vital building block, a module in the mass which is the organization.[27] The principal advantage of the small group as an object of study is its tractable size. Thus, it is sometimes assumed that the small group possesses the properties of larger units, but because of its size confines the number of interactions to manageable levels for study. On the other hand: "We simply cannot extrapolate conclusions from the small group studies when we are dealing with groups in large organizations."[28] Yet, it would appear that small group analyses would be most useful for understanding organizational behavior, although undoubtedly other variables are also significant in the explanation of the larger entity.

The study of small groups has, in large part, been conducted along two broad lines of research. The first of these has emanated from the pioneering work of Kurt Lewin, and is centered mainly in the area of group dynamics. The second grew out of the sociometric principles and methodology of J. L. Moreno, and emphasizes group structure.[29] Research in group dynamics has investigated problems associated with group decision making, group cohesiveness, leadership, equilibrium, and problem solving. On the other side, sociometric analysis combines mathematical and statistical techniques with topics such as change and growth, communication nets, social distance, power, and organizational size and shape. In recent years these two wide bands have tended to converge as group structure and cohesiveness has been examined through interaction analysis, the techniques of communication net research, and other mixtures.

Group dynamics. A great deal of the research in group dynamics has focused on two features of the viability of groups and their inducement-contributions balance. These features are cohesiveness and locomotion. Cohesiveness has been defined as "the total field of forces which act on members to remain in the group."[30] Some scholars view cohesiveness as an independent variable operating on other properties of the group.[31] Thus, it is often argued that cohesiveness is a factor which strengthens the group as it is increased. It is also claimed that the conformity of members in the group grows as the group becomes more cohesive.

More frequently, cohesion is considered to be a dependent variable, affected by a number and variety of internal and external forces. For example, cohesion has been found to be enhanced by cooperation among group members, and to be lessened by competition; to be increased by a democratic atmosphere and decreased by authoritarian or by a laissez-faire environment; to improve with a growth in friendship among the members of the group, with mounting group prestige, and with task interest.

The concept of locomotion is sometimes applied to the group as an entity, and sometimes to its individual members alone. In both cases locomotion, as the name suggests, refers to change; to goal seeking behavior; to movement toward attractive ends and away from repellent ones. Group locomotion implies a degree of cohesiveness, that is, the group has to possess some inducements that bind its members together as they move toward common goals. Studies of locomotion often concentrate on the obstacles that tend to impede movement. Obstacles such as ignorance, the lack of communication, ineffective leadership, status differences, and presence of a vociferous minority may block the problem-solving or goal-seeking abilities of the group. The most fruitful applications of the concept of locomotion have been made to the entire group. There have been a few excellent studies of individual locomotion —most notably those by Lippitt and White into the styles of leadership— but these have become diffused into the examination of member roles, and often seem to be disassociated from the behavior of the group.

Critics have remarked that the concept of cohesion is "too general to explain anything in particular and so general as to describe anything one may wish it to designate."[32] Similarly, the concept of locomotion has been criticized as including only those variables which *appear* to be relevant for the accomplishment of group tasks, and neglecting other variables which, in other situations or to other observers, *might be* relevant. As Olmstead has pointed out:

> Enthusiasm, seriousness, and a fondness for mathematics do not a science make. What is required, of course, is a knowledge of what to look for and an understanding of how the variables selected for observation constitute the framework of a functioning whole. This is a big order, and one which none of us is prepared to fill. Grim pursuit of a few handy variables on the one hand, or essentially wistful talk about "total fields" on the other, do not quite measure up to this implacable demand.[33]

Sociometric analysis. An application of sociometrics that is relevant to viability is found in the study of communication nets within small groups. Much of the research conducted in this area consists of variations based on the models originally designed by A. Bavelas.[34] The way in which communication takes place within the group, its pattern and efficiency, facilitates or retards group locomotion, and is of vital importance in maintaining the viability of the group.

Most of the research on communication nets has been empirical, and has consisted of the observation and evaluation of small groups formed temporarily for the purposes of the experiment.[35] Through the manipulation of the structure of these groups, researchers have examined member satisfactions and group performance under a variety of experimental conditions. Small groups have been organized in a number of ways, and communication nets have been altered in order to determine the effects of different structures on contributions and inducements. Group structures, typical of those analyzed in communication net experiments, are illustrated in Figure 38. The points in each diagram represent individual

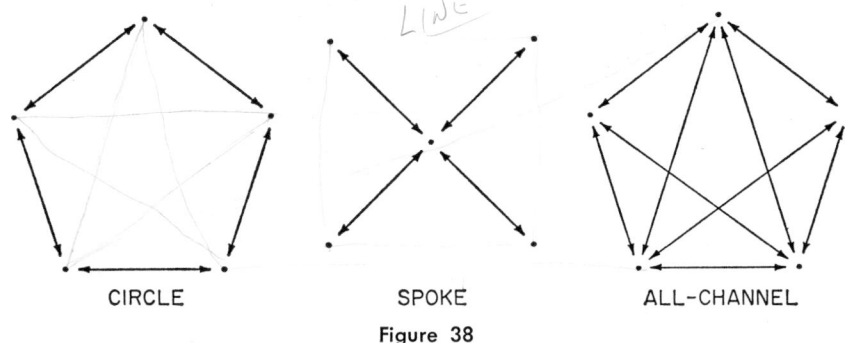

CIRCLE   SPOKE   ALL-CHANNEL

Figure 38

members of the group. The arrows indicate the channels through which communications flow. As shown by the two-pointed arrows, communications in these groups flow in both directions between the designated participants.

The groups designed for each experiment are assigned common tasks involving, usually, the solution of some problem and the transmission of information along prescribed communication channels. Occasionally the task is simply assigned to the group, and the manner in which the group organizes itself to perform the task, and the way in which labor is divided among the members of the group are the focus for research. More often, however, communication nets, as illustrated in Figure 38, are pre-established, and the observer notes the effects of different structures upon group efficiency, accuracy, satisfactions, and the changes in productivity that occur when the position of the leader within the net is altered. Guetzkow and Simon, for example, conclude: "The communication nets affected the efficiency with which the groups performed only through the influence they exerted upon the ability of the group to develop adequate organizations.[36] Other scholars have found that accuracy is enhanced through increased feedback. It has also been found that member satisfactions and group efficiency typically move in opposite directions, and that it is most difficult to increase both simultaneously.

The Homans-Simon theory of small group interactions. George C. Homans has systematized a number of the more significant concepts observed by other investigators in their studies of small groups, and has integrated them into a theory of group behavior.[37] Herbert A. Simon, utilizing many of the propositions in Homans' system, set these forth within the framework of a mathematical model, and derived new, additional propositions.[38] It is a part of Simon's model, based largely upon Homans' work, which we shall examine briefly here.

The variables included in the Homans-Simon model are:

I = average rate of interaction among group members
F = level of friendliness among group members
A = activity carried on within the group by group members
E = the extent of the tasks imposed on the group by forces external to it.[39]

Furthermore, because such variables are difficult to measure with exactitude, Simon uses an ordinal rather than cardinal scale of measurement (for example, less or more; increasing, decreasing).

The Homans-Simon model postulates the following hypotheses, from which nonlinear equations are drawn, as indicated:

(A) The average rate of interaction among group members is a function of both the level of friendliness and the amount of activity within the group.

(1) $$I = f(A, F)$$

(B) Changes in group friendliness are dependent upon the level of friendliness which exists and the extent of interaction. Thus, friendliness will grow as interaction increases; but if the group is especially friendly and the amount of interaction decreases over time, friendliness will also diminish, so that

(2) $$\frac{dF}{dt} = g(I, F)$$

(C) If the group is friendlier than the level of activity demands, and if the external tasks imposed by the environment require a level of activity higher than currently exists, the amount of activity will tend to increase.

(3) $$\frac{dA}{dt} = \psi(A, F, E)$$

By substituting the value of I from equation (1) into equation (2) we obtain

(4) $$\frac{dF}{dt} = g[f(A, F), F] = \phi(A, F)$$

where $f, g, \psi,$ and ϕ are unspecified functions. If E is regarded as a constant we can obtain the rate of change of F relative to A for paired values of F and A by dividing (4) by (3)

$$\text{(5)} \qquad \frac{dF}{dA} = \frac{dF/dt}{dA/dt} = \frac{\phi(A, F)}{\psi(A, F, E)} = \frac{\phi}{\psi}$$

If we set dA/dt as in equation (3) equal to zero, A is not changing over time. Because A is a constant and ψ equal to zero, dF/dA in equation (5) will have a vertical path, illustrated in Figure 39(a). As $\phi > 0$ or < 0 this path will be either upward or downward. Similarly, if in equation (4) dF/dt is set equal to zero a curve with a horizontal path will be produced as in Figure 39(b), which will move either to the right or left as ψ is either larger or smaller than zero, respectively.

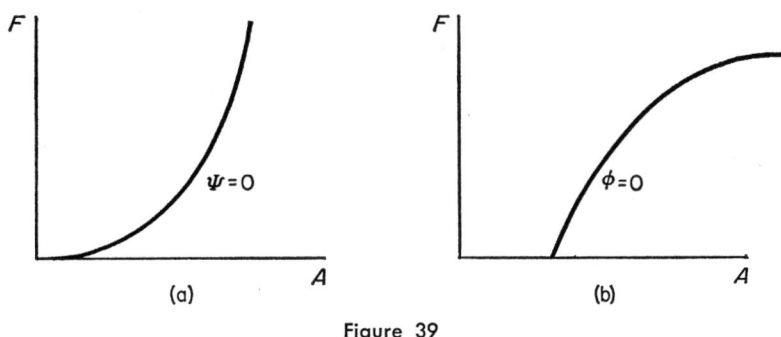

Figure 39

By combining the curves of Figure 39 into a "direction field" we can depict two points of equilibria where the curves intersect, as in Figure 40. In this diagram, with both ψ and ϕ equal to zero, K is a stable and L an unstable equilibrium position. K is stable because the paths move toward it, whereas L is unstable, because the paths move away from this position.

The shapes and positions of the ψ and ϕ functions in Figures 39 and 40 have empirical significance. Thus, it is assumed that, for a given value of E, greater friendliness will result in greater activity, so that the

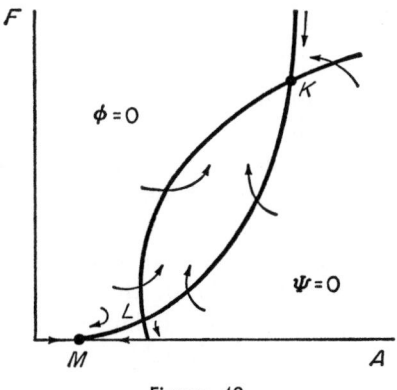

Figure 40

equilibrium value of A must increase with increases in F. After some level of A, however, as F continues to rise dA/dt will increase at a decreasing rate so that the curve $\psi = 0$ is concave upward. It is also assumed that greater activity brings about greater friendliness up to some saturation level so that curve $\phi = 0$ is concave downward. Both $\phi = 0$ and $\psi = 0$ cut the A axis to the right of the graph origin to indicate that there will be some group activity even in the absence of friendliness given a positive E.[40]

From this model three propositions are drawn. Suppose that the system is at K, a position of stable equilibrium, and that E, the external forces (for example, the tasks assigned to the group by the foreman) are reduced. Through equation (3) the equilibrium value of A also is lowered, which means that the curve $\psi = 0$ moves to the left. As $\psi = 0$ moves to the left, the point of intersection with $\phi = 0$, K, also moves downward and to the left. Thus, the first proposition is:

"As E is decreased the equilibrium levels of A and F will be decreased."[41]

As E continues to be reduced and K falls, the two curves are finally tangent only at point E_t. This leads to the second proposition, which is:

"As E is decreased below some critical level, E_t, F will go to zero; and for some sufficiently small value of E [equal to or less than E_t depending on the location of the intersection of ψ (A, F, E_t) with the x-axis] A will go to zero."[42]

In other words, as E falls below the critical value E_t, the dissolution of the group takes place, and there is a separation of the $\phi = 0$ and $\psi = 0$ curves.

The third and final proposition is:

"The level of E required to bring a group into existence is greater than the minimum value, E_t, required to prevent the group, once formed, from dissolution."[43]

The Homans-Simon model of small group interactions has, of course, been introduced mainly as an illustration of some aspects of small group theory. Although the variables in this model, such as friendliness, are not common in organization theory, there are many similarities between the two areas, and the problems and analyses are often identical. Concepts of equilibria in the Homans-Simon model are also found in a number of organizational theories, and a similar framework for explaining the cohesiveness, structure, and activity of the organization could be employed. The inducement-contribution balance is also common to both sets of theories, and we can obtain insights into the factors affecting inducements, and producing increased contributions, from the Homans-Simon model.

Modern Theory:
Equilibrium and Viability

The theories we have examined thus far have been essentially viability models.[44] These theories have emphasized either the requirements which permit the system to exist; or that pattern of relationships which makes the organization effective. They have not, however, stressed what it is—its goal or goals—that the organization is existing for or the objective of its effectiveness. Modern organization theory is still largely concerned with viability. Nevertheless, the very complexity of this theory results in the introduction of additional variables such as goals and motivations not basic to theories discussed previously in this chapter. In this section we shall look primarily at the equilibria and viability elements in the mainstream of modern organization theory, and defer the discussion of other variables to a later section. This compartmentalization does not necessarily destroy the homogeneity of modern theory, for as James G. March and Herbert A. Simon have pointed out:

> The Barnard-Simon theory of organizational equilibrium is essentially a theory of motivation—a statement of the conditions under which an organization can induce its members to continue participation, and hence assure organizational survival.[45]

Our interest here, therefore, will be in the inducement-contribution balance and equilibrium concepts found in prominent organization theories. These theories are not completely separated from those noted earlier or from others which we have not, and will not, examine. Nevertheless, there exists a series of still more closely connected and related works—starting perhaps with the studies of Mary Parker Follet,[46] given a schematic and systematized foundation by Chester Barnard,[47] and subsequently embellished and refined by Herbert Simon[48]—which have been set forth as a complete theoretical structure by March and Simon.[49] Although this lineage describes a straightforward accumulation of theoretical assumptions about organizations, it should be noted that the junctions between this line of organizational concepts and other studies have occurred frequently.

The central hypotheses of the Barnard-Simon theory of organizational equilibrium have been set forth as follows:

1. An organization is a system of interrelated social behaviors of a number of persons whom we shall call the *participants* in the organization.

2. Each participant and each group of participants receives *from* the organization *inducements* in return for which he makes *to* the organization *contributions*.
3. Each participant will continue his participation only so long as the inducements offered him are as great or greater (measured in terms of *his* values and in terms of the alternatives open to him) than the contributions he is asked to make.
4. The contributions provided by the various groups of participants are the source from which the organization manufactures the inducements offered to participants.
5. Hence, an organization is "solvent"—and will continue in existence—only so long as the contributions are sufficient to provide inducements in large enough measure to draw forth these contributions.[50]

The theory of equilibrium in organizations presupposes an underlying organizational structure. This structure, however, is not defined precisely in terms of participation. For example, the participants in the structure encompassed by the firm obviously include all employees and active owners, but there are groups which contribute to the organization, such as suppliers, shareholders, and consumers, and receive inducements from it. Should these "fringe" groups be considered to be part of the organization? The answer is not clear.[51]

It is, despite the difficulty of ascertaining the margins of the organizational entity, possible to state meaningful hypotheses about inducements, contributions, and organizational equilibrium. Both contributions and inducements can be expressed in terms of utilities to the individual participant. The assignment of utilities to inducement components, especially in the business organization where inducements are often expressed monetarily, offers no conceptual difficulties. The utility of a contribution, however, is defined as ". . . the value of the alternatives that an individual forgoes in order to make the contribution."[52]

Given the definition of inducements and contributions in utility terms, it is evident that as inducements exceed contributions ($I > C$) the individual's satisfactions increase, and continue to expand as the difference between I and C grows.

In Figure 41 are depicted the conditions of organizational survival or organizational equilibrium. The horizontal axis (P) is participation, and the vertical axis (U) utilities. The diagram greatly oversimplifies the picture of contributions and inducements, in that their utilities are represented as being related linearly with participation. Nevertheless, it enables us to portray most of the significant features of the Barnard-Simon model. At the line OP satisfactions to the individual are zero; above this line the individual receives positive satisfactions, below it he is increasingly dissatisfied. His participation is terminated (that is, he leaves the organization) where the P, I, and C lines intersect the vertical axis. In the short run, therefore, as indicated in Figure 41, the individual may

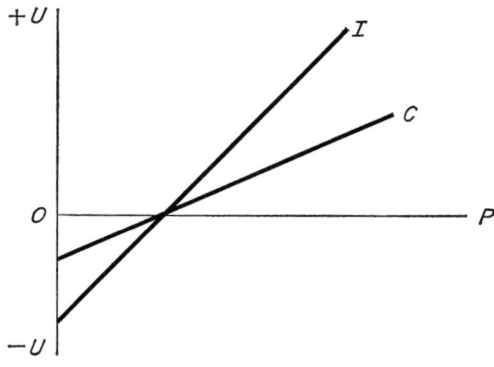

Figure 41

be dissatisfied, but still not leave the firm. Dissatisfaction leads to the search for alternatives, but adjustment to alternatives, or a lowering of the OP line as search fails (somewhat as aspiration levels are reduced) takes time. In the long run the difference between inducements and contributions would have to be positive or zero, or the individual would leave the organization.

From this model we can, with March and Simon, hypothesize that (1) "increases in the balance of inducement utilities over contribution utilities decrease the propensity of the individual participant to leave" [53] and that the inducement-contributions balance is a function of (2) "the perceived desirability of leaving the organization and the perceived ease of movement from the organization." [54] To maintain organizational viability, then, management (or other organization members) may have to initiate adjustments within the firm in order to maintain the $I \geq C$ balance. Changes may have to be instigated to keep the $I \geq C$ balance for particular members of the organization, for example, higher wages to retain skilled workers or a new dividend policy to keep shareholders satisfied. The $I \geq C$ balance, however, also depends, as in point (2) above, upon forces external to the organization, so that wages may not only have to be higher absolutely than what they were, but they must also produce an inducement-contributions balance of utilities higher than that which the organizational member perceives elsewhere. March and Simon emphasize the following variables as important in the maintenance of participation: (a) Viability of alternatives, that is, the fact that real markets are not "perfect"; (b) search propensities, for example, organization members are often resistant to change; (c) satisfaction, which is a function of the expectations and perceptions of organization members; and (d) alternatives to movement.[55] Finally, dissatisfaction with the organization does not necessarily cause the participant to leave the organization, for through bargaining, satisfactions may be increased.

Two features of this analysis should be noted. First, the movement toward precision. The notion of inducements and contributions has been refined compared with, for example, that given by Mayo. The expression of these variables in terms of utilities has given them a quantitative content, at least in theory, which has been interpreted in terms of empirical factors by March and Simon. Consequently these authors have made the concepts of inducements and contributions considerably more sophisticated than in theories of their predecessors. Second, the concept of organizational equilibrium still differs from the idea of equilibrium in traditional economic theory. Equilibrium traditionally is a point toward which (if it is stable) variables tend to gravitate. In the March-Simon model, equilibrium appears to exist so long as inducements are at least equal to contributions in the long run. However, this analysis indicates that equilibrium exists when $I > C$ as well as when $I = C$. Thus, participants may receive a surplus of satisfactions as well as minimal satisfactions (in terms of perceived alternatives), and still equilibrium is maintained. In other words, even though the concept of organizational equilibrium has been made more precise in the theory of March and Simon, it still remains a relatively indefinite zone ($I \geq C$) in which only the lower limits are established.

RATIONALITY AND DECISION MAKING

In this section we shall examine the centrality of decision making in modern organization theory. The decision-making process, of course, has been examined previously in Chapter 5, but not as an important feature in the organization. In connection with this subject we shall also scrutinize two related topics: roles and rationality. Role theory, as we shall observe, plays a significant part insofar as it explains those social forces which affect choice. Rationality, with its associated assumptions of maximizing or satisfying, forms one of the parameters within which decision making takes place.

Role Theory

Harvey Leibenstein has written that:

> (Decision making) . . . is also central to the concept of an organization that we shall develop. But decisions are not made by individuals with entirely undefined parts to play in an organization. In other words, it seems quite natural to view decisions as being made within the roles played by individuals who are members of an organization.[56]

Our primary concern with the concept of role will be with its significance for, and relationship with, the decision-making process, as set forth above by Leibenstein. It should be noted, however, that role theory, stimulated by the work of Mead,[57] and elaborated upon by Linton,[58] has long been an integral part of sociological and psychological theories. The sociologist has been confronted with the problem of clarifying the relation between the informal organization and the formal organization and status positions ordained by organizational roles.[59] In solving this problem some sociologists have utilized the concept of the social role as the focal point for the forces of the external culture, the formal organization, and the internal interpersonal relationships.

Although the concept of the role has become central in the study of sociology, it is used rather loosely, and there is little agreement as to its precise definition.[60] Simon has defined the role as "a social prescription of some, but not all, of the premises that enter into an individual's choices of behavior."[61] Shibutani has written: "Where the division of labor is clearly defined, the contributions expected of the various participants may be called roles."[62] Turner defines role to be ". . . a collection of patterns of behavior which are thought to constitute a meaningful unit and deemed appropriate to a person occupying a particular status in society, occupying an informally defined position in interpersonal relations, or identified with a particular value in society."[63] We could continue to present role definitions, all of which differ somewhat; but the three given illustrate adequately the general concept and suggest the semantic difficulties involved.[64]

A role affects to some degree the behavior of the person enacting it. A role, however, is ordinarily considered as a normative concept which refers to that behavior which is appropriate or expected, rather than the behavior of a specific actor in a specific situation. Thus, a role is a prescription for action, but it does not necessarily restrain the activities of all individuals to the same extent. Because a role fails to confine and direct an actor within a narrow channel, it does not permit the accurate prediction of behavior by itself.[65] Nevertheless, the concept of role may be of considerable utility, for it enables us to understand some of the institutionalized pressures which are brought to bear upon the decision maker.

It is often assumed that organizational viability is contingent, in part at least, on the durability of certain basic roles in the organization. Such underlying roles might include, for example, those which facilitate organizational tasks and those which function to build and maintain the organization.[66] The stability of the organization also may be dependent upon an aggregate role structure in which roles acquire considerable rigidity and are not easily altered by the actions of individual participants. Such stability may result in an equilibrium of roles and/or of role structure. "A role is in equilibrium if in the absence of changes external to the role it does not itself change."[67] In an equilibrium role structure the organization operates on the basis of a mutual acknowledgement of the status, function, authority, and responsibilities of each role, which in turn reinforces and legitimizes organizational expectations. It is evident that the movement toward organizational goals may be assisted or impeded by the nature and efficacy of its role structure. If actors in the organization disclaim their role responsibilities or refuse to recognize the role authorities of others it is likely that the organization will be inefficient and ultimately cease to exist. Even where actors do their best to conform to the demands of the role, the role may be so confused, because it is poorly defined or perceived by the individual or by others in the organization, that it cannot be satisfactorily enacted.[68]

> There is clear evidence . . . that the members of experimental groups find it necessary to develop a recognized role structure before they can devote their efforts to effective task achievement. . . . The high status member of a group occupies a position of centrality in that he acts as a coordination center and is able to control the flow of information. His ability to control reinforcement is an important factor in the development of the role structure.[69]

The role structure then, as Stogdill points out in the passage above, may be a basic ingredient in organization theory—essential to decision making, to viability, and to the formulation and attainment of goals. In fact, many sociologists conceive the organization to be a role structure or system. Despite the vagueness of the role concept and the looseness of its directives for action, roles are perceived and played, deferred to and acted upon, and as a consequence are significant for the study of business behavior.

Rationality

The conventional economic theory of the firm, it will be recalled, assumed perfect rationality on the part of the decision maker (entrepreneur, firm). In order to possess such perfectly objective rationality it is necessary that the decision maker be omniscient prior to his decision, so that he is perfectly aware of the entire range of alternative choices open to him and of all their possible outcomes. It is also essential that such a superhuman figure have a clear cut goal or other criterion, so that he is enabled to select that one best course of action from all those which confront him which will permit him the maximum movement toward his goal. In the conventional economic theory of the firm the entrepreneur has as his goal the maximization of profits, and it is in the light of this criterion that he evaluates, in an objectively rational manner, his alternatives and the consequences of his actions, and makes his decisions. The theory of the choosing mechanism in economics is completely uninformative on internal structure. The postulates of rationality and goal are given, and behavior is contingent upon environmental or external factors. Economic man, therefore, is an automaton, stripped bare of any of the human characteristics that all real men possess. This is not to say, of course, that economic man may not be useful for certain purposes of economic analysis, but such a concept is not very useful for organization theory, the essence of which demands an interest in behavior of persons and groups within the firm.

Because of the limited utility of the assumption of perfect rationality to organization theory, then, scholars in the latter discipline have turned to more qualified rationality concepts. Herbert Simon, who has been the leading figure in this movement, has suggested that the term "rationality" should be employed only when modified by descriptive adverbs. Thus, he has suggested that:

> ... a decision may be called "objectively" rational if *in fact* it is the correct behavior for maximizing given values in a given situation. It is "subjectively" rational if it maximizes attainment relative to the actual knowledge of the subject. It is "consciously" rational to the degree that the adjustment of means to ends is a conscious process. It is "deliberately" rational to the degree that the adjustment of means to ends has been deliberately brought about (by the individual or by the organization). A decision is "organizationally" rational if it is oriented to the organization's goals; it is "personally" rational if it is oriented to the individual's goals.[70]

Those modifiers establish limits or parameters within which rationality resides. Even should all these parameters tend to coincide, the very psychological characteristics of the decision maker, and the structure of the environment which confronts him, further limits his rationality. Real behavior cannot be objectively rational (except perhaps by chance). Behavior in reality is affected by personal, social, and external factors. Man does not have the complete knowledge of all the alternative courses of action open to him or of the outcomes of his decisions. He can anticipate the future consequences of his act, but only in an imperfect manner. Uncertainty, therefore, affects his decision and blemishes his perceptions. In a business firm, furthermore, the presence of others may result in outcomes which are the products of conflicts of "rationality" so that the result does not seem to be "rational" to any of the participants. Finally:

> *The capacity of the human mind for formulating and solving complex problems is very small compared with the size of the problems whose solution is required for objectively rational behavior in the real world —or even for a reasonable approximation to such objective rationality.*[71]

This principle Simon calls bounded rationality. It implies that man can try to be rational, that rationality may be intended, but that he is forced by the complexity of the real world to construct a simplified model of reality. This is not to say that man must be irrational, but the very fact that he is human implies that he is fallible. To remove the bounds from rationality, and to presume that man is objectively rational is to reduce the subject matter of behavioral theory to an exercise in logic, a tautological study without basis in fact and without realistic content.

Satisficing and Maximizing

In earlier chapters we examined briefly the notion of satisficing. This idea, for example, formed part of the theories of Margolis and Chamberlain. Satisficing, as we shall see, also plays an important role in organization theory, where it flows naturally from the assumption of bounded rationality. Satisficing consists of ascertaining a course of action that is "good enough"—that is satisfactory although it is not optimal.

Man must satisfice rather than maximize because he possesses bounded rationality. As Herbert Simon has observed: "Administrative theory is peculiarly the theory of intended and bounded rationality—of the behavior of human beings who *satisfice* because they have not the wits to *maximize*." [72] The administrative man of organization theory, therefore, is one who aspires to make a "normal profit," to charge a "fair price," and to maintain his "share of the market." When administrative man makes a decision he bases his choice upon relatively few alternatives. Furthermore, he may not even realize that he has not explored all courses of actions, and he may use rules of thumb, tricks of the trade, or act in a habitual manner.

The concept of satisficing man differs from that of maximizing man insofar as constraints, both "internal" and "external," limit the global rationality and consequently the decision processes and behavior of the latter. Herbert Simon has set forth certain "classical" concepts of rationality, and then introduced a series of assumptions and limitations to illustrate clearly how maximizing differs from satisficing.[73] We shall examine some of these differences in the following paragraphs of this section.

The "classical" concepts of rationality include such straightforward choice procedures as the max-min rule of game theory, the explanations of maximization under conditions of certainty, and the rules for making optimum choices where probabilities are known (that is, the maximization of expected values). In each of these choice situations it is assumed that the decision maker knows the precise nature of the outcomes of his decision, and that he is able to assign pay-offs to each outcome. As a result of these assumptions it is clear that the decision maker is able to order all possible outcomes in a hierarchy of preferences.

There is no evidence that persons perform the computations demanded by classical concepts, at least where the choice situation is somewhat complex. It is more likely that decision makers employ a variety of simplifications in making choices. Simon suggests some of the simplifications which such a person might employ. Assume that a situation exists wherein an individual is selling an item for which he has reserved an "acceptable" price. He aspires to this price level. Anything over this price is "satisfactory," anything less is "unsatisfactory."[74] The problem is, of course, that the concept of satisfactory has one open end. It is bounded by the acceptable price (x) as a minimum, but obviously within its range $x + 1$ is more satisfactory than x, and $x + 2$ is more satisfactory than $x + 1$.

In a real life situation the answer to a simple decision problem within a fixed interval of time would be for the seller to select the best $x + n$ price that was above his acceptable minimum price. Or he might decide to accept or reject each price offer as it was made prior to considering the next offer (or offers) if these were made sequentially (with the number of sequences uncertain) over time. In neither case, however, is it necessary that the optimum solution, the unique solution, or even an existing solution be attained.

In classical theory, furthermore, payoffs must be ordered, and, therefore, comparable. In actual decision processes, however, it may be impossible for payoffs to be compared. Simon notes three instances where payoffs might not be comparable: (1) Where decisions are made by a group, and where the payoff preferences of individual group members differ, (2) Where the individual is confronted with a choice situation in which the important bases for decision consist of a variety of incomparable items, that is, salary, climate, prestige, and so on, (3) Where each alternative has an indeterminate number of possible payoffs. These problems have been handled in a variety of ways—n-person games, indifference curves, and probability techniques—but they have not all been amenable to analysis. Simon has suggested the use of vector payoff functions to handle these situations. Graphically a vector analysis would successfully depict the conflict of opposing forces or alternatives, and suggest the strength of the factors involved, but it would be most difficult to quantify vector lengths empirically.[75]

The notion of satisficing is often contingent upon certain attributes possessed by the individual, for example, his aspiration levels, his persistence, his perceptions. The emphasis on reality in theorizing and on the characteristics of the individual enhances the descriptive utility of the satisficing concept, but at the same time results in a more complex model for predicting behavior. It is a weaker assumption, although it has greater propriety, than maximization. Certainly, in terms of the number and nature of the variables that have to be known before it is possible to predict the behavior of the decision maker, the requirements of maximization are no less demanding than are those of satisficing.

Finally, although the empirical evidence is far from conclusive, several investigations appear to substantiate the satisficing model of business behavior. G. P. E. Clarkson, for example, has developed an iterative problem-solving program to simulate trust investment behavior.[76] Through the use of multiple acceptable level rather than maximizing goals based upon the appraisal of certain characteristics of individual investors, Clarkson was able to predict the list of securities that would be selected for these individuals by investment trust officers with remarkable accuracy. This model, it should be emphasized, assumes acceptable-level goals and the sequential consideration of alternatives until the first satisfactory one is reached. Cyert and March, as well as others, have reported on a number of experiments in which aspiration level models are used. The predictions made are relatively weak, but they should be strengthened as we learn more ". . . about the parameters of the relation between achievement and aspiration . . ."[77] Nevertheless, some of these predictions are quite helpful, and satisficing appears to be supported more firmly by the empirical evidence than maximizing.

Organizational Decision Making

Much of organization theory emphasizes, as we have observed in earlier sections of this chapter, the processes and structures of the organization, that is, the formal and informal relationships, the bureaucratic form, dysfunctional consequences, communications nets, and interactions between organizational members. A major concern of modern organization theory, however, has been the decision-making process. The aim has been to construct a theory that explains how decisions are made in organizations.

The theories of decision making that have emerged have not agreed upon all the elements that are significant, and even the approaches to the decision-making process sometimes differ. For example, as Mason Haire observes, Jacob Marschak has treated the decision process as an independent variable, whereas Rapoport, and Cyert and March make it a dependent variable in their theories of organization.[78] In this section we shall examine briefly the essentials of the decision-making theory constructed by Cyert and March. Despite the differences that exist between decision-making models, there are also many similarities and the Cyert-March theory contains elements that have been widely accepted as important by organization theorists.

The skeleton of the Cyert-March theory of organizational decision making is based upon four factors. (1) Multiple, changing, acceptable level goals. (2) The sequential examination of alternatives, with the acceptance of the first satisfactory alternative. (3) The avoidance of uncertainty wherever possible through the use of routine procedures. The firm, as a consequence, tries to rely upon policies that are reactive rather than anticipatory. (4) Standard operating procedures and rules of thumb are used in most choice situations in the short run.[79]

Cyert and March conceive the organization to be a coalition. Individuals in the organization have goals, and through a bargaining process among these individuals organizational goals arise. These goals change in response to pressures in the short run, and adapt gradually to changes in coalition structure in the long run. Cyert and March conclude, finally:

> . . . because of the form of the goals and the way in which they are established, conflict is never fully resolved within an organization. Rather, the decentralization of decision making (and goal attention), the sequential attention to goals, and the adjustment in organizational slack permit the business firm to make decisions with inconsistent goals under many (and perhaps most) conditions.[80]

Organization theory does not, of course, neglect the importance of an organizational goal or goals. As we noted, however, there may be good reasons why goals may be confused, directional only rather than quantitative (for example, more profit instead of x dollars of additional profit), and thus act as constraints upon the propriety of individual, group, and organizational behavior. The fact that organizations have goals, and that these may differ from those of individuals within them, produces an environment for conflict.

Within the framework of goals man attempts to satisfice. Satisficing and goal setting and goal attainment are interrelated. Goals will not be established without regard to the probability of their attainment. Goals may also be step functions contingent upon prior behavior. Thus, a realistic profit level reached in period one may very well result in the setting of a higher profit plateau in period two.

The selection of a satisfactory alternative, as Cyert and March explain this process, involves a number of component parts. Perhaps the most central of these is search activity, which arises in response to problems. Search occurs when existing decisions are not satisfactory. It takes place through the sequential examination of alternatives, and increases in intensity as the need for a satisfactory solution mounts. Other elements of significance in the choice of a satisficing alternative are: The computation of decision criteria (for example, calculation of net returns and costs); the communication system of the organization, which might bias information on relevant variables; and a complex mixture of individual and organizational expectations.[81]

Cyert and March argue, much as in Alchian's theory discussed earlier, that the business firm is an adaptive organization that undergoes a learning process on the basis of its experiences. As such it "reacts" when possible to the external environment, and does not try to anticipate or forecast change unless forced to do so. Wherever it can the enterprise attempts to avoid uncertainty, to maintain the rules that have brought it satisfactory results in the past, and to make these rules simple.[82]

From these elements Cyert and March move on to a more detailed construction of their theory of the firm. This theory is discussed more at length in Chapter 10. In this section, however, we have observed how the decision-making process is a central feature of their theory, and have examined some of the elements which enter into this process.

Given somewhat ambivalent and conflicting goals and satisficing behavior, men in business organizations must choose between alternative courses of action. The decision process which they use may vary widely, dependent upon the importance of the decision, its historical antecedents, and similar variables. Nevertheless, it is likely that the decision process of organization man will include certain common elements. For example, the decision maker(s) may well try to simplify the forces affecting the choice to be made, and to reduce the number of variables and alternatives involved so that they are understandable and tractable. In fact, the attempt to make the environment more manageable is another common element in decision making. Thus, businessmen often try to reduce uncertainty through habitual behavior, or through emulation and imitation of other successful enterprises. The fact that habits in industry are so strong, and that imitation is so common and major innovation relatively rare, would seem to substantiate some of the premises of uncertainty reduction and satisficing behavior.

Finally, decision making in organizations often seems to be a learning, or groping, or searching process whereby decisions, like feelers, are tentatively extended and then, depending upon the feedback which occurs, are withdrawn or confirmed.

This sort of description of the decision-making process in organization, and of some of the variables which affect this process, is not ascribable to any one theorist, but is composed of elements from several theories. Its main weakness, perhaps, lies in its descriptive nature. Nevertheless, it is a step in the direction of understanding organizational behavior.

SUMMARY

In this chapter we have examined several of those fragments of organization theory which have attracted the attention of many scholars interested in business behavior. At times these pieces have appeared disconnected, but it may be observed that they are related to much of the theoretical work presented in Chapter 4, in that they emphasize organizational viability and equilibrium. These theories also have in common an attempt to touch reality more closely than the more traditional economic theory. In so doing they reduce abstractions of global rationality to more limited but more realistic notions, and maximization to satisficing. These theories recognize the frailty of man and endeavor to account for it. Although this ambition is laudable, organization theory has been weakened by it, and often these theories have been oriented toward description and analysis rather than prediction. Nevertheless, two features of organization theory are indicative of its promise: (1) That it is grounded in empiricism to a large extent and (2) that it has made rapid advances in a relatively brief span of years. Finally, organization theory, with much of the recent work having as its focus the decision-making process, seems on the verge of producing an acceptable theory of business behavior; one that is more complex, but yet more realistic and more useful for our understanding and prediction of the activities of the firm and its members than more traditional theories.

Notes and References

1. Albert H. Rubenstein and Chadwick J. Haberstroh, editors, *Some Theories of Organization* (Homewood, Ill.: Richard D. Irwin, Inc. and The Dorsey Press, Inc., 1960), p. 2.

2. The general nature of scientific management can be obtained from such books as the following: Frederick W. Taylor, *The Principles and Methods of Scientific Management* (New York: Harper & Row, Publishers, 1911); Alvin Brown, *Organization of Industry* (Englewood Cliffs, N. J.: Prentice-Hall, Inc., 1947); James D. Mooney, *The Principles of Organization* (New York: Harper & Row, Publishers, 1947); and Luther Gulick and L. Urwick, *Papers on the Science of Administration* (New York: Columbia University Institute of Public Administration, 1937).

3. Elton Mayo, *The Social Problems of an Industrial Civilization* (Boston: Division of Research, Harvard Business School, 1945), p. 21. This statement, of course, is typical of the disdain which the empiricist, the pragmatist, and the "doer" feel for "theory" and theorists.

4. Reported in: Fritz J. Roethlisberger and William J. Dickson, *Management and the Worker* (Cambridge: Harvard University Press, 1939), and in other books by the "Harvard" or "human relations" group.

5. Elton Mayo, *The Human Problems of an Industrial Civilization,* Second Edition (Boston: Harvard Graduate School of Business Administration, 1946), p. 173.

6. Roethlisberger and Dickson, *op. cit.,* p. 365.

7. Fritz Roethlisberger, *Management and Morale* (Cambridge: Harvard University Press, 1942), p. 192.

8. Roethlisberger and Dickson, *op. cit.*, p. 590.

9. Mayo, *Social Problems* . . . , *op. cit.*, pp. viii-ix.

10. Cf. Alvin Gouldner, "Reciprocity and Autonomy in Functional Theory," in Llewellyn Gross, ed., *Symposium on Sociological Theory* (New York: Harper & Row, Publishers, 1959) and Sherman Krupp, *Pattern in Organization Analysis: A Critical Examination* (Philadelphia: Chilton Company, 1961), Chapter 3.

11. *Ibid.*, p. x.

12. Elton Mayo's Foreword to Roethlisberger, *op. cit.*, p. xix.

13. See Krupp, *op. cit.*, Chapter 5. Weber does go beyond the solely mechanical model in particular areas, such as in his discussion of the relationships between officials and offices. See: H. H. Gerth and C. Wright Mills, *From Max Weber* (New York: Oxford University Press, A Galaxy Book, 1946).

14. Max Weber, *The Theory of Social and Economic Organization*, translated by A. M. Henderson and Talcott Parsons (New York: Oxford University Press, 1947), p. 331.

15. See comment by Peter M. Blau, *Bureaucracy in Modern Society* (New York: Random House, Inc., 1956), pp. 28-29.

16. Robert K. Merton, "Bureaucratic Structure and Personality," *Social Forces*, Vol. 17 (1940), p. 561, published by The University of North Carolina Press.

17. Gerth and Mills, *op. cit.*, p. 340.

18. Merton, *op. cit.*, p. 560.

19. For an interesting treatment of the effects of dysfunctional elements on organizational goals, see: Leo Spier, "Graph Theory as a Method for Exploring Business Behavior," in Joseph W. McGuire, editor, *Interdisciplinary Studies in Business Behavior* (Cincinnati: Southwestern Publishing Company, 1962), pp. 70-98.

20. Cf. Philip Selznick, "Foundations of the Theory of Organization," *American Sociological Review*, Vol. 13 (February, 1948), pp. 25-30; and Philip Selznick, *TVA and the Grass Roots* (Berkeley: University of California Press, 1953), especially the final chapter.

21. Cf. Talcott Parsons, *The Structure of Social Action* (New York: McGraw-Hill Book Company, Inc., 1937), p. 752.

22. Selznick, "Foundations . . . ," *op. cit.*, p. 26.

23. *Ibid.*, p. 25.

24. *Ibid.*, p. 34.

25. See the tabulation on number of small group articles by periods in Fred L. Strodbeck, "The Case for the Study of Small Groups," *American Sociological Review,* Vol. XIX (December, 1954), p. 651.

26. Robert T. Golembiewski, *The Small Group: An Analysis of Research Concepts and Operations* (Chicago: The University of Chicago Press, 1962), p. 9.

27. See John W. Thibaut and Harold H. Kelley, *The Social Psychology of Groups* (New York: John Wiley & Sons, Inc., 1959) which uses a framework analogous to game theory to explore interactions in small groups, especially in dyads, but which speculates briefly on the effects of increasing size.

28. William F. Whyte, "Small Groups and Large Organizations," in John H. Rohrer and Muzafer Sheriff, editors, *Social Psychology at the Crossroads* (New York: Harper & Row, Publishers, 1951), p. 297.

29. Robert A. Dahl, Mason Haire, and Paul F. Lazarsfield, editors, *Social Science Research on Business Product and Potential,* chapter by Mason Haire, "Psychology and the Study of Business: Joint Behavioral Sciences" (New York: Columbia University Press, 1959), pp. 74ff.

30. Leon Festinger, Stanley Schachter, and Kurt Bock, *Social Pressures in Informal Groups* (New York: Harper & Row, Publishers, 1950).

31. Stanley Schachter, Norris Ellertson, Dorothy McBride, and Davis Gregory, "An Experimental Study of Cohesiveness and Productivity," Darwin Cartwright and Alvin Zander, editors, *Group Dynamics* (New York: Harper & Row, Publishers, 1953), pp. 401-411.

32. Robert Albert, "Comments on the Scientific Function of the Concept of Cohesiveness," *American Journal of Sociology,* Vol. LIX (November, 1953), p. 233.

33. Michael S. Olmstead, *The Small Group* (New York: Random House, Inc., 1959), p. 117.

34. A. Bavelas, "Communication Patterns in Task-Oriented Groups," *Journal of the Acoustical Society of America,* Vol. 63 (1950), pp. 725-730.

35. Cf. H. J. Leavitt, "Some Effects of Certain Communications Patterns on Group Performance," *Journal of Abnormal and Social Psychology,* Vol. 46 (1951), pp. 38-40; G. H. Rothschild, "Some Effects of Prolonged Experience in Communication Nets," *Journal of Applied Psychology,* Vol. 40 (1956), pp. 281-286; Harold Guetzkow and Herbert Simon, "The Impact of Certain Communication Nets Upon Organization and Performance in Task Oriented Groups," *Management Science,* Vol. 1, Nos. 3 and 4, April-July, 1955.

36. Guetzkow and Simon, *Ibid.*

37. George C. Homans, *The Human Group* (New York: Harper & Row, Publishers, 1950).

38. Herbert A. Simon, "A Formal Theory of Interaction in Social Groups," *American Sociological Review*, Vol. 17 (1952), pp. 202-211; Reprinted in Herbert A. Simon, *Models of Man* (New York: John Wiley & Sons, Inc., 1957), pp. 99-114; and in A. Paul Hare, Edgar F. Borgatta, and Robert F. Bales, *Small Groups, Studies in Social Interaction* (New York: Alfred A. Knopf, Inc., 1955), pp. 132-148. All references are to pagination in *Models of Man*.

39. *Ibid.*, p. 100.

40. Points *A* through *C* are found on p. 101, whereas the formulae and diagrams are on pp. 107-109 in *Ibid*.

41. See *Ibid.*, p. 110.

42. *Ibid.*, p. 111.

43. *Ibid.*

44. See Amitai Etzioni, "Two Approaches to Organizational Analysis: A Critique and a Suggestion," *Administrative Science Quarterly*, Vol. 5 (September, 1960), pp. 257-278.

45. James G. March and Herbert A. Simon, *Organizations* (New York: John Wiley & Sons, Inc., 1958), p. 84.

46. See Mary Parker Follet, *The New State* (New York: Longmans, Green & Co., 1923); *Creative Experience* (New York: Longmans, Green & Co., 1924); and *Dynamic Administration*, Henry C. Metcalf and L. Urwick, eds. (New York: Harper & Row, Publishers, 1942).

47. Chester I. Barnard, *The Functions of the Executive* (Cambridge: Harvard University Press, 1958).

48. Herbert A. Simon, *Administrative Behavior*, Second Edition (New York: The Macmillan Company, 1958).

49. March and Simon, *op. cit.*

50. Herbert A. Simon, D. W. Smithburg, and V. A. Thompson, *Public Administration* (New York: Alfred A. Knopf, Inc., 1950), pp. 381-382.

51. See March and Simon, *op. cit.*, pp. 89-90.

52. *Ibid.*, p. 85.

53. *Ibid.*, p. 93.

54. *Ibid.*

55. *Ibid.*, p. 108.

56. Harvey Leibenstein, *Economic Theory and Organizational Analysis* (New York: Harper & Row, Publishers, 1960), p. 120.

57. G. H. Mead, *Mind, Self and Society* (Chicago: University of Chicago Press, 1934).

58. R. Linton, *The Study of Man* (New York: Appleton-Century-Crofts, Inc., 1936).

59. Leonard Reissman, "A Study of Role Conceptions in Bureaucracy," *Social Forces*, Vol. 27 (March, 1949), p. 305.

60. Lionel J. Neiman and James W. Hughes, "The Problem of the Concept of Role: A Resurvey of the Literature," *Social Forces*, Vol. XXX (1951), pp. 141-149.

61. Herbert A. Simon, "Theories of Decision-Making in Economics and Behavioral Sciences," *The American Economic Review*, Vol. XLIX, No. 3 (June, 1959), p. 274.

62. Tamotsu Shibutani, *Society and Personality* (Englewood Cliffs, N. J.: Prentice-Hall, Inc., 1961), p. 46.

63. Ralph H. Turner, "Role-Taking, Role Standpoint, and Reference Group Behavior," *American Journal of Sociology*, Vol. 61 (January, 1956), p. 316.

64. The controversy on definition is discussed in Neiman and Hughes, *op. cit.*; F. L. Bales, "Position, Role, and Status: A Reformation of Concepts," *Social Forces*. Vol. 34 (1956), pp. 313-321; and Neal Gross, W. S. Mason, and A. W. McEachern, *Explorations in Role Analysis* (New York: John Wiley & Sons, Inc., 1958).

65. Cf. Herbert A. Simon, *Administrative Behavior*, Second Edition (New York: The Macmillan Company, 1957), pp. xxxff.

66. K. D. Benne and P. Sheats, "Functional Roles of Group Members," *Journal of Social Issues*, Vol. 4, No. 2 (1948), pp. 41-49.

67. Leibenstein, *op. cit.*, p. 209.

68. Cf. E. J. Roethlisberger, "The Foreman: Master and Victim of Doubletalk," *Harvard Business Review*, Vol. 23 (1945), pp. 283-298 and S. A. Stouffer, "An Analysis of Conflicting Social Norms," *American Sociological Review*, Vol. 14 (1949), pp. 706-717.

69. Ralph M. Stogdill, *Individual Behavior and Group Achievement* (New York: Oxford University Press, 1959), pp. 162-163.

70. Simon, *Administrative Behavior, op. cit.*, pp. 76-77.

71. Simon, *Models of Man, op. cit.*, p. 198. Italics are his.

72. Simon, *Administrative Behavior, op. cit.*, p. xxiv.

73. Simon, *Models of Man, op. cit.*, "A Behavioral Model of Rational Choice," Chapter 14.

74. This notion of "acceptable" price as a boundary is similar to the opportunity cost concept of Chapter 3 and the aspiration level boundary discussed in the next chapter.

75. This paragraph is based on Simon, *Models of Man, op. cit.*, pp. 250-252.

76. B. P. E. Clarkson, *Portfolio Selection: A Simulation of Trust Investment* (Englewood Cliffs, N. J.: Prentice-Hall, Inc., 1963).

77. Richard M. Cyert and James G. March, *A Behavioral Theory of the Firm* (Englewood Cliffs, N. J.: Prentice-Hall, Inc., 1963), p. 35.

78. Mason Haire, *Modern Organization Theory* (New York: John Wiley & Sons, Inc., 1959), p. 9. The papers by Marschak, Rapoport, and Cyert and March are contained in this symposium volume.

79. Cyert and March, *op. cit.*, p. 113.

80. *Ibid.*, p. 43.

81. *Ibid.*, Chapter 4.

82. *Ibid.*, p. 103.

9

PSYCHOLOGY AND BUSINESS BEHAVIOR

Although the term business behavior has been employed frequently in earlier chapters, it has never been defined precisely. Implicit in our discussions of business behavior has been the central theme of choice. Thus, theories of business behavior consist primarily of hypotheses about the basis upon which, and the framework within which, processes of choice are carried out.

There are many variables which enter into business decisions, and which affect the selection of one alternative over other possible alternatives. One such variable, certainly, is the character of the decision maker. Another important force is the situation in which the decision must be made. These are gross variables, however, and are too broad to permit intensive analytical treatment. Social scientists, therefore, have most frequently broken apart such elements into smaller components. The forces "within" the decision maker, for example, may include such items as goals, degree of rationality, and amount of information possessed. The situation may encompass, among other factors, the group or organization within which the decision maker operates, the importance of the rewards that may be attained, and a host of other environmental pressures. Each of these subdivisions may be further atomized for scrutiny—and often are—into the forces that shape or affect them. The amount of information available, for instance, is often a function of the operation of some sort of formal or informal feedback mechanism, so that uncertainty in *this* choice situation might be reduced because of the known consequences of earlier, similar, choices. Goals and the degree of rationality possessed by the decision maker may be conditioned by, and contingent upon, personality and cultural forces.

The study of business behavior, therefore, consists of a thorough blending of a large part of the more significant concepts and principles of all the social sciences insofar as these help us to understand the choice process in a business context. In earlier chapters we examined those variables drawn largely from economics and organization theory as they focused upon business decisions. In this chapter we shall concentrate mainly upon constructs from psychology that, directly or indirectly, help us to understand more fully the circumstances surrounding choice in business. As we shall see, some of the theories discussed in earlier chapters—especially those that make use of such concepts as the aspiration level and of bounded rationality—have their bases in psychology. The subject matter of this chapter, therefore, is not entirely new, nor is most of it completely different from other theories presented previously. This chapter has as its purpose to illustrate still some other approaches and additional ways in which psychology is—or might be—pertinent to the study of business behavior.

Psychology has as its object the study and understanding of human nature as it interacts with and adjusts to the environment. It covers a broad spectrum of subject matter, ranging from experimental psychology at the one extreme to social psychology at the other. The principal focus for the psychologist is the individual, although his interest ranges over to animal and group behavior at the extremes. Furthermore, psychologists are concerned with human behavior of all kinds, and in all settings. There are, for example, such specialties as child psychology, abnormal psychology, animal psychology, psychophysics, and industrial psychology, wherein specific and selected aspects of individual behavior, or certain restricted environments, are singled out for study.

Although there are, therefore, many diverse areas of concentration within the field of psychology, certain central fields are of particular relevance to the study of business behavior. In this chapter we shall examine three of these—personality theory, learning theory, and behavioral decision theory. Each of these topics (and many others from psychology which should be noted, but are not because of space limitations) is closely related to the subject of business behavior, and could play an important role in business theories. In most instances the relations between psychological and business theories should be evident, although occasionally these will be made explicit.

PERSONALITY THEORY

J. L. McCary has noted that developments in the field of personality have been marked by the "new theories (which) sprang up in numbers directly proportional to the number of psychologists interested in experimentation."[1] In recent years there has been some consolidation of theories, and some recognition of similarities among the various systems. Nevertheless, in comparison with economics, with its hard core of the theory of the firm, or with decision theory, the theory of games, or even organization theory, personality theory remains a morass of conflicting hypotheses with little connection between them.

Personality theory represents an effort to explain the total functioning of the individual. Personality has been defined as "the fundamental organization of the individual which determines the unique nature or individuality of his interactions with himself and with his environment."[2] Personality is a holistic concept which is all inclusive of those integrated qualities, impulses, habits, interests, ideals, and other characteristics that compose the individual as he exists in society.[3]

Because the scope of personality theory is so broad, because the variables involved are so numerous, because of a lack of homogeneity in research methods, and because of the introspective nature of many of the forces studied, it has been difficult to obtain unanimity even as to what factors should be emphasized in the study of personality. Calvin Hall and Gardner Lindzey, for example, list at least eighteen elements that have been stressed to some degree by the most important personality theorists, but no one of these elements is emphasized to the same extent in all seventeen theories noted.[4] Ronald Taft has attempted to cluster these theories into a smaller number of broad groups with similarities which, in his opinion, make them fit together fairly well.[5] The problem of simplification and categorization of personality theories still remains acute.[6] Nevertheless, because these theories do bring to bear a stream of psychological analysis upon the nature of decision makers, we shall point out some of their more important features. We shall accomplish this end by examining a few of the more important variables in personality theory.

The Holistic Schema of Personality

There has been in recent years an increasing emphasis upon the interrelated nature of the forces within the individual and external to him (the environment).[7] Theories in which the individual is viewed as entirely separate and isolated from society and from culture have become less important, whereas personality, culture, and society are more and more observed as parts of a holistic schema of interacting forces. William Stern has pointed out that man is "self-contained" but at the same time "open to the world about him." Increasingly, conceptualizations of personality recognize that behavior is a function of what F. H. Allport has called an "inside" and "outside" view of personal structure.

It is evident that not all of man's behavior can be explained by what lies under his skin. In 1935 Muzafer Sheriff experimented with subjects confronted with a pinpoint of light in complete darkness. This light source, which was stationary, appeared to move, and could not be localized without other points of reference. The subjects were asked to estimate the direction of light movement and its distance. When each subject was alone his judgment of direction and distance was uncertain and erratic. When the same subjects performed together they tended to reach agreement on the direction of movement and the distance of the light.[8] This experiment, and others like it, indicates that perception and judgment are strongly influenced by external sources.

The increasing emphasis on the environment in personality theory since 1935, in fact, has perhaps gone too far.[9] Nevertheless, this trend is indicative of the widening perspectives of personality theory, and its consequent concern with forces that are both inside and outside the individual.[10] Of course, this integration should not prevent the abstract or theoretical treatment of the separate parts of the personality field, so long as its holistic nature is recognized. Finally, the integrative forces in psychology have not yet proved adequate to erect a synthesis of personality theories acceptable to a majority of theorists in the field.

Biological, Unconscious, and Hereditary Forces

Second, the biological, unconscious, and hereditary factors, which in the past have been preeminent in personality theories, currently seem to have lost some of their luster as environmental forces have been increasingly emphasized.

The first relatively comprehensive theory of personality was constructed by Sigmund Freud who, in his psychoanalytic theory, stressed such concepts as internal conflict, unconscious motivation, and defense mechanisms.[11] More specifically, Freud argued that (1) man is dominated by unconscious emotions and motives and (2) that the early stages of childhood form the most important bases for adult personality. Neither of these hypotheses fit well into the format of rational decision making advanced by theorists from most of the other disciplines examined in earlier chapters.

Freud postulated two basic drives: the life instincts, which consist of all activities that are positive and constructive; and the death instincts, or hate instincts, which are destructive.[12] Man's behavior is typically ambivalent, based upon a mixture of these instincts. Life and death instincts, furthermore, are made operational through the personality structure composed of the id, the ego, and the superego. The id contains the basic drives for pleasure and aggression in their pure form. The ego, while acting in the service of the id, is its link with external reality. It is the rational part of man's psychic system which tries to satisfy the desires of the id while operating within the limits of the real world.[13] The superego is the social and moral arbiter of the psychic system. Whereas the id, therefore, is primarily biological, and the ego determined by physical reality, the superego is basically affected by society and culture. These three components are engaged in continual conflict which is normally resolved through mechanisms that strive to bring about a return of homeostasic equilibria. These mechanisms are conscious or unconscious adjustments which tend to reduce tensions, such as rationalization (the unconscious substitution of favorable for real motives), introjection (guilt feelings), displacement (a search process for satisfaction) and other processes. Many of these are defense mechanisms of the ego, for example, identification (imitation and emulation) and suppression, by which the ego tries to relieve tension and to avoid anxiety.

The Freudian system, therefore, is composed of continually interacting forces within the individual, and between the individual and the environment.[14] Because it is concerned with the external and internal stimuli which act and react upon the personality structure, and with the relationships and conflicts among the components of this structure, psychoanalysis is commonly considered to be a dynamic theory. The ideal adult Freudian personality would consist of a harmonious balance between its parts and external reality, no regressive traits, life instincts predominant, and the resolution of all conflict.

Freud's theory has often been criticized on both methodological and theoretical grounds. It is said, for example, that his experiments were not controlled; that they are subject to a wide variety of interpretations, and that they are based largely upon unreliable statements by troubled patients. Furthermore, the theory is too vague to permit behavioral predictions. Finally, the emphasis upon sexual and similar drives, upon the unconscious, and upon hereditary forces has often been criticized. Nevertheless, Freud's theory is significant for its impact upon the development of subsequent personality theories.

Freud influenced the theories of many of his contemporaries and a whole neo-Freudian school of personologists. Carl G. Jung, for example, originally was a close friend and colleague who deviated from strict Freudian thought largely because of the latter's emphasis upon sexuality as the principal motivating force of man. Jung's theory is, in general, quite similar to Freud's, for the unconscious is still stressed and conflicts within the organism remain of vital importance.[15] Nevertheless, the components of the unconscious are considerably altered, and the elements producing conflict are changed (for example, introversion-extroversion). Jung believed, furthermore, that man progresses toward more complete stages of development—a much more optimistic idea than that possessed by Freud.

The neo-Freudians have altered Freud's theory more than did Jung. Many of the modifications and changes made by the followers of Freud have resulted from the movement away from the biological structure and the sexogenic forces which play such a prominent role in Freud's theory. Alfred Adler, the first of Freud's Vienna group to split away from the basic theory, deemphasized the concept of inborn instincts and of unconscious drives.[16] Adler stressed the conscious sources of action and the importance of social forces in the development of personality. He placed economic and social goals among the principal motivating forces of man, but thought that underlying all behavior was the drive for self-assertion rather than sexuality. All men have inferiority complexes, Adler claimed, which force them toward compensation—to domination and superiority. Finally, Adler believed that although men try to strive for superiority in common, the *manner* in which they reach for this goal gives each person a unique style of life.

Other well-known neo-Freudians—Karen Horney, Harry Stack Sullivan, and Erich Fromm—each utilize several Freudian concepts, but each departs uniquely from the basic theory and from the others.[17] Nevertheless, the direction of change in each case is the same, because it is away from the biological, sexual, and unconscious forces motivating the individual and toward an emphasis upon the importance of social and cultural factors in the determination of personality and behavior.

Common Traits and Unique Individuality

Are there common traits or types among all men? Or is each person a unique individual, marked more by the differences which exist between him and his fellows than by the similarities which exist between them? Some psychologists stress the common nature of man; others emphasize the differences.

The trait approach to personality is significant because it has as its goal the prediction as well as the understanding of behavior. A trait is a consistent pattern of action and reaction. If an observer knows an individual's traits it is presumed that the subject's future activities can be anticipated. Traits have been classified along a number of dimensions. Trait terms (for example "aggressiveness") are called common traits. Allport and Odbert found nearly 18,000 such terms.[18] There are also unique traits, possessed by only one person.[19] Unfortunately, the very uniqueness of such traits makes them defy description. Cattell has differentiated between surface traits (for example, tact, aggression) and depth traits, such as intellectual capacity.[20] Other trait divisions also exist.[21]

Out of the trait approach to personality has evolved factor analysis, which is basically a technique for analyzing correlations among traits. Cattell, for example, has developed the concept of "psychological characters" which he views as homeostasic-like tendencies.[22] H. J. Eysenck has tried to isolate behavioral dimensions by reducing the covariation among samples of behavior to the lowest number of independent factors.[23] He believes he has accumulated evidence for "types" in which broad aggregates of personality traits may be classified. In factor analysis, then, scholars are trying to reduce a large and untractable number of traits into a relatively small and manageable number of basic and independent factors.

The great advantage of factor analysis is that it classifies and categorizes an unwieldy number of traits. On the other hand, this type of approach fragments the human personality into a number of isolated and independent variables while ignoring the cohesive substance that integrates and organizes these factors into a single entity.

Whereas trait psychologists have attempted to ascertain what elements personalities share in common, other psychologists have argued that the unique features of the individual should be the chief concern of personality investigations. Obviously, it is claimed, personality would not exist if all persons thought, acted, and felt alike.[24]

Gordon W. Allport, perhaps more than any other American psychologist, has emphasized individuality.[25] He has worked toward explanations of uniqueness. Cultural and societal forces, to Allport, bring about conformity of behavior. However, one must explore the factors that make each person different from others really to understand individual personality. These factors, which Allport calls the "propriate" functions, include self-identity, self-esteem, self-image, a "sense of importance," and rational thought.[26] He has written that a mature person has a future-oriented philosophy of life, a "becoming" personality, which gives meaning to his behavior.[27]

Although the trait school of psychology is popular today, there is little agreement on substance. Although personality is often described in terms of traits, few psychologists are in accord as to what particular or specific traits are significant. Also, the trait approach tends to abstract the individual from his environment, to study primarily the former and to deemphasize the latter. Thus, "traditional" trait theories of personality are not wholly in accord with the trends toward attention to external stimuli which were observed in an earlier section.

Phenomenological Approaches

Phenomenologists belong to a school of psychology which believes that the individual's apprehension of objects and events, rather than the stimuli themselves, is the most important determinant of human behavior. Boulding, for example, has advanced the thesis that man's behavior depends upon his image of the world.[28] Miller, Galanter, and Pribram, using data from cybernetics and information theory, have extended Boulding's hypothesis to include plans, which they feel are essential to exploit the image.[29]

The best known and most influential phenomenologist was Kurt Lewin.[30] Lewin referred to his approach as "field theory." The field is a complex psychological representation of an individual's perceptions of reality which includes the interactions of forces internal and external to the person. The field in each situation is the life space of the individual, containing both the person and the environment as he is experiencing it. Life space contains all the psychological facts—conscious and unconscious—that the individual perceives. The life space contains all the forces operating in the present that determine present behavior. Because the life space is continually changing, Lewin's theory is dynamic.

Lewin used topology, a pseudo-mathematical descriptive terminology, to represent the life space and its forces and other features. Forces are motivations, and have positive or negative valences (attractions). The individual's behavior is directed by the strongest positive valences toward certain goals and away from others by negative valences. Conflicts often arise for a variety of reasons. Thus, a person may be both hungry and sleepy; he must work at a hated task or lose his income. Such conflicts may be resolved perhaps through sequential actions (eat, then sleep), through vacillation (quit job, reduce income, obtain another job, increase income), or through day dreaming. Conflict may also occur because one is both attracted and repelled by the same goal (sex and sin;

football vs. study) which may result in frustration.[31] Barriers or constraints, which prevent the subject from locomotion toward the desired goal, may bring about repression. Barriers may also enhance the positive valences of some objects (for example, goals which appear difficult to attain may have a greater attraction).[32]

Lewin hoped to uncover genotypical (general and ideal) situations that would explain phenotypical (observable and specific) events.[33]

Gibson has noted that field theory might be applied to the study of business behavior, but not without difficulty. He has suggested:

> If field theory is to be applied to the study of business behavior, we may have to begin with those firms which failed and those firms which are prosecuted under the legal structure before we can begin to indicate motives that could be considered as normal. We might then construct a maze of all socio-legal barriers (topological diagrams) to which a business might be subject in its routine existence, and from its selection of paths and successive states of lack of tension, construct or determine motives for those actions as inferred from studies of case histories. Which goals are attained? Which motives are changed? What does the business perceive from its life space in a certain environment, and how does it adjust? When is the firm in a state of lack of tension? The scientific observer and experimenter must construct a maze before observation of behavior of the rat in that maze. Thus, field theory could offer some valid possibilities for observing business behavior.[34]

Lewin's theoretical framework has aroused a considerable amount of controversy in the social sciences.[35] It has been criticized as merely a cumbersome methodological structure containing little original substance.[36] The terms borrowed from physics and mathematics are vaguely defined and sometimes misused.[37] The objective environment is completely ignored in field theory, although it must have some impact upon behavior.[38] Finally, the theory is primarily descriptive, and does not have great utility as a predictive device.[39]

Henry A. Murray's theory of personality might be classified under a number of headings. It is termed phenomenological largely because Murray used the concept of "press" to refer to the items that the individual abstracts from the environment as being of special significance or relevance for facilitating or obstructing his needs. The objective environment, *per se*, Murray termed the "alpha press," or alpha situation, whereas the perceived reality, and thus the basis for behavior, is the "beta press." [40] A person's environment, therefore, is his image of the environment ("a stable organization in the brain"), and his behavior is a function of his needs and his beta situation.[41]

One of Murray's chief contributions to personality theory is his listing, categorizing, and analyzing of needs. Need is examined as a motivating force which institutes a search pattern toward satisfaction. Needs may be primary or secondary, overt or covert (latent). They may be focal (specific) or diffuse. The 13 primary needs Murray lists are largely biological. The 28 secondary needs are influenced by societal and cultural factors, and include aggression, autonomy, recognition, achievement, acquisition, and others.[42]

Psychologists with an organismic orientation toward personality: (1) observe behavior as contingent upon individual perceptive images of reality; (2) argue for the study of personality as a coherent entity which cannot, and should not, be separated into isolated parts; and (3) claim that all organisms are motivated by one drive—self actualization. The chief proponents of organismic theory are Kurt Goldstein, Andras Anygal, Prescott Lecky, and A. H. Maslow, of whom Maslow is probably best known to scholars in business.[43]

Maslow places his emphasis upon psychological health rather than on conflict or pathology. He finds that healthy individuals (who are difficult to discover, evidently) are motivated by self-actualizing drives, which means that they are resistant to the pressures to conform, and that they are independent, realistic, problem-oriented, creative, spontaneous, and acceptant of self and of others. Maslow is familiar to students of business primarily because of his hierarchy of needs; wherein needs are ranked from survival needs (for example, hunger) up through the needs for safety, belongingness and love, esteem, self-actualization, cognition, and aesthetic needs. The lower the need in this hierarchy the more demanding it is, and needs higher than it will be ignored until it is satisfied. A normal person is one who can satisfy his needs at the highest level of which he is capable.

Before closing this section on phenomenological approaches to personality mention should be made of self theory, because one of the few books relating psychological and business theory utilizes its hypotheses.[44] Carl Rogers, one of the leading advocates of self theory, believes that each person is at the center of his psychological field, and reacts to what he perceives in this field.[45] He is motivated by the need to preserve and enhance his "self," and conflict results from changes in the self and its perceived relationships to the field.

n-Achievement

We began this chapter by pointing out that theories of business behavior are concerned primarily with the choice processes. In the light of this statement the foregoing discussion of personality theories may seem somewhat irrelevant. However, we shall argue that these theories are in fact closely allied to theories of business behavior, and that the associations, furthermore, may be conceptualized in several ways.

First, it is evident that an integral part of any decision-making process is the nature of the decision maker. The decision maker is a human being. Personality theory attempts to explain human behavior. Ergo, the more we know about personality the better we understand business behavior.

Second, personality theories have been used directly in some theories of business behavior. Phenomenological approaches, such as those employed by Lewin, Maslow, and Rogers, for example, have been allotted important roles in some business theories.

Third, personality theory may be thought of as a background for more "applied" concepts of behavior. We can imagine, in this view, that personality theory constitutes a "pool" or "reserve" of concepts that can be selected and made operative in their application to specific behavioral environments. It is in this light that we want to examine personality theories here. We shall do this by using achievement theory for our illustration.

In a comprehensive and important recent volume, David C. McClelland has drawn upon a wide variety of the behavioral sciences to describe the "Achieving Society." [46] At the core of this study is McClelland's contention, based upon a great deal of empirical evidence collected in a number of countries, that the successful entrepreneur possesses a unique personality dominated by what he calls the achievement motive. This motive, as the title suggests, is the drive to achieve, that is, an insatiable desire to accomplish challenging tasks successfully.

McClelland measures the need for achievement (called the n-Achievement) primarily by relying upon Freudian methods whereby he (and others) analyzes the fantasies and free associations of individuals.[47] Through a series of carefully programmed tests McClelland and his associates are able to ascertain individual n-Achievement scores, and have hypothesized that individuals with high scores are predisposed toward business success and tend to look with favor upon entrepreneurial endeavors. McClelland reports on the results of a number of psychological studies, and then states:

> If we can assume, as all our evidence indicates, that Western capitalists were actually motivated primarily by the achievement motive, we can now understand why they were so interested in money and profit, although not, paradoxically, for its own sake. Money to them was the measure of success. It gave them the concrete knowledge of the outcome of their efforts that their motivation demanded. . . . What gallons of ink and acres of paper might have been saved if economic and political theorists had understood this distinction sooner.[48]

The central position of the achievement motive in McClelland's model is buttressed by a vast array of evidence drawn from a great number of sources. It is also reinforced by a member of subsidiary behavioral and personality traits. For example, a person with a high n-Achievement score is oriented toward informational feedback on his behavior; he obtains his satisfactions from initiating successful actions rather than from public adulation for his accomplishments; he is (in America, at least) optimistic and conscientious, he prefers moderate risks to certainty or extreme risks.[49] The businessman, with these and other personality characteristics, becomes a complex and yet a more human individual in McClelland's schema than in more traditional theories. Yet, McClelland, through a careful documentation of his hypotheses and the skillful use of a blend of personality, social, and cultural theories and empirical evidence, builds an excellent—if somewhat diffuse—case in support of his premise that achievement motivation and business behavior are closely related.

Personality Theory in Retrospect

We have examined, in a rather cursory and much too brief fashion, only a few elements in some of the many prevalent personality theories. Nevertheless, the features of personality theories that we have observed point up the sorts of things psychologists consider significant in their explanations of human behavior.

There appears to be a tendency for personality scholars to view personality as an interrelated and interacting mixture of personal and environmental forces. Yet, there is little agreement on the relative strength of internal and external factors, on which forces are important, or even on what the words "internal" and "external" or "environmental" mean. Freud, for example, maintained that much of man's psychological development resulted largely from an unfolding of his biological processes. Yet, the neo-Freudians have tended to move ever closer to an emphasis upon the environment. Trait approaches to personality have been primarily descriptive, although through factor analysis a few independent variables which appear basic may be uncovered. Phenomenological psychologists believe that the image of the world (internal and external) as viewed by the individual is the pertinent environment which plays a vital role in explaining behavior. Finally, most personality theorists are organismic to a large degree, because the individual is no longer considered to be self-contained.

Thus, personality theory at present is in a state of flux, with the field composed of unifying and disparate forces. Nevertheless, a close examination of these theories provides the business scholar with insights into behavior, as is illustrated by McClelland's theory. Business behavior is individual behavior in business situations. Personality theory reinforces this conclusion for it is, above all, a "personal" theory in which the central focus of attention is the person.

LEARNING THEORY

A second field which has been vigorously cultivated in recent decades by psychologists, perhaps even more assiduously than the area of personality, is learning theory. There have been several attempts to combine the two fields, and because they do tend to blend together, these have met with some success.[50] Nevertheless, it has appeared more fruitful to keep the two apart, and in recent years especially, this separation has resulted in considerable progress in learning theory, largely because of the use of mathematical tools and concepts in the area.

In his excellent review of theories of learning, Ernest R. Hilgard presents the following definition:

> Learning is the process by which an activity originates or is changed through reacting to an encountered situation, provided that the characteristics of the change in activity cannot be explained on the basis of native response tendencies, maturation, or temporary states of the organism (for example, fatigue, drugs, and so on).[51]

Everyone has many encounters with instances of learning in everyday life. It should be noted, however, that learning psychologists do not ordinarily concern themselves with these instances. Most frequently the observations upon which learning theories are based have involved laboratory arrangements in which such items as the lever-pressing behavior of pigeons, the movements of white rats through a maze, the salivary response of dogs, and the wink of the human eyelid have made up the observed phenomena. Learning theories, then, have not very often been related to real life "learning" situations.

The fundamental concepts in learning theory are: (1) drive; (2) stimulus or cue; (3) response; and (4) reinforcement or reward. Learning consists of the acquisition of responses to stimuli, and theorists customarily have investigated the relationships between those and other variables.

Early learning theorists were often concerned with finding the relationship between quality of task performance and repetition.[52] This relationship was termed the "learning function." It was generally found that the repetition of a task will result in improved performance, but the exact nature of the function which best described this relationship was a subject of much debate among psychologists. Until the late 1940's, however, learning theorists rarely utilized mathematical models or tools. They were concerned largely with the mean measures of performance.[53]

In contrast, during the last decade, learning theorists have concentrated on the construction of models involving the process of acquisition. These are of the utmost significance to business scholars, for they involve the whole question of choice. R. Duncan Luce has written:

> Most acquisition experiments are readily considered to be choice situations. A person or an animal is confronted with a choice between two or more responses on each trial of a long sequence. For example, on each trial a rat turns right or left, a person guesses yes or no, or the dog jumps soon enough to avoid shock or it does not. These responses have certain specifiable outcomes for the subject, and behavior on future trials is altered as a result. If acquisition in fact occurs, one response becomes more frequent and others less so, but not in all experiments does one response tend to occur on 100 per cent of the trials asymptotically. The relative frequency may tend to stabilize at some other value.
>
> On each trial of a learning experiment, the animal or human subject is exposed to a fixed stimulus situation—a piece of apparatus in an experimental room with constant lighting, temperature, and sounds—but only some of the stimuli are perceived by the subject on any given trial. In stimulus-response theories, stimuli become conditioned to certain responses: that is, they tend to evoke those responses. The mechanism by which this conditioning occurs marks the differences among the several theories, but all agree that somehow stimuli and responses do get connected or associated as a habit is acquired.[54]

Although psychological learning theories are typically derived under experimental conditions, they unquestionably have a great deal of relevance to business situations. Obviously both individuals and organizations adapt themselves to their environments. Rules are established, based upon experience, whereby men and firms survive and, under certain circumstances, thrive. Both individuals and organizations have to go through some sort of a learning process in order to be viable or successful. Both have to adapt—to learn to cope with the environment of which they are a part.

We shall examine two "types" of learning theory in this section. First, we want to look at contiguity theory, as illustrative of a whole school of mathematical learning theories. Second, we shall discuss a more recent model developed by Julian Feldman. Both of these are based upon the binary choice experiment, in which subjects must predict which of two mutually exclusive events will occur on each of a series of trials.

Contiguity Theory

In recent years several psychologists have combined learning theory and probability concepts to construct stochastic models.[55] One such model, originated by E. R. Guthrie, has been put into mathematical form by W. K. Estes.[56] Guthrie introduced a principle known as association by contiguity which means (in a learning theory context) that the outcome of any one trial alters the probabilities of subsequent responses by the subject in following trials.

In its simplest form, the theory of contiguity says that the probability that the subject in a binary choice experiment will predict that event E_1 rather than E_2 will occur on trial $n+1$ is increased if E_1 occurred on trial n. The probability that E_1 will be selected on trial $n+1$ is decreased if event E_2 occurred on trial n. Contiguity theorists assume that the probabilities of the response given on trial $n+1$ are completely determined by the response given on trial n and its outcome. This assumption is known as the "independence-of-path" assumption.[57] Past events, prior to n, do not influence future events, except insofar as they have influenced n, and in this way are related to $n+1$.

In Estes' model E_1 and E_2 are considered as mutually exclusive and exhaustive events of each of a sequence of trials. $p_1(n)$ is the probability that E_1 will be selected (for example, that a red rather than a green light will flash if the subject presses button 1 rather than button 2), and $p_1(n+1)$ is the probability that E_1 will be selected in the very next trial.

These preliminary remarks may be summarized in the "fixed point" formula:[58]

$$p_1(n+1) = p_1(n) + \theta[1 - p_1(n)]$$

where $0 < \theta < 1$, and is an empirically derived constant. If $\theta = 0$ we can see that

$$p_1(n+1) = p_1(n)$$

so there would be no change in probabilities between two successive trials. On the other hand, if $\theta = 1$, then

$$p_1(n+1) = 1$$

so that E_1 will be selected regardless of the outcome of trial n. In both of these cases the contiguity principle is inoperative, for the outcome of trial n has no effect on $n+1$. If the contiguity principle does work, then, θ must be a fraction.

If E_1 does occur on trial n the increase in probability of its being chosen on trial $n+1$ can be set forth as:

$$p_1(n+1) - p_1(n) = \theta[1 - p_1(n)]$$

Suppose that those trials where E_1 occurs are expressed as a fraction π of the total number of trials, and the fraction where E_1 does not occur by $(1 - \pi)$. π and $(1 - \pi)$, then, are in effect the relative frequencies of E_1 and E_2, and

$$p_1(n+1) - p_1(n) = \{\theta[1 - p_1(n)]\} + (1 - \pi)[-\theta p_1(n)]$$

or, multiplying through and combining terms:

$$p_1(n+1) - p_1(n) = \theta[\pi - p_1(n)]$$

The difference equation for E_1 is now dependent upon the relative frequency of E_1 rather than 1. From this analysis Estes derives a learning curve equation indicating that the probability of E_1 being selected on any trial n (starting at trial zero) is

$$p_1(n) = \pi - [\pi - p_1(0)](1 - \theta)^n$$

where π is a limit that $p_1(n)$ approaches asymptotically.

This sort of model is related closely to the decision theories discussed in Chapter 6. Estes' theory, to be sure, predicts how the decision maker will behave in a choice situation wherein there are only two alternatives. It is oversimplified. Yet, it does set forth rules for choice behavior. It states that choices made in a current problem are conditioned by the outcome of an identical problem in the recent past. Furthermore, contiguity theory has been tested many times, and has predicted accurately the empirical results.[59] Subjects do tend to select E_1 at a rate approaching π, the relative frequency with which E_1 occurs. This is not the result that would be expected from a "rational" decision maker. If E_1 occurs 75 per cent of the time it would be rational to choose E_1 every time rather than to try to match the stimulus probabilities. The fact that subjects do indeed seem to act in the fashion predicted by mathematical learning theories would appear to be one more indication that traditional choice theories based upon the omniscient rationality of the decision maker are inappropriate foundations for explanations of business behavior.

The general format of contiguity theory has been applied in broad fashion to organizational learning. Cyert and March have argued, for example, that organizations "learn," because they adapt to situations by drawing upon their past experiences. As part of their learning process, organizations . . . "change their goals, shift their attention, and revise their procedures for search . . ." [60] Cyert and March observe that goals, which they define as aspiration levels, change with experience. They assume that in any particular time period organizational goals are a function of ". . . (1) organizational goals of the previous time period, (2) organizational experience with respect to that goal in the previous period, and (3) experience of comparable organizations with respect to the goal dimension in the previous time period." [61] The authors describe these relationships as

$$G_t = a_1 G_{t-1} + a_2 E_{t-1} + a_3 C_{t-1}$$

where G is the organizational goal, E organizational experience, C the experience of comparable organizations, and where $a_1 + a_2 + a_3 = 1$. The t's *and* $t-1$'s refer to current and prior time periods. a_3 is a parameter reflecting organizational sensitivity to environmental change, and a_1 and a_2 connote organizational speed in adapting to change.

The Cyert and March description of the organizational learning process is more complex than the simple Estes theory. It contains more variables. It is less formalistic and is not as well supported by empirical evidence. Nevertheless, the links between this newly developed model of organizational learning and the mathematical learning theories of psychology seem to be clear.

Feldman's Problem-Solving Model

Mathematical learning models, such as that constructed by Estes, do not consistently predict all the characteristics of behavior included in binary choice experiments. One difficulty is that often subjects, after one event has occurred several times in succession, tend to switch to the other event.[62] Such behavior, referred to as the "gambler's fallacy" is frequently also observed in nonexperimental situations. Needless to add, this pattern is not consistent with the learning model described above. Also, when the subject is supposed to predict events in a series that contains conditional probability relationships there is some evidence that mathematical learning theories are inadequate.[63] Therefore, mathematical learning models are not entirely satisfactory in predicting behavior in all binary choice experiments.

Julian Feldman has constructed a model for predicting binary choice behavior based upon evidence that subjects form hypotheses concerning patterns in a series of events.[64] Feldman states:

> The subject is apparently not a passive mechanism being conditioned to make responses with a certain probability. He is more adequately depicted as an active information-processing mechanism that views the binary choice task as the problem of finding the structure of the event series.[65]

The Feldman model involves recording the subject's verbal comments as he "thinks aloud" while making his choices. This record is called a "protocol." Through the use of the protocol, information is obtained on the cognitive processes of the subject, and Feldman was able to construct a model that made the same predictions as the subject, and for the same reasons.

> A hypothesis is generated about the structure of the event series on the basis of the preceding events. This hypothesis is used to obtain a prediction of the next event. The prediction performs the role of a test

of the hypothesis. If the prediction is correct, the hypothesis is retained unless a decision is made that the pattern of events will be interrupted ("negative recency"). If the prediction is incorrect, either the event is explained as an interruption of the pattern . . . or a new hypothesis is generated.[66]

Basic to the model, therefore, is the hypothesis held by the subject. This hypothesis has a pattern component, that is, the subject believes that event E_1 will continue, that E_1 and E_2 will alternate, and so on. Some hypotheses contain also a second component which Feldman calls a negative or "guess-opposite" component. If this second component is present the prediction of the hypothesis is the opposite of the prediction of the pattern component.[67]

Feldman's model consists of simulating the cognitive processes of the subject on the computer, and of establishing a machine protocol which is an approximate image of the subject's protocol. Feldman has been quite successful in accomplishing this task, and the model should form a basis for a more complete understanding of human behavior in learning and problem-solving situations.

BEHAVIORAL DECISION THEORY

Psychologists have become increasingly concerned with explorations in decision making in recent decades. To some extent their investigations have overlapped with those conducted by mathematicians, economists, and others. However, they have brought to the study of decision making the background of a discipline which differs from the others, and thereby contributes to our understanding of the choice process. Ward Edwards has noted some of the sub-fields in behavioral decision theory with which psychologists have been preoccupied—utility, subjective probability, stochastic theories of choice, variance preferences, and personality variables.[68] Most frequently, however, the work of psychologists in decision theory has been marked by the approach they take to the problems involved rather than by the different nature of the subjects they study. To illustrate the psychological contributions to decision theory let us examine briefly the level of aspiration and motivational determinants of risk-taking behavior as discussed in the recent literature.

It should be emphasized that the treatment of aspiration levels by psychologists does not imply *different* theories simply because the theorists involved are from a discipline that differs from that of economists or organization theorists. In fact, there is a close relationship between the concept of aspiration levels in all these areas.

Aspiration Levels

Many decision theorists assume that choice is a function of utility and subjective probability, so that an individual tries to maximize

$$SEU = \sum_i p_i^* u_i$$

where SEU is the subjectively expected utility, p_i^* refers to the subjective probability corresponding to the objective probability of the ith outcome and u_i is utility. Sidney Siegel has employed this concept in his discussion of aspiration levels.[69]

Business theorists have been dissatisfied with most analyses of levels of aspiration, for they find these too vague as a conceptual limit toward which behavior tends. Siegel has tried to give this concept precision. He bases his discussion of aspiration levels upon the work of Kurt Lewin, et al.[70] Lewin's approach stressed the level of aspiration as a function of three forces: (1) a striving toward success, (2) an avoidance of failure, and (3) the "cognitive factor of a probability judgement." [71]

Siegel translates these features of Lewin's work into terms of decision theory. The last factor, thus, is subjective probability, and success and failure are placed on an achievement scale or continuum. Also on this scale is a "point" which represents a level of aspiration.[72] Success, redefined in decision-theory terms, is a position on the achievement scale with positive utility, whereas failure has negative utility.

Suppose, continues Siegel, that a one-person game with a choice between two alternatives is constructed. The outcome of this game is decided by the toss of a coin. Figure 42 sets forth this game. Assume

	Alternative (a)	Alternative (b)
If heads occurs	4	3
If tails occurs	0	3

Figure 42

further that the individual involved has an aspiration level of 4, and that any smaller number connotes failure to him. In this case he will select alternative (a) because it has greater expected *utility* for him, even though alternative (b) has a greater expected *value*. Given aspiration level 4, then, the choice of alternative (a) tells us that "for this individual the difference in utility between 4 and 3 is greater than the difference between 3 and 0." [73] Zero utility lies somewhere between numbers 3 and 4, with 4 or more items all possessing positive utility for this individual, and less than 4 items having negative utility.

Siegel then defines the level of aspiration of an individual as:

> . . . a point in the positive region of his utility scale of an achievement variable; it is at the least upper bound of that chord (connecting two goals) which has maximum slope; that is, the level of aspiration is associated with the higher of the two goals between which the rate of change of the utility function is a maximum.[74]

There is some experimental evidence which confirms Siegel's aspiration level model.[75] Siegel suggests, finally, that the SEU model might be altered to incorporate these findings on aspiration levels. Thus, if LA equals the level of aspiration, and if R is reinforcement effects (that LA rises with attained success in the immediate past), then the individual will still choose to maximize.

$$SEU = \sum_i p_i {}^* u_i$$

but this will be modified so that

$$u_i = f(LA, R)$$

John W. Atkinson has constructed a model utilizing aspiration levels which he uses to examine the motivational determinants of risk-taking behavior.[76] Atkinson's model involves six variables: the subjective probability of success (Ps); the subjective probability of failure (Pf); the incentive value of success (Is); the negative incentive value of failure (If); the achievement motive (Ms); and the motive to avoid failure (Mf). Ps and Pf depend upon the degree of difficulty of the task to be performed, so that Ps is lowered as the difficulty of the task is increased. Atkinson also argues that Is is a positive function of the degree of difficulty so that $Is = 1 - Ps$, that is, low for easy and high for difficult tasks. On the other hand, $If = -Ps$, so that the humiliation of failing a very easy task is great.[77]

Atkinson combines the aforementioned variables to obtain a resultant motivation, so that:

Resultant Motivation = $(Ms \times Ps \times Is) + (Ms \times Pf \times -If)$

If the achievement motive (Ms) is greater than that to avoid failure (Mf) for a person, it is likely that he will desire a task with moderate difficulty, that is, where $Ps = .50$. At this point the uncertainty of the outcome is greatest, for as the tasks become too difficult the subject becomes more convinced he will fail, whereas for easier tasks it becomes more and more likely he will be successful. Such a person, with a strong achievement motive, should, therefore, set his level of aspiration so that he voluntarily chooses activities that *maximize* his anxiety about failure.

On the other hand, the person in whom the motive to avoid failure is stronger should select either the easiest of the alternatives or should be extremely speculative and set his goal where there is virtually no chance for success. These are activities which *minimize* his anxiety about failure.[78]

The (Ms) person, then, will set his level of aspiration at the point where his positive motivation is strongest, where the odds seem to be 50-50. The (Mf) person, on the other hand, in his desire to avoid failure, sets either very low aspiration levels, so that he cannot fail, or very high ones, so that failure will not result in self-blame or embarrassment. Through this analysis it is possible to plot the relative attractiveness of tasks which differ in the subjective probability of success (that is, in difficulty).

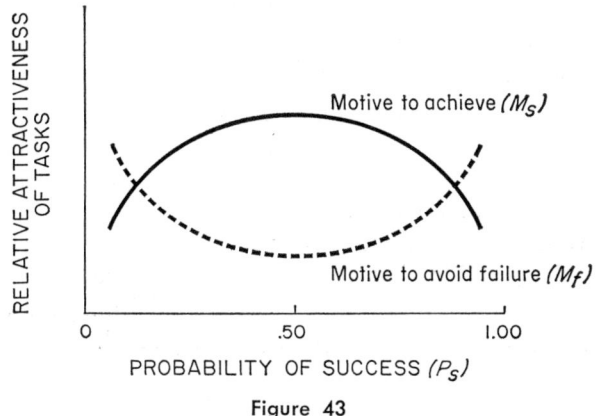

Figure 43

Using this model, what effects will success and failure have upon the level of motivation? Atkinson argues that the (Ms) person, with a desire to achieve, will proceed along the following lines: His first goal is at a level where $(Ps) = .50$, as noted above. If such a person succeeds at this first task he will take on a more difficult project on his next attempt. If he is forced to repeat the same task over and over again with continued success, he will gradually lose interest in his work, for the subjective probability of success is so high that the incentive value approaches zero. If the (Ms) subject fails at his first task where $Ps = .50$ he will shift to lower and lower levels of difficulties. This is called a lowering of level of aspiration. If he continues to fail he will sooner or later find that his motivation to achieve (Ms) begins to diminish.

If a person has a desire to avoid failure (Mf) his behavior may take several forms. To illustrate: If such an individual initially selects a very easy task and fails, and there exists no easier task, he may next select the most difficult task. In other words, his aspiration level may jump simply to minimize the expected pain of failure after a failure at the easiest task. If the (Mf) person is successful at the easiest task his (Ps) increases and his (Pf) decreases so that the task becomes less and less unpleasant.

The results of several experiments would seem to bear out many of the points contained in Atkinson's article.[79]

Atkinson's model differs widely from Siegel's in several respects. One important consideration to Siegel is the nature of the goal, that is, its utility. On the other hand, Atkinson emphasizes the value which the individual places upon the achievement of the goal rather than upon its utility. The significant variable in Atkinson's model is the value which the individual places upon the achievement of the goal rather than upon its utility. The significant variable in Atkinson's model is the value of a goal object as affected by its difficulty of attainment. This variable of difficulty might very well be incorporated usefully into *SEU* models, and reflected in the concept of subjective probability.[80] Both Siegel's and Atkinson's models seek to constrain maximizing behavior in choice situations. Both models contain their flaws, nevertheless. One important misconception, especially noticeable in the Atkinson model, is that subjective probabilities must add up to 1. People do not behave this way. Subjective probabilities do not necessarily have to add up to 1.[81] Furthermore, it may be possible that utility and subjective probability interact.[82] If this interaction does occur, Siegel's model and, for that matter, *SEU* models, may have to be completely reevaluated.

SUMMARY

In this chapter we have examined three areas of modern psychology which are closely related to, and which could be most useful for, the study of business behavior. Unfortunately, it has been possible only to outline superficially some of the features of theories drawn from personality, learning, and decision-making fields. The treatment of these fields, in itself, has been a choice problem, not only of deciding which theories from each area to include, but even of deciding which areas in the broad study of psychology to discuss. The three fields which have been examined herein were selected on the basis of three criteria: (1) Their relevance to the problem of choice; (2) Their importance in modern psychology; and (3) The fact that they impart to the reader some of the flavor of the discipline of psychology.

The problems with which psychologists are concerned are most pertinent for the study of business behavior. Personalities behave, in business as elsewhere. The more completely that we can understand the decision maker—the workings of that "black box"—the better we can understand and predict behavior. Furthermore, it is evident that personalities change. That they acquire or forget information. That they adjust and react. That they are motivated differently by the same or different stimuli, and respond differently, over time. That they learn—for indeed life is a learning process. Finally, it is also clear that the choice situation itself requires more intensive investigation. How persons decide between alternatives—indeed how they even establish alternatives or define alternatives—remains a matter of considerable debate.

As this chapter is concluded, it is apparent how much more could and should be said about the importance of psychology for the study of business behavior. The relationships between these two fields will undoubtedly become clearer in future years as more and more of these interactions are recognized.

Notes and References

1. J. L. McCary, editor, *Psychology of Personality* (New York: Logos Press, 1956), p. xi.

2. Floyd L. Ruch, *Psychology and Life,* Fourth Edition (Chicago: Scott, Foresman & Company, 1953), p. 30.

3. James Drever, *A Dictionary of Psychology* (Baltimore: Penguin Books, Inc., 1955), p. 203.

4. Calvin S. Hall and Gardner Lindzey, *Theories of Personality* (New York: John Wiley & Sons, Inc., 1957), p. 548.

5. Ronald Taft, "A Statistical Analysis of Personality Theories," *Acta Psychologica,* Vol. XVII, No. 1, pp. 80-88.

6. Many authors have tried to categorize personality theories, but very few have placed these into similar groupings. See, for example, H. Brand, editor, *The Study of Personality; A Book of Readings* (New York: John Wiley & Sons, Inc., 1954), wherein are classified individual behavior theories (uniqueness); general behavior theories (common features); and functional behavior theories (characteristic methods of choice). E. Brunswik, "The Conceptual Framework of Psychology," *International Encyclopedia of Unified Science,* Vol. I, No. 10 (Chicago: University of Chicago Press, 1952), which classifies theories in terms of responses desired. R. A. Littman and E. Rosen, "Molar and Molecular," *Psychological Review,* Vol. 57, pp. 58-65, which categorizes theories into the two headings given in the article's title. G. W. Allport, *Becoming: Basic Considerations for a Psychology of Personality* (New Haven, Conn.: Yale University Press, 1955), and many, many others.

7. McCary, *op. cit.*, pp. xiv-xv.

8. Muzafer Sheriff, "A Study of Some Social Factors in Perception," *Archives of Psychology*, Vol. XXVII, No. 187 (1935).

9. Gordon W. Allport, "European and American Theories of Personality," in Henry P. David and Helmut von Bracken, eds., *Perspectives in Personality Theory* (New York: Basic Books, Inc., 1957), pp. 12-14.

10. Some psychologists have serious misgivings about this trend, cf. Gordon W. Allport, "The Historical Background of Modern Social Psychology," in Gardner Lindzey, ed., *Handbook of Social Psychology* (Cambridge: Addison-Wesley Publishing Co., 1954), Vol. I, pp. 3-56; and John Gilden, editor, *For a Science of Social Man* (New York: The Macmillan Company, 1954), pp. 160-256.

11. The best biography of Freud, which also contains a detailed treatment of his theoretical contributions, has been written by his former student and associate Ernest Jones, *The Life and Work of Sigmund Freud* (New York: Basic Books, Inc., 1955), 3 volumes. Freud's psychoanalytic theory of personality is briefly explained in a number of books, among which are: Hall and Lindzey, *op. cit.*, Chapter 2; Charles M. Harsh and Harry G. Schrickel, *Personality, Development and Assessment*, Second Edition (New York: The Ronald Press Company, 1959), Chapter 14; and Richard S. Lazarus, *Adjustment and Personality* (New York: McGraw-Hill Book Company, Inc., 1961), Chapter 6.

12. The best known of the life instincts are the sexual instincts, with which psychoanalytic literature has been greatly preoccupied. However, Freud also thought that the death instincts were extremely important to the understanding of human behavior, although these were not as conspicuous. Thus he wrote: "the goal of all life is death." S. Freud, "Beyond the Pleasure Principle," in J. Strachey, editor, *The Standard Edition of the Complete Psychological Works*, Vol. XIII (London: Hogarth Press, Ltd., 1955), p. 38. Because the death instincts often take the form of aggression, these are perhaps more significant for explanations of business behavior than the life instincts. The death instincts concepts, however, have not been widely accepted by psychologists. See, for example, O. Fenichel, *The Psychoanalytic Theory of Neurosis* (New York: W. W. Norton & Co., Inc., 1945). Cf. Hall and Lindzey, *op. cit.*, Chap. 2.

14. Very little has been done to relate Freudian theory directly to business behavior. However, see: Geraldine Pederson-Krag, "A Psychoanalytic Approach to Mass Production," *Psychoanalytic Quarterly*, XX (July, 1951), pp. 434-451; and Merlin Thomas, "Sexual Symbolism in Industry," *International Journal of Psychoanalysis*, XXXII (1951), pp. 128-133.

15. Jung was a prolific writer, and this brief paragraph does him a grave injustice. For a more comprehensive view, see: C. G. Jung, *Collected Works* (New York: Pantheon Books, Inc., 1953).

16. This résumé of Adler's ideas is based largely upon H. L. and Rowena R. Ansbacher, editors, *The Individual Psychology of Alfred Adler* (New York: Basic Books, Inc., 1956).

17. See, among other works by these authors, Erich Fromm, *Escape from Freedom* (New York: Holt, Rinehart & Winston, Inc., 1941; Karen Horney, *Neurosis and Human Growth* (New York: W. W. Norton & Co., Inc., 1950); H. S. Sullivan, *The Interpersonal Theory of Psychiatry* (New York: W. W. Norton & Co., Inc., 1953). For an excellent survey of the Freudian school, see Ruth L. Munroe, *Schools of Psychoanalytic Thought* (New York: The Dryden Press, 1955).

18. G. W. Allport and H. S. Odbert, "Trait-Names: A Psycholexical Study," *Psychological Monographs*, Vol. 47, No. 211 (1936).

19. G. W. Allport, *Personality: A Psychological Interpretation* (New York: Holt, Rinehart & Winston, Inc., 1937).

20. R. B. Cattell, *Personality: A Systematic, Theoretical, and Factual Study* (New York: McGraw-Hill Book Company, Inc., 1950).

21. Cf. D. C. McClelland, *Personality* (New York: W. Sloane Associates, 1951).

22. Cf. R. B. Cattell, *Description and Measurement of Personality* (New York: Harcourt, Brace & World, Inc., 1946); *Factor Analysis: An Introduction and Manual for the Psychologist and Social Scientist* (New York: Harper & Row, Publishers, 1952); and R. B. Cattell and D. R. Saunders, "Interrelation and Matching of Personality Factors from Behavior Rating, Questionnaire, and Objective Test Data," *Journal of Abnormal Social Psychology*, Vol. 54, pp. 143-159.

23. H. J. Eysenck, "The Organization of Personality," *Journal of Personality*, Vol. 20 (1951), pp. 101-118; and, *The Scientific Study of Personality* (London: Routledge & Kegan Paul, Ltd., 1952).

24. M. Schoen, *Human Nature* (New York: Harper & Row, Publishers, 1930).

25. Cf. G. W. Allport, *Personality: A Psychological Interpretation, op. cit.*; and "Motivation in Personality," *Psychological Review*, Vol. 47 (1940), pp. 533-554.

26. G. W. Allport, *Becoming, op. cit.*

27. *Ibid.*, pp. 90ff.

28. Kenneth E. Boulding, *The Image* (Ann Arbor: University of Michigan Press, 1956).

29. George A. Miller, Eugene Galanter, and Karl H. Pribram, *Plans and the Structure of Behavior* (New York: Holt, Rinehart & Winston, Inc., 1960).

30. Cf. Kurt A. Lewin, *A Dynamic Theory of Personality*, translated by K. E. Zener and D. K. Adams (New York: McGraw-Hill Book Company, Inc., 1935); *Resolving Social Conflicts: Selected Papers on Group Dynamics*, edited by Gertrude W. Lewin (New York: Harper & Row, Publishers, 1948); *Field Theory in Social Science: Selected Theoretical Papers*, edited by D. Cartwright (New York: Harper & Row, Publishers, 1951).

31. This paragraph leans heavily on the discussion in Clifford T. Morgan, *Introduction to Psychology* (New York: McGraw-Hill Book Company, Inc., 1956), pp. 251-253.

32. H. F. Wright, "Influence of Barriers upon Strength of Motivation," *Contributions to Psychological Theories*, Vol. I, No. 3 (Durham, N. C.: Duke University Press, 1937).

33. For an illustration oriented toward business behavior, see Joseph Clawson, "Lewin's Vector Psychology and the Analysis of Motives in Marketing," in Reavis Cox and Wroe Alderson, editors, *Theory in Marketing* (Homewood, Ill.: Richard D. Irwin, Inc., 1950), pp. 46-48.

34. Mark J. Gibson, "Field Theory and Business Behavior," in Joseph W. McGuire, editor, *Interdisciplinary Studies in Business Behavior* (Cincinnati: Southwestern Publishing Company, 1962), pp. 186-187.

35. For an excellent and much more complete discussion of field theory, see Hall and Lindzey, *op. cit.*, pp. 206-256; and Robert W. Leeper, *Lewin's Topological and Vector Psychology: A Digest and Critique*, University of Oregon Monographs, Studies in Psychology, No. 1 (Eugene, Ore.: University of Oregon Press, 1943).

36. H. E. Garrett, "Lewin's 'Topological' Psychology: An Evaluation," *Psychological Review*, Vol. 46 (1939), pp. 517-524.

37. I. D. London, "Psychologist's Misuse of the Auxiliary Concepts of Physics and Mathematics," *Psychological Review*, Vol. 51 (1944), pp. 266-291.

38. E. C. Tolman, "Kurt Lewin, 1890-1947," *Psychological* Review, Vol. 55 (1948), pp. 1-4.

39. Even Lewin seemed to recognize this point. See Kurt Lewin, *Field Theory in Social Science: Selected Theoretical Papers, op. cit.*, p. 20.

40. H. A. Murray and Clyde Kluckhohn, "Outline of a Conception of Personality," in C. Kluckhohn, H. A. Murray, and D. Schneider, editors, *Personality in Nature, Society, and Culture*, Second Edition (New York: Alfred A. Knopf, Inc., 1953), pp. 3-52.

41. Henry A. Murray, et al., *Explorations in Personality* (New York: The Oxford University Press, 1938), p. 110; and C. Kluckhohn and H. A. Murray, *Personality in Nature, Society and Culture* (New York: Alfred A. Knopf, Inc., 1948), p. 10.

42. Murray, *Explorations in Personality, op. cit.*, pp. 79-83.

43. Representative works by these scholars are: Kurt Goldstein, *Human Nature in the Light of Psychopathology* (London: Cambridge University Press, 1940), and *The Organism* (New York: American Book Company, 1939); Andras Anygal, *Foundations for a Science of Personality* (New York: Commonwealth Fund, 1941); P. Lecky, *Self-Consistency* (New York: Island Press, 1951); A. H. Maslow, *Motivation and Personality* (New York: Harper & Row, Publishers, 1954) and "A Dynamic Theory of Human Motivation," *Psychological Review*, Vol. 1 (1943), pp. 370-396.

44. The book referred to is C. A. Hickman and M. H. Kulen, *Individuals, Groups and Economic Behavior* (New York: The Dryden Press, Inc., 1956).

45. Carl R. Rogers, *Client-Centered Therapy* (Boston: Houghton Mifflin Company, 1951), especially pp. 480ff. Cf. D. Snygg and A. W. Combs, *Individual Behavior* (New York: Harper & Row, Publishers, 1949); and M. A. Sheriff and H. Cantril, *The Psychology of Ego-Involvements* (New York: John Wiley & Sons, Inc., 1947).

46. David C. McClelland, *The Achieving Society* (Princeton, N. J.: D. Van Nostrand Co., Inc., 1961).

47. See *Ibid.*, Chapter 2.

48. *Ibid.*, pp. 236-237.

49. *Ibid.*, Chapter 6.

50. Cf. Donald K. Adams, *et al.*, *Learning Theory, Personality Theory, and Clinical Research*, The Kentucky Symposium (New York: John Wiley & Sons, Inc., 1954), and, especially J. Dollard and N. E. Miller, *Personality and Psychotherapy* (New York: McGraw-Hill Book Company, Inc., 1950), a widely accepted blend of Freudian personality concepts and learning theory.

51. From: *Theories of Learning*, 2nd edition by Ernest R. Hilgard. Copyright © 1956 by Appleton-Century-Crofts, Inc. Reprinted by permission of Appleton-Century-Crofts.

52. Cf. H. J. Ettlinger, "A Curve of Growth Designed to Represent the Learning Process," *Journal of Experimental Psychology*, Vol. 9 (1926), pp. 409-414, and L. L. Thurstone, "The Learning Curve Equation," *Psychological Monographs*, Vol. 26 (1919), pp. 1-51.

53. See R. Duncan Luce, ed., *Developments in Mathematical Psychology* (New York: The Free Press of Glencoe, Inc., 1960), especially Part 2, pp. 125-130, for a brief historical summary of learning theory.

54. *Ibid.*, p. 130.

55. Stochastic is used here in its modern sense, meaning probabilistic.

56. In W. K. Estes, "Toward a Statistical Theory of Learning," *Psychological Review*, Vol. 57 (1950), pp. 94-107 credit is given (107) especially

to E. R. Guthrie, "Psychological Facts and Psychological Theory," *Psychological Bulletin*, Vol. 43 (1946), pp. 1-20.

57. Robert R. Bush and Frederick Mosteller, *Stochastic Models for Learning* (New York: John Wiley & Sons, Inc., 1955), p. 17.

58. See *Ibid.*, pp. 29-33.

59. Cf. D. A. Grant, H. W. Hake, and J. P. Hornseth, "Acquisition and Extinction of a Verbal Conditioned Response with Differing Percentages of Reinforcement," *Journal of Experimental Psychology*, Vol. 42 (1951), pp. 1-5.

60. Cyert and March, *op. cit.*, p. 123.

61. *Ibid.*

62. M. E. Jarvik, "Probability Learning and a Negative Recency Effect in the Serial Anticipation of Alternative Symbols," *Journal of Experimental Psychology*, Vol. 41 (1951), pp. 291-297.

63. N. H. Anderson and D. A. Grant, "A Test of a Statistical Learning Model for Two-Choice Behavior with Double Stimulus Events," *Journal of Experimental Psychology*, Vol. 54 (1957), pp. 305-317.

64. Harold Borko, editor, *Computer Applications in the Behavioral Sciences*, Chapter 15 by Julian Feldman, "Computer Simulation of Cognitive Processes" (Englewood Cliffs, N. J.: Prentice-Hall, Inc., 1962), pp. 337-359.

65. *Ibid.*, p. 340.

66. *Ibid.*, p. 342.

67. *Ibid.*

68. Ward Edwards, "Behavioral Decision Theory," in Paul R. Farnsworth, Alga McNemar, and Quinn McNemar, eds., *Annual Review of Psychology* (Palo Alto, California: Annual Reviews, Inc., 1961), pp. 463-498.

69. Sidney Siegel, "Level of Aspiration and Decision Making," *Psychological Review*, Vol. 64, No. 4 (July, 1957), pp. 253-261.

70. Kurt Lewin, T. Dembo, L. Festinger, and P. S. Sears, "Level of Aspiration," in J. McV. Hunt, editor, *Personality and the Behavior Disorders*, Vol. I (New York: The Ronald Press Company, 1944), pp. 333-378.

71. *Ibid.*, p. 376.

72. Siegel, *op. cit.*, p. 254.

73. *Ibid.*, p. 256.

74. *Ibid.*, p. 257.

75. Cf. *Ibid.*, 256-260; P. M. Hurst and S. Siegel, "Prediction of Decisions from a Higher Ordered Metric Scale of Utility," *Journal of Experimental Psychology,* Vol. 52 (1956), pp. 138-144; D. Davidson, S. Siegel, and P. Suppes, "Some Experiments and Related Theory in the Measurement of Utility and Subjective Probability," in D. Davidson, *et al.,* eds., *Decision-Making: An Experimental Approach* (Stanford, Calif.: Stanford University Press, 1957), pp. 19-81; H. A. Simon, "A Behavioral Model of Rational Choice," *Quarterly Journal of Economics,* Vol. 69 (1955), pp. 99-118.

76. John W. Atkinson, "Motivational Determinants of Risk-Taking Behavior," *Psychological Review,* Vol. 64, No. 6 (1957), pp. 359-372.

77. *Ibid.,* p. 362.

78. *Ibid.,* p. 364.

79. D. C. McClelland, "Some Social Consequences of Achievement Motivation," in M. R. Jones, editor, *Nebraska Symposium on Motivation* (Lincoln, Neb.: University of Nebraska Press, 1955); D. C. McClelland, J. W. Atkinson, R. A. Clark, and E. L. Lowell, *The Achievement Motive* (New York: Appleton-Century-Crofts, Inc., 1933).

80. See N. T. Feather, "Subjective Probability and Decision Under Uncertainty," *Psychological Review,* Vol. 66, No. 3 (May, 1959), pp. 150-162, for an interesting comparison of the Atkinson and *SEU*—as well as other—models.

81. Ward Edwards, *Subjective Probability in Decision Theories,* Report No. 2144-361-T, Project MICHIGAN, Willow Run Laboratories, University of Michigan (March, 1959).

82. The evidence is conflicting. Cf. H. C. A. Dale, "*A Priori* Probabilities in Gambling," *Nature,* Vol. 183 (1959), pp. 539-546; and F. W. Irwin, "Stated Expectations as Functions of Probability and Desirability of Outcomes," *Journal of Personality,* Vol. 21 (1953), pp. 329-335.

10

THE INTERACTIONS BETWEEN CULTURE AND BUSINESS

The decision process within business is never entirely unrestricted. Instead, business behavior is a function of a host of variables. The individual personality, the organizational context for action, the situation, and environmental forces all place constraints upon business operations and decisions. We have observed how some of these personal and institutional factors might, in theory, affect the behavior of men in business. In addition to the variables previously discussed there are also other factors which are important to our understanding of how and why businesses and businessmen perform as they do. In this chapter we shall examine, as one of these other factors, the culture of business; and less extensively, the related variables of environment and society.

Business behavior takes place within a cultural matrix. It occurs within a societal framework, and affects and is affected by the environment within which it operates. Although cultural investigations are often merely descriptive, they do enable man to understand, and frequently to predict, the activities of his fellow man. As the well-known anthropologist, Clyde Kluckhohn, once wrote:

> A good deal of human behavior can be understood, and indeed predicted, if we know a people's design for living. Many acts are neither accidental nor due to personal peculiarities nor caused by supernatural forces nor simply mysterious. Even those of us who pride ourselves on our individualism follow most of the time a pattern not of our own making. We brush our teeth on arising. We put on pants—not a loin cloth or a grass skirt. We eat three meals a day—not four or five or two. We sleep in a bed—not in a hammock or on a sheep pelt. I do not have to know the individual and his life history to be able to predict these and countless other regularities, including many in the thinking process, of all Americans who are not incarcerated in jails or hospitals for the insane.[1]

Many of the "countless other regularities" of individual behavior may be found in business, and a knowledge of the culture within which the enterprise operates will enable us to understand and predict these regularities. A cultural approach to business behavior uncovers the obvious patterns and interwoven structures which serve as guidelines for and limits to business actions, and often discloses those subtle and underlying means and goals of behavior. Such an approach to the enterprise indicates that men in all cultures do not act in the same way, nor for the same reasons, nor to the same ends. As we shall observe, it may be correct to assume that businessmen, like all individuals, tend to maximize their satisfactions in terms of the choices they make and the alternatives they perceive, but the crux of the cultural approach is that the perceptions and satisfactions of one culture may differ substantially from those of another.[2] In underdeveloped nations, for example, for many individuals business may be only a way to earn money essential for life, so that an increase in income leads to a decrease in effort.[3]

In this chapter, then, we shall discuss several concepts and theories drawn principally from the discipline of cultural anthropology. These ideas, in general, may be utilized to explain how business behavior is conditioned by the culture in which it exists. Cultural theories may, therefore, be used to explain the context for business activities, that is, culture is another variable which acts as a restraint on business behavior —it is a parameter within which operations must take place. More than this, however, cultural theories strive to reinforce as well as limit the decision process in business. Culture is an active variable and a dynamic one. It underlies behavior in a positive fashion just as it limits it negatively.

The sequence of topics in this chapter will be as follows: We shall briefly examine some definitional material, and then move on to some of the theoretical approaches to the study of culture. We shall then discuss the process of innovation and change. Finally, we shall look at rationality, goals, the entrepreneurial function, and the problem of universals.

CULTURE, SOCIETY, AND ENVIRONMENT: DEFINITIONS

Definition of Culture

In anthropology, as in all the social sciences, it is an easy matter to become lost in a morass of semantics. There are hundreds of definitions of culture. Kroeber and Kluckhohn, in an investigation of almost two hundred of these definitions and statements, found that the vast majority differed but slightly in their comprehensiveness and in their cultural properties.[4] There were a few definitions that were completely bizarre, but there also appeared to be a historical trend in definitional fashions. It was concluded, however, that most behavioral scientists in recent years would agree with the following definition.

> Culture consists of patterns, explicit and implicit, of and for behavior acquired and transmitted by symbols, constituting the distinctive achievement of human groups, including their embodiments in artifacts; the essential core of culture consists of traditional (that is, historically derived and selected) ideas and especially their attached values; culture systems may, on the one hand, be considered as products of action, on the other as conditioning influences upon further action.[5]

Culture, as Ralph Linton has emphasized, is a continuing process.[6] At any point in time it may be seen as the product of accumulated traditions and customs; of cultural elements which have been altered, and it has within it the potential for continuing change. Culture is always changing, although it contains configurations, that is, more or less basic values and beliefs which tend to make it integrated and unified. The American culture has certain basic configurations, but it is also highly diversified and dynamic, encompassing a variety of subcultures, which exist as continually shifting enclaves within the larger entity. Other cultures, such as the Ainu of Japan, were more highly patterned or structured than ours is now, and consequently were better defined and more homogeneous. Cultures, in our modern world, most often come into contact with one another. In these instances elements of one will become "diffused" into the other. If this sort of diffusion and contact continues over a considerable time period, the transfer process is termed acculturation. Acculturation, then, is one way in which cultures change. A more basic cause of change is usually considered to be innovation, which is then diffused culturally and distributed geographically.

The Meaning of Society

Society, on the other hand, is generally defined as an aggregate of individuals, animals, or even institutions (as in the case of business firms) structured and organized into populations and groups. The origin of societies and the bonds which hold populations together have been a matter of considerable speculation. The social contract doctrine, for example, propounded the idea that society was created by the mutual and "rational" activities of those individuals who compose the society. The theory of Darwin led Westermarck to believe that western society had evolved from monogamous marriage practices, and Marx to the assumption that communism would eventually evolve from capitalism. Tonnies, the German sociologist, differentiated between *Gemeinschaft* societies, with small memberships, homogeneous populations, and traditional beliefs; and *Gesellschaft* societies, which are larger and vaguely defined.[7] Tonnies theorized that the modern *Gesellschaft* societies had evolved historically from the *Gemeinschaft* types.

Caryl P. Haskins, the famous scientist and social philosopher, has related society and culture (as, of course, have many other scholars). Man, in Haskins' view, is a biological and ideational component which combines with other idea complexes to form a cultural society.[8] This entity, like all living organisms, is subject to mutation, inheritance, and selection. Modern societies, as opposed to more primitive ones, are marked by their integrative character, that is, they tend to have permanence, and all members are functionally related. The binding tie in society is the human mind, which permits integration and the creation of communication, trade, and business systems. Some sociologists, on the other hand, believe that the tie that binds individuals into paths of conduct which are societal rather than individualistic, and makes modern societies *Gesellschaft* rather than *Gemeinschaft,* is the mass media.

> Mass society is categorically distinct, according to this concept, from premodern societies in a number of dimensions. It is composed of very large numbers of socially unrelated individual members; it is held together by impersonal communications via the mass media; and, most distinguishing of all, it operates on the basis of one-way communication rather than "interaction."[9]

It is evident that societies and their cultures are closely related. In fact, both may be observed as but different abstractions of the same phenomena.[10] Societies must have internal consistencies which tightly or loosely hold their members together. Social organization is based upon cultural patterns. The way in which a society is formed and continued, and that which gives it form and substance, and which distinguishes and separates it from other societies is culture. Society, then is more than a simple aggregate of individuals. It encompasses, instead, those populations which share in, and manifest, the same cultural attributes.

The Environment

The environment consists of that external world in which men carry out their activities. This world includes both the natural habitat and the artifacts which are created by man. At the beginning of the twentieth century habitat and culture were linked by theories of geographic determinism. Huntington, for example, attributed the dynamics of civilization to climate.[11] Although environment undoubtedly influences technology and material culture—and thus business operations—it does not determine the uses to which materials and resources will be put. The habitat may be restrictive upon behavior, but it also allows alternatives. The environment is only one variable which affects man's activities, and even the richest resources will be unimportant until men utilize them. As Forde has observed, between the environment and human activity there is always ". . . a middle term, a collection of specific objectives and values, a body of knowledge and belief: in other words, a cultural pattern.[12]

Many scholars have emphasized the influence of the environment upon man and his culture rather than the mutual influence of the earth and its peoples upon one another.[13] Many of the field investigations into primitive economies have attempted to relate the culture of a community in a functional manner to its environment.[14] In fact, some of the more recent research by economist-anthropologist teams has concentrated primarily upon the cultural-environmental relationships.[15]

Thus, it is evident that there is a triumvirate of external forces—culture, society, and environment—that are intimately and inextricably interwoven into a fabric within which behavior, including business behavior, takes place. In the next section we shall examine some of the approaches to the study of these external variables—in particular culture—to see how business activities might be confined or perhaps altered or initiated by them.

THEORIES OF CULTURE

Most of the theories of culture employed by cultural anthropologists are methodological. They constitute conflicting approaches to the study of culture, but very few are actually concerned with explanations of culture *per se*. Although cultural theories do differ substantially from the behavioral theories examined in earlier chapters, they do give us some insight into the approaches and thought processes of anthropologists, and in some instances into culture itself. The major schools of cultural theory are often summed up by general descriptive terms: "evolutionism," "historicalism," "functionalism," and so on. Several of these approaches to culture will be examined briefly in this section.

Cultural Evolution

Theories of cultural evolution are predicated on the work of Darwin, and assume that cultures have passed through three great stages of savagery, barbarism, and finally civilization. Some primitive societies today have not yet evolved to the second, and certainly not to the third stage. The primary notion of evolutionism, therefore, is that the nations of the West represent the high end of cultural evolution, whereas the savage tribes are at the lower extreme.[16] Some theorists trace the evolution of particular aspects or institutions of modern culture from prehistoric times. For example, it has been suggested that present-day political organizations, which are tied together territorially, have evolved from kinship relationships. Evolutionists also argued that business practices, economic organizations, and patterns of business behavior progressed to their present sophisticated and complex levels from primitive economic origins.

The early theories of cultural evolution were most widely held prior to the turn of the twentieth century. The idea that western civilization is the final repository of a series of past and lower stages of culture is unsupported by field research. It is also somewhat naive, for this concept looks upon evolution as a unilinear thread which holds cultural stages together over time. In fact, however, cultures do not necessarily evolve from within. There is no inherent tendency for the native Indians of the Brazilian jungles to evolve culturally in the direction of modern American culture. To be sure, an acculturation process, whereby the cultures of modern man rub against the native cultures, may result in "progress." But such a progress is imposed from external sources, and is not inborn within the primitive culture itself.

A more sophisticated approach to cultural evolution has been advanced during the past twenty years by Leslie White, whose views have since been supported by several other anthropologists. Thus, White has written:

> Cultures must be explained in terms of culture . . . culture is a continuum. Each trait or organization of traits, each stage of development, grows out of an earlier situation. The steam engine can be traced back to the origins of metallurgy and fire. International cartels have

grown out of all the processes of exchange and distribution since the Old Stone Age and before. . . . Culture is a vast stream of tools, utensils, customs, and beliefs that are constantly interacting with each other, creating new combinations and syntheses. New elements are added constantly to the stream; obsolete traits drop out. The culture of today is but the cross section of this stream at the present moment, the resultant of the age-old process of interaction, selection, rejection, and accumulation that has preceded us. . . . The culture of the present was determined by the past and the culture of the future will be but a continuation of the trend of the present. Thus, in a very real sense culture makes itself.[17]

White's views have been termed "universal evolution" to distinguish them from those held by his predecessors. Modern evolutionists often assume that there are parallels in historically separate cultural traditions, and seek to explain these parallels by identical but independent causes.[18] Unfortunately, none of the evolutionary theories of culture correspond closely with the results of empirical research. The very fact that cultural traditions are often distinct, and that they vary from locality to locality is dismissed by the evolutionists as irrelevant. Nevertheless, it has proved very difficult for these theorists to account for the divergent cultures which so obviously exist—even in the same stages—without moving outside the evolutionary framework.

Historical Theories of Culture

The first major anthropologist to advocate historicalism was Franz Boas, the "father of American ethnology." Historical theories arose originally as a part of the revolution against naive evolutionism and environmental determinism. For the first thirty years of this century historicalism dominated anthropological thought. Scholars utilizing the historical method tend to deal with the traits of a people, and appear to regard culture in a descriptive way as the sum of these traits. This approach, which usually employs an ethnographic survey, results in nonpredictive descriptions of culture, wherein economic, religious, artistic, and other traits are added to make the whole. These traits are observed as of a moment of time, and from the observer's own perspective. Often the descriptions of artifacts or traits are well done, with an effort at the analysis and comparison of trait trends from one subculture to another.[19] Frequently, however, as Lord Hailey has noted:

> In the early years of this century anthropologists usually followed the method of "survey work," in which the inquirer travelled over a wide area recording for each tribe the broad characteristics of physical type, social organization, and material culture. In River's survey work . . . in Melanesia (1901-2) he spent a short time on each island, and sometimes questioned not more than one informant.[20]

Often, too, the traits discussed are unrelated one to the other, or when they are, as in Linton's work, they are related primarily in a historical manner. Clark Wissler, for example, grouped traits into patterns, so that the American culture was composed of such traits as rapid communication and compulsory education.[21] Historical anthropologists became collectors of cultural attributes and artifacts, most of which were isolated and (because these are not seen as part of a whole) were usually unable to impart to the reader a sense of cultural vitality or cultural unity. Nevertheless, historicalism did contribute to an understanding of cultures because it emphasized objective observation and field research. However, there has been little attempt made to apply the findings of historicalism in any systematic way to the solution of practical problems.

Functional Approaches to Culture

The functional approach to culture stems largely from the work of two scholars working separately in Britain, Bronislaw Malinowski and Alfred Radcliffe-Brown. These functionalists emphasized the interrelationships between cultural elements, and integrated these into a holistic cultural system. They concentrated in particular upon those parts of the culture which contributed in a significant functional way toward the maintenance and operation of the entire system. This emphasis has led Thompson to remark that:

> The main contribution of the so-called "functionalists" to anthropology was . . . that they introduced into anthropological field research the effective use of an explicit, modern systems approach. In other words, they were the first in the discipline to exploit systematically the idea that the basic unit of field research in relation to the problem might fruitfully be treated as though it were a system wherein all the parts were functionally related to one another and to the whole.[22]

Malinowski stressed organizations or institutions as the proper unit for anthropological research.[23] He believed every institution was established to satisfy a need within the culture, and distinguished three levels of imperatives which were universal, because they were found in all cultures. These need levels are (1) biological, such as the needs for food, shelter, and defense, (2) derived, which include such institutions as law, education, and business, and (3) synthetic, which consist of those integrative imperatives such as religion, art, and play.[24] Malinowski generalized from his observations of the elements of culture to the interactions between these elements and their *raison d'être*. He continually wrote as an observer located outside the culture observed, and described institutional systems as they existed in their environment. That is, he did not try to isolate or abstract institutions from their setting, but rather tried to study them as part of the wider culture of which they were part. Malinowski believed that culture bound individuals tightly within its confines, and that only occasionally could they break out of its institutionalized regulations.

Radcliffe-Brown centered his analysis around the concept of society rather than culture. He attempted to describe in an exhaustive manner the general mechanisms of social systems. Institutions were appraised in the light of what they contributed to the viability of the social structure. Radcliffe-Brown, to even a greater extent than Malinowski, advocated a systems approach wherein the components are tied together, and, therefore, separated from the environment or other variables external to the system. He wrote:

> A natural system . . . is a conceptually isolated portion of phenomenal reality (the system separated from the rest of the universe which is then the total environment of the system), consisting of a set of entities in such relation to one another as to make a naturally cohering unity.[25]

Radcliffe-Brown has been termed a social anthropologist, because of his emphasis on the relation of culture and society. His pioneering work led to a number of studies of the minutiae of social interaction. His followers, such as Lloyd Warner and Arensberg and Kimball, studied the organization of behavior and the institutions of modern society.[26] This sort of work has focused upon human relations, and has strayed quite far from the more traditional anthropological stress upon history and evolution.

Configurational Approaches to Culture

Two of the best known proponents of the configurational approach to the study of culture are Edward Sapir and Ruth Benedict. Boas has written, in his introduction to *Patterns of Culture:*

> Dr. Benedict calls the genius of culture its configuration. In the present volume the author has set before us this problem and has illustrated it by the example of three cultures that are permeated each by one dominating idea. This treatment is distinct from the so-called functional approach to social phenomena in so far as it is concerned rather with the discovery of fundamental attitudes than with the functional relations of every cultural item. It is not historical except in so far as the general configuration, as long as it lasts, limits the directions of change that remain subject to it.[27]

Sapir likewise defined culture as "nearly synonymous with the 'spirit' or 'genius' of a people."[28] It consists of ". . . those general attitudes, views of life, and specific manifestations of civilization that give a particular people its distinctive place in the world." [29]

Anthropologists of the configurational school, then, look for those features of a culture which seem to them to form the essence or core of the life of a people. Thus, Benedict wrote about "patterns" and "mainsprings." Most of these deeply rooted aspects of culture are closely related to psychology. For example, she observed that man's paramount aim in American culture is to amass private possessions and to multiply occasions for display, which in turn affect a variety of activities ranging from the modern position of the wife to rivalry and waste.[30] Of course, there are more themes than this in our complex culture, as Benedict recognizes. In fact Opler isolated about twenty major themes in his study of the culture of the Apache Indians, which is certainly less complex than that of modern America.[31]

The analysis of cultural configurations has become of considerable importance in modern social anthropology. However, there are still many scholars who believe that configurationalism tends to produce results which are more artistic than scientific, and that the method is more subjective than objective.

Other Cultural Approaches

In recent decades there has been increasing interest in cross-disciplinary approaches to the study of culture and society. Anthropologists have exhibited a mounting concern with psychological and sociological data. Margaret Mead, for example, was one of the first anthropologists to investigate the relationships between the individual, personality, character, and culture.[32] These studies have led Mead, and others, to an analysis of the modern American character, and in some instances to the changes which have occurred in this national portrait.

Margaret Mead has stressed the unstable nature of the modern American, resulting largely from the behavioral patterns produced in childhood by the conflict between parental and peer group standards.[33] Others have examined the modern American character, and have found different variables and relationships to be of greater significance than those noted by Mead.[34] Mead stressed child development, others have found immigration, the rate of population growth, repression, work, and the social ethic to be more important in explaining American character.

Kluckhohn, in collaboration with the psychologist Henry A. Murray, explored the theoretical relationships between culture and personality.[35] They tried to isolate the universals common to all mankind, such as biological structure and growth, the fact that man is affected by his environment, culture, and society. Men differ from their fellows, because their environments, cultures, and societies vary; but other men in the same settings should be affected similarly, and, therefore, behave similarly. It is still other variables, therefore, such as his role, situation, and constitution, that make the individual unique. The individual, then, is seen by Kluckhohn and Murray as affected both by culture and by environment and yet behaving individualistically because of the ". . . endless variation within the general patterning due to the organism's constitutionally-determined peculiarities of reaction and to the occurrence of special situations."[36]

Anthropologists in recent decades have come to work in the realm of learning theory as well as with personality theories. Culture, in this context, becomes habit and custom learned from others and from the environment.[37] The culture offers cues to the individual, evokes his response, establishes sanctions for his misdeeds and errors, and sets goals and rewards.

Following the lead of Radcliffe-Brown, anthropologists have crossed over to, and intermingled with, the work of sociologists. Chapple, for example, has analyzed human relations in terms of interactions and equilibria, much as we discussed behavior in Chapter 8.[38]

Cultural Approaches in Review

The comments above are but a brief summary of the main features of some of the approaches employed by anthropologists in the study of culture. One general trend which stands out is the movement away from what is called "unilinear" explanations of culture, and toward interdisciplinary approaches which bring into focus the individual, the society, and the environment. Another is the movement toward approaches which compare the traits, characters, personalities, and so on, of two or more cultures—what has been generally described as the "cross-cultural" approach.

Perhaps the most important feature of these cultural theories or approaches—at least for the study of business—lies in their underlying but implicit characteristics. Anthropological methodology, regardless of the specific approach utilized, would seem to be a rewarding way to examine the business enterprise. The firm may be conceived as a sub-cultural matrix within wider cultural settings, somewhat as the first circle in water into which a stone is thrown remains within but still affects the concentric ripples which surround it. A part of the firm's culture is identical with that in which it exists, but there are some differences which bring about conflicts and confusion with the societal culture.[39] This sub-culture, in turn, is a fabric of industrial, occupational, and group cultures. Through a cultural approach to business behavior it might be possible to isolate those elements which separate business from other societal activities, and perhaps even to compartmentalize those features which are unique to individual industries or occupations or levels. As Jean Boddewyn has concluded:

> (1) The cultural approach and its cross-cultural, historico-cultural, and subcultural versions offer a multidimensional picture of the economic "genus" in place, time, and species. As such, it helps one to perceive the broadness and diversity of economic behavior above and beyond the simplified models of economic theory.
>
> (2) Yet, the cultural approach is insufficient by itself. Not only does it require a socio-psychological theory to explain the interaction of individuals and their culture, but it cannot even claim to interpret satisfactorily all economic phenomena. Other theories are needed to refine gross cultural concepts or to explain culture itself.
>
> (3) Graver still: are cultural explanations too amorphous or atomized to be of any use? The search for a general theory of business attempts to replace simple economic models by something more substantial—yet of general application. The fact is, however, that . . . the cultural approach proposes instead a variety of explanations to fit particular times, places, and circumstances.
>
> But, is that bad?
>
> It may well be that a realization of the diversity of economic and business behavior is exactly what is needed before business theory gets into "simplified" models of its own! [40]

INNOVATION AND CULTURAL CHANGE

Most students of business and economics are acquainted with the theory of innovation set forth by Joseph A. Schumpeter.[41] Fewer, perhaps, know of the institutional concepts of change and progress, as described, for example, by Wesley Mitchell.[42] And even further removed from typical fare for business students are those discussions of cultural change and innovation as presented by such social scholars as H. G. Barnett and Julian H. Steward.[43] Schumpeter, of course, attributed innovations, which are new ways of doing things, or better, unique combinations of the factors of production, to the efforts of entrepreneurs. In other words, he advocated a hero theory of innovations and progress. Mitchell and others, on the other hand, held to an environmental theory of innovation, wherein the individual is of secondary importance and the accumulation of knowledge and the "times" become the prime forces bringing about change. Barnett, and to some extent Steward, would be between Mitchell and Schumpeter, although their theories are much more complex, and even their definitions of innovation differ considerably from those advanced by their economic colleagues.

Barnett takes an unusually broad definition of innovation, which he terms . . . "any thought, behavior, or thing that is new because it is qualitatively different from existing forms." [44] In this sense innovation can include all types of changes—technological, religious, economic, social, industrial, and cultural. The general elements in each of these types of change are similar, and are invention (innovation) and diffusion. Invention, of course, is popularly limited to things, but in a restricted way may be synonymous with innovation in that it involves novelty. For example, the American constitution may be thought of as a social invention which synthesizes American colonial experiences and a thread of western European philosophy which extends back to ancient Greece.[45] Diffusion may be considered simply as the spread of innovation. Thus, the Industrial Revolution, which resulted from the introduction of modern business techniques, consisted of a series of inventions and innovations which were diffused (and are still spreading) throughout the world.[46] The radio and movies have had a great impact upon the nonliterate peoples of the Middle East.[47] Thousands of changes in business behavior have occurred which over time and space have become diffused throughout society.

There are, according to Barnett, two primary sources of innovation.[48] First, there is the existing culture and the way that it is concentrated and distributed within society. This cultural milieu encompasses the accumulation of ideas in the culture. Thus, there must be a culture which contains those elements conducive to innovation.[49] Second, innovation cannot be forthcoming without individuals who possess certain unique attributes.[50]

The growth of material culture has progressed at an accelerated rate, in part because of the expanded, and expanding, base of cultural elements.[51] Another factor of some import in the development of modern innovations is the evolution of ideas in research organizations and the education of thousands of scientists and technicians.[52] Technological change has, in itself, mounted cumulatively and thereby set the climate for still further change and stimulated the institutions and men which produced still more changes. As Alfred North Whitehead once pointed out, the greatest invention has been the invention of the method of invention.[53]

In modern societies the process of diffusion does not have to move spatially outward step-by-step from the center of innovation. Because of the linkages between communities through rapid communications and transportation facilities it is possible for innovation to be diffused quickly throughout the western world at least, and to leap-frog over some areas in transit. Cultural diffusion may follow class, wealth, or industry patterns so that persons far removed geographically from the source may be aware of, or use, an innovation before its existence is even known in its own neighborhood.[54]

The impact of diffusion is closely related to the society and culture in which it occurs. Material innovations are ordinarily more easily diffused in alien cultures than nonmaterial elements, and the former may be accepted even though they are not completely understood. In fact, the transference of cultural elements is normally in terms of form alone, without the accepting society caring or knowing about the original cultural context within which the innovation was used.[55] As innovations are diffused they have derivative effects whereby the behavior of a people is altered in ways only indirectly related to the introduction of the innovation.[56] Thus, the automobile had not only direct effects upon business institutions, but it also had an impact upon family relationships, on government, religion, and sex.[57]

Technological innovations, therefore, can produce cultural and social changes which are far reaching in their effects upon behavioral patterns. Many of these effects spread slowly, and diffusion may occur in such minute increments that its derivative effects are absorbed without people being aware of the changes which take place. However, the innovation must truly offer a more satisfying means to cultural ends than that which it seeks to replace, or it will not be diffused throughout the society. This, certainly has been the history of cultural change in America, where slowly, over time, innovations and their diffused and derivative effects have altered our society, and in turn have changed the institutions and practices of businessmen and business firms. In other words, we would go one step further than Ogburn, who has written:

> Technology changes society by changing our environment to which we, in turn, adapt. This change is usually in the material environment, and the adjustment we make to the changes often modifies customs and social institutions.[58]

For we would point out that technology works in a circular manner, having its first impact upon the industrial structure of a nation, then moving on to society, but then finally reacting back again upon business.

However rapidly technological change occurs, and regardless of how it is diffused, it is evident that the changes in institutional structures and value systems take place more slowly. The thesis that all parts of modern culture do not change together and that some adjust more slowly than others is generally called the cultural lag.[59] There are several causes of cultural lag. For example, the values of a culture are embodied and reflected in the personalities of its population. Change often disrupts these values, and causes people to be fearful of and anxious about innovation. Many business changes have caused, and are causing, personal anxiety, both in and outside of the enterprise, which leads individuals to seek the security of the old, and to defend themselves against the new. The social and cultural climate for change is also an important factor helping or hindering the diffusion of innovation. In the United States this climate usually has been considered receptive to technological change —at least during the last fifty years, for there appears to be a tradition developed which has led the public to expect technological change.[60] On the other hand, Americans, including businessmen, are not receptive to basic alterations in social, economic, religious, and other important institutions, contributing to a cultural lag. Finally, the resistance of vested interest groups tends to produce an uneven setting for innovations.

Now, what does all this have to do with the theory of business behavior? The firm may be looked upon as the crucible within which technological change occurs. In fact, this may be its chief and most important product, not the material goods or intangible services which are termed output, but rather the making of change. However, as it produces change it itself is also changed. The firm is peopled by personalities who are part of society, and as innovations are diffused there is a feedback (possibly with a cultural lag) to the firm which modifies its attitudes and values. The theory of the firm as the creator and creature of change is a dynamic theory, having as its focus change *per se*. Management in such a theory becomes both innovative and adaptive, causing change and being changed. The essentials of such a theory of business behavior, then, become those elements which explain the causes of change and the factors which accompany it. Whereas in part these elements are social and psychological, they are also cultural, and must include the setting in which the firm exists as well as the firm and its inhabitants.

CULTURAL ASPECTS OF BUSINESS BEHAVIOR

It is evident that business behavior is conditioned by the culture in which it exists. In this section we shall illustrate this principle by examining two features of business theory from a social and cultural point of view.

Rationality and Maximization

Adam Smith, in his construction of the edifice which became classical economics, remarked "It is not from the benevolence of the butcher, the brewer, or the baker, that we expect our dinner, but from their regard to their own self-interest."[61] Smith, like most economists since, assumed that man has an inherent propensity to forward his own interest, but did not delve into the nature of this propensity. The conclusion that man is motivated by his self-interest is acceptable to most anthropologists, but they would argue that such a statement is meaningless unless it is imbedded in some sort of cultural context. Furthermore, they would argue that rational behavior—the maximization of satisfactions in terms of choices—varies considerably in different cultures. Andreas Papandreou, an economist, recognized this fact when he wrote:

> It is not sufficient to postulate the rational norm. We must further make commitment to value-systems which are "ideally typical" in the culture under analysis.[62]

Men in a variety of cultures may act to forward their self-interest, and may choose among alternatives in accord with this objective, but *what* alternative they select, and *why* they select it is often culturally determined. Thus, to argue that men behave rationally is to say little unless there is knowledge of the cultural determinants and restraints—the cultural prescriptions and patterns—on behavior.

In this light, then, the maximization of profits is a manifestation of culture, and business behavior as it is known is a product of western civilization. Certainly the habits of the well-documented Kwakiutl tribe of Northwestern America, which contained "potlatches" in which goods were given away, are hardly compatible with the doctrine of maximum profits. Nor is it necessary to go to primitive societies for illustrations of this point. For example, David Landes, in his examination of modern business practices in France notes:

> The business is not an end in itself, nor is its purpose to be found in any such independent ideal as production or service. It exists by and for the family, and the honor, the reputation, the wealth of the one are the honor, wealth and reputation of the other.[63]

And, he goes on to state:

> In such a system the compulsive urge toward growth inherent in business for the sake of business is either diluted or absent. The family firm, large or small, is run like a household or, more specifically, a bourgeois household. The primary concern is to live well within one's means, saving as much as possible. Translated into business terms, the main objective is to avoid use of credit and to make the highest rate of profit possible on a given turnover; to amortize expenses rapidly and build up huge reserves; and to finance expansion out of such reserves. . . .[64]

Even in modern France, therefore, the concept of profits and business behavior differs from that in the United States. It is still further removed in those societies such as the Sioux which stressed endurance and prowess in war, or in that of the Zuni Indians, where fertility held a central place, or even in those modern nations where the teachings of Confucius, which emphasize the importance of loyalty, hold sway.

Cultural studies are replete with societies in which the goals, the concept of work, and those activities which enhance personal prestige differ from those normally held in Europe and America. As Herskovits has observed:

> The principle of maximizing satisfactions by the conscious exercise of choice between scarce means is valid because we find that this does occur in all societies. The cross-cultural perspective, however, gives us pause when defining "rationality." We are tempted to consider as rational the behavior that represents only the typical reactions to be expected of those who order their lives in terms of the economic systems of Europe and America, where it is rational to defer the gratification of wants, to accumulate resources, to produce more goods and multiply services. Yet, . . . there are many cultures, if not a majority of them, where the deferment of wants is held to be disadvantageous, where best judgment dictates that resources be expanded, where there is a tradition of expanding production and increasing services. None the less, in societies having traditions of this sort, choices are not only made, but debated.[65]

Choice processes and the maximization of satisfactions may, therefore, have a universality not possessed by business organizations, business behavior, or profit maximization. A study of cultures indicates that there is no innate predisposition on the part of mankind to maximize profits, to conduct business activities in firms, or to make similar choices (or even to consider similar alternatives) in business situations.

The Entrepreneurial Function

Over time, and in different societies, there has evidently been a substantial change in entrepreneurial types, and presumably in the entrepreneurial function. These differences can be seen most clearly by an examination of different cultures. In some underdeveloped nations, for example, an entrepreneur normally will prefer to invest in real estate or purchase prestige goods rather than reinvest profits to promote the rapid rate of growth of his firm.[66] Conspicuous consumption is preferable to savings in many of these societies. In many primitive cultures there are no persons capable of distinguishing profitable actions, or of taking business risks. In such societies there may be few, if any, entrepreneurs as they exist in the technically advanced nations of the West.

In the United States many commentators have remarked upon the changing nature of the entrepreneur. Thorstein Veblen long ago noted that the captain of industry, who emerged from the Industrial Revolution, had disappeared as his function shifted from a creative, adventuresome, and insightful interest in technology and enterprise, and as he became more and more a business manager and technician.[67] Joseph A. Schumpeter has written that the social process has undermined the role and social position of the capitalist entrepreneur, routinizing his function and producing a new type of bourgeois businessman.[68] William H. Whyte, Jr. claims that the character of the American businessman has been altered as the Protestant ethic of frugality, individualism, and hard work has been superseded by the social ethic of group norms, teamwork, and conformity.[69] David Riesman has remarked the shift from "inner directed" types to "other directed" types of businessmen, summed up in his phrase, "from invisible hand to glad hand." [70]

All of the evidence, and all the speculation, then, would appear to bear out the assertion that entrepreneurial types and executive behaviors have been altered over time, and are not necessarily closely related in different societies.

It is a basic essential of an anthropological approach to business behavior, therefore, to recognize that the typical theoretical explorations of business are limited to behavior in that sort of exchange economy which is familiar in the Western Europe and North America of our time. These studies cannot be taken as having universal application. Papandreou, in commenting about economics, advanced this point of view very succinctly in the following passage:

> The very attempt of economic analysis to build a theory of universal validity, to avoid any and all psychological and sociological commitments takes it into the path of operational meaninglessness. . . . we should extricate ourselves from the shackles of economic universalism and experiment with less general but often more useful construction.[71]

SUMMARY

In this chapter we have surveyed several aspects of cultural theories, and have attempted to apply these theories to a variety of areas within business. The very difficulty that has been encountered in making such applications is indicative of the amorphous nature of cultural theory. It would seem to be a truism that business behavior is affected by its culture, by the society of which it is a member, and by the environment in which it operates. It is also a fact that businessmen and business firms affect culture, society, and environment. The course of innovation and the lack of business universals also appear to be well documented. All these features, and more, are brought out by an anthropological approach to the business enterprise.

Yet, cultural theories rest uneasily in the hands of the business theorist. In many ways they appear to be too broad to be useful for predicting business behavior. It is, of course, true that many choices in business contain cultural parameters, and that even the range of alternatives confronting the decision maker is limited by cultural elements. Nevertheless, cultural theories are informative only of "proper" or "normal" cultural behavior, and do not serve as precise guidelines for action. In any given business situation there may be several alternative courses of action which are satisfactorily within the cultural framework. There even may be many which are culturally respectable. Nevertheless, through a study of culture alone it will be most difficult, if not impossible, to pinpoint that alternative which will be selected—or even with what probability one of a limited number will be chosen.

The failure of anthropology to produce theories wherein the course of business activity is spelled out and predicted does not, of course, mean that anthropologists and their approaches have nothing to offer business scholars. As this chapter makes clear, there is a great deal that cultural theories can contribute to the study of business. In order to arrive at a well-rounded theory of business behavior, however, it will be necessary to forge a blend or mix of cultural theories and those from other social disciplines.

Notes and References

1. Clyde Kluckhohn, *Mirror for Man* (New York: McGraw-Hill Book Company, Inc., 1949), p. 21.

2. Cf. Melville J. Herskovits, *Economic Anthropology* (New York: Alfred A. Knopf, Inc., 1952), pp. 18-24.

3. Robert Theobald, *The Rich and the Poor* (New York: The New American Library of World Literature, Inc., A Mentor Book, 1961), p. 36.

4. A. L. Kroeber and Clyde Kluckhohn, *Culture: A Critical Review of Concepts and Definitions*, Papers of the Peabody Museum of Archaeology and Ethnology, Vol. 47, No. 1, Harvard University (1952).

5. Reprinted in Clyde Kluckhohn, *Culture and Behavior*, edited by Richard Kluckhohn (New York: The Free Press of Glencoe, Inc., 1962), p. 73.

6. Ralph Linton, *The Study of Man* (New York: Appleton-Century-Crofts, Inc., 1936).

7. Tonnies, *Fundamental Concepts of Sociology: Gemeinschaft and Gesellschaft*, translated by C. P. Loomis (New York: The American Book Company, 1940).

8. Caryl P. Haskins, *Of Societies and Men* (New York: W. W. Norton & Company, Inc., 1951), especially Chapter 12.

9. Richard T. LaPiere, *A Theory of Social Control* (New York: McGraw-Hill Book Company, Inc., 1954), p. 19.

10. C. Geertz, "Ritual and Social Change: A Javanese Example," *American Anthropologist*, Vol. 59, No. 1, pp. 32-54.

11. Ellsworth Huntington, *Principles of Human Geography* (New York: John Wiley & Sons, Inc., 1957).

12. C. Daryll Forde, *Habitat, Economy and Society: A Geographical Introduction to Ethnology* (London: Methuen & Co., Ltd., 1934), p. 464.

13. Cf. the remarks by Amer Stewart in R. F. Spencer, editor, *Method and Perspective in Anthropology. Papers in Honor of Wilson D. Wallis* (Minneapolis: University of Minnesota Press, 1954), pp. 223ff.

14. For example, Bronislaw Malinowski, *Coral Gardens and Their Magic: A Study of the Methods of Tilling the Soil and of Agricultural Rites in the Trobriand Islands* (New York: The American Book Company, 1935); Raymond W. Firth, *Primitive Polynesian Economy* (London: Routledge & Kegan Paul, Ltd., 1939); and Richard Thurnwald, *Economics in Primitive Communities* (London: Oxford University Press, 1932).

15. See, for example, Karl Polanyi, C. M. Arensberg, and E. Pearson, *Trade and Market in the Early Empires: Economics in History and Theory* (New York: The Free Press of Glencoe, Inc., 1957).

16. E. B. Tylor, *Primitive Culture* (London: John Murray, Publishers, Ltd., 1871), pp. 26-27.

17. Leslie A. White, *The Science of Culture* (New York: Farrar, Straus & Company, 1949), pp. 339-340.

18. Julian H. Steward, *Theory of Culture Change* (Urbana: University of Illinois Press, 1955), p. 14.

19. See, for example, Ralph Linton, *The Material Culture of the Marquesas Islands* (Honolulu: Bishop Museum, 1923).

20. Lord Hailey, *An African Survey*, Rev. ed. (London: Oxford University Press, 1956), p. 44.

21. Clark Wissler, *Man and Culture* (New York: Thomas Y. Crowell Company, 1923).

22. Laura Thompson, *Toward a Science of Mankind* (New York: McGraw-Hill Book Company, Inc., 1961), p. 9.

23. Bronislaw Malinowski, *A Scientific Theory of Culture and Other Essays* (Chapel Hill, N. C.: University of North Carolina Press, 1944), p. 39.

24. See Bronislaw Malinowski, *Magic, Science and Religion and Other Essays* (New York: Doubleday Company, Anchor Books, 1955).

25. A. R. Radcliffe-Brown, *A Natural Science of Society* (New York: The Free Press of Glencoe, Inc., 1957), p. 20.

26. W. Lloyd Warner and P. S. Lunt, *The Social Life of a Modern Community*, Yankee City Series, Vol. I (New Haven, Conn.: Yale University Press, 1941); Conrad M. Arensberg and S. Kimball, *Family and Community in Ireland* (Cambridge, Mass.: Harvard University Press, 1940).

27. Ruth Benedict, *Patterns of Culture* (Boston: Houghton Mifflin Company, 1948), introduction by Franz Boas, n.p.

28. Edward Sapir, *Culture, Language and Personality*, selected essays edited by David G. Mandelbaum (Berkeley: University of California Press, 1956), p. 84.

29. *Ibid.*, p. 83.

30. Benedict, *op. cit.*, pp. 226-228.

31. Morris E. Opler, "Themes as Dynamic Forces in Culture," *American Journal of Sociology*, Vol. 51, pp. 198-206.

32. Margaret Mead, *Coming of Age in Samoa* (New York: Morrow Publishing Company, 1927).

33. Margaret Mead, "Social Change and Cultural Surrogates," *Journal of Educational Sociology*, Vol. 14, No. 2, pp. 92-109.

34. Cf. Gregory Bateson, "Morale and National Character," in *Civilian Morale*, G. Watson, editor (Boston: Houghton Mifflin Company, 1942), pp. 71-91; Geoffrey Gorer, *The American People* (New York: W. W. Norton & Company, Inc., 1948); David Riesman, et al., *The Lonely Crowd* (New Haven: Yale University Press, 1950); among others.

35. Clyde Kluckhohn and Henry A. Murray, *Personality in Nature, Society and Culture* (New York: Alfred A. Knopf, Inc., 1948).

36. *Ibid.*, p. 47.

37. Cf. John Whiting, *Becoming a Kwoma: Teaching and Learning in a New Guinea Tribe* (New Haven, Conn.: Yale University Press, 1941); and John P. Gillin, editor, *For a Science of Social Man: Convergence in Anthropology, Psychology, and Sociology* (New York: The Macmillan Company, 1954).

38. E. D. Chapple and C. S. Coon, *Principles of Anthropology* (New York: Holt, Rinehart & Winston, Inc., 1942).

39. For an interesting discussion of how the behavior of the enterprise may be related to the behavior of the industry within which it resides, see, Almarin Phillips, "A Theory of Interfirm Organization," *Quarterly Journal of Economics*, (November, 1960), pp. 602-613.

40. Jean Boddewyn, "The Cultural Approach to Business Behavior," in Joseph W. McGuire, ed., Interdisciplinary Studies in Business Behavior (Cincinnati: Southwestern Publishing Company, 1962), pp. 203-204.

41. Joseph A. Schumpeter, *Capitalism, Socialism and Democracy*, 2nd ed. (New York: Harper & Row, Publishers, 1947).

42. Wesley C. Mitchell, *Lecture Notes on Types of Economic Theory* (New York: Augustus M. Kelley, 1949).

43. H. G. Barnett, *Innovation* (New York: McGraw-Hill Book Company, Inc., 1953), and Julian H. Steward, *Theory of Culture Change* (Urbana: University of Illinois Press, 1955). An interesting volume on invention which contains several different sorts of stimulating discussions and utilizes a variety of approaches has been published by the National Bureau of Economic Research, *The Rate and Direction of Inventive Activity: Economic and Social Factors*, A conference of the Universities-National Bureau Committee for Economic Research and the Committee on Economic Growth of the Social Science Research Council (Princeton, N. J.: Princeton University Press, 1962).

44. Barnett, *op. cit.*, p. 7.

45. See Edward Rose, "Innovations in American Culture," *Social Forces*, Vol. 26 (March, 1948), pp. 255-272.

46. Cf. George A. Theodorson, "Acceptance of Industrialization and Its Attendant Consequences for the Social Patterns of Non-Western Societies," *American Sociological Review*, Vol. 18 (October, 1953), pp. 477-484.

47. Daniel Lerner, *The Passing of Traditional Society* (New York: The Free Press of Glencoe, Inc., 1958), pp. 49-53.

48. Barnett, *op. cit.*, p. 10.

49. Cf. Simon Kuznets, "Inventive Activity: Problems of Definition and Measurement," *The Rate and Direction of Inventive Activity . . . , op. cit.*, pp. 19-43, and Kenneth J. Arrow, "The Economic Implications of Learning by Doing," *The Review of Economic Studies*, Vol. XXIX, No. 80 (June, 1962), pp. 165-173.

50. Barnett, *op. cit.*, p. 10.

51. Hornell Hart, "Technological Acceleration and the Atomic Bomb," *American Sociological Review*, Vol. 11 (June, 1946), pp. 277-293.

52. Alfred B. Stafford, "Is the Rate of Invention Declining?," *American Journal of Sociology*, Vol. 57 (May, 1952), pp. 539-545.

53. Alfred North Whitehead, *Science and the Modern World* (New York: The Macmillan Company, 1925), p. 137.

54. Cf. E. C. McVoy, "Patterns of Diffusion in the United States," *American Sociological Review*, Vol. 5 (April, 1940), pp. 219-227.

55. Ralph Linton, *The Tree of Culture* (New York: Alfred A. Knopf, Inc., 1955), p. 45.

56. William F. Ogburn, "The Process of Adjustment to New Inventions," in William F. Ogburn, editor, *Technology and International Relations* (Chicago: University of Chicago Press, 1949).

57. S. C. Gilfillan, "The Prediction of Inventions," in National Resources Committee, *Technological Trends and National Policy* (Washington, D.C.: The National Resources Committee 1937).

58. William F. Ogburn, "How Technology Changes Society," *Annals of the American Academy of Political and Social Science*, Vol. 249 (January, 1947), p. 81.

59. Cf. the original statement of cultural lag in William F. Ogburn, *Social Change* (New York: B. W. Huebsch Inc., 1922), pp. 200-201.

60. Barnett, *op. cit.*, p. 56.

61. Adam Smith, *The Wealth of Nations* (New York: The Modern Library, Inc., 1937), p. 14.

62. Andreas Papandreou, "Economics and the Social Sciences," *The Economic Journal*, Vol. LX (1950), p. 721.

63. David S. Landes, "French Business and the Businessman: A Social and Cultural Analysis," in Edward Mead Earle, ed., *Modern France* (Princeton, N. J.: Princeton University Press, 1951), p. 336.

64. *Ibid.*, p. 338.

65. Herskovits, *op. cit.*, p. 24.

66. Theobald, *op. cit.*, p. 36.

67. Thorstein Veblen, *The Portable Veblen*, Max Lerner, editor (New York: The Viking Press, Inc., 1948), especially pp. 377-395.

68. Joseph A. Schumpeter, *Capitalism, Socialism and Democracy*, 3rd ed. (New York: Harper & Row, Publishers, 1950), especially Chapter 12.

69. William H. Whyte, Jr., *The Organization Man* (New York: Simon and Schuster, Inc., 1956), especially Part I.

70. Riesman, *et al.*, *op. cit.*, Chapter 6.

71. Papandreou, *op. cit.*, p. 723.

11

BUSINESS THEORIES: AN APPRAISAL

The multitude of theories presented in earlier chapters, drawn from a number of the social sciences, with an uneven emphasis upon a widely diversified range of variables, and employing a variety of terminologies and techniques, has probably created a chaotic image of the present state of the study of business behavior. Yet, as we shall again stress in this chapter, the divergencies between theories are in most instances more apparent than real. All efforts to construct meaningful theories of business behavior are confronted by similar problems: Most contain elements that are closely related. It is this communality of features that we want to focus upon in this chapter. We shall do this in two ways. First, we shall single out specific areas—whether these be problems, parameters, variables or whatever—that seem to possess a large degree of universality in business theories. Second, we shall examine a few more theories of business behavior. These differ from most of their predecessors discussed in prior chapters in that they tend to contain many of the ideas presented earlier in their theoretical structures. These theories also illustrate how some business scholars are combining fragments from a number of disciplines to construct models of behavior.

COMMON FEATURES IN THEORY

The theories we have examined contain many common elements. Not all of them may be neatly categorized into a small number of theoretical boxes, of course, but yet the similarities seem often to be more striking than the differences. In this section we shall point out several of these similarities.

Problems in Theory Construction

Ideally any theory of business behavior should be both realistic and tractable. It should be compatible with the factual evidence as provided by business activities, but yet should contain a relatively small number of variables that can be easily manipulated and that are inclusive of a wide range of business situations. The prescription of realism and tractability is a difficult one for the theorist to take, for most often both ends are in conflict. If the theory is too realistic it loses its universality. If it is too tractable—if it contains too few elements—it becomes too abstract, and is unrealistic. The line between realism and tractability, therefore, is a narrow one in any theory, and often a work may be criticized as being too oriented to one side, to the neglect of the other.

This sort of problem in theory construction is found to be common to most of the theories we have discussed. The great appeal of the economic theory of the firm, for example, and of many other theories in this tradition, is its tractability. At the same time, much of the revolt against tradition has stemmed from the belief that these theories have sacrificed so much realism for tractability that they are irrelevant for explaining typical business behavior. On the other hand, some alternative theories, especially those with an organizational or cultural foundation, have tended to be too descriptive. Their realism has in some instances become so burdensome that they defy manipulation, and their theoretical content and import are lost.

The choice often, therefore, seems to be between a theory that is elegant but empty, and one that is too full of detail to be elegant. This sort of Hobson's choice often confronts business theorists, for it is a common problem. It would appear, however, that, if the choice must be made, it had better be made on the pragmatic basis of predictability rather than elegance. This conclusion, it will be recalled, is identical to that reached in Chapter 1.

A similar problem, stressed particularly in Chapter 2, but running through many of the theories presented, involves the dichotomy between individual and organizational decision making. Implicit in such theories as the economic theory of the firm (and all others we termed "holistic") is the assumption that the organization in some way "chooses" alternatives. Behavioral theories, on the other hand, emphasize the role of the individual in the decision-making process. The latter theories are ordinarily more complex, but yet more revealing, for through some mechanism (for example, conflict, compromise, bureaucratic hierarchy) individual choice has to be translated into organizational behavior.

Holistic theories of business behavior contain the implicit assumption that the decisions of the firm are basically individual decisions, or that these closely resemble the individual decision-making process, and are subject to the same restraints. Given a goal and alternative courses of action, the firm chooses that course which will move it nearest to its goal. Because the firm is ordinarily considered, in holistic theories, to be rational, the further assumption that it is consistent in ordering its preferences in the light of its goal is also needed. In other words, the firm in holistic theories will always select that one alternative that will bring it closest to its objective; it will judge all its decisions in the light of some constant criterion. In rare instances a holistic theory will recognize that business firms do not have consistent preference orderings, and, as in psychological learning theories, will postulate that the outcome of a current decision is causally related to some prior decision or outcome. Through this sort of mechanism the holistic theorist is enabled to retain his firm decision-maker identity, and still is able to account for and predict behavior which would otherwise appear inconsistent.

Behavioral theories generally probe more deeply into the decision-making process than do holistic theories. A common assumption inherent in these theories, for example, is that there is conflict within the groups that inhabit the firm, and that decisions are the product of conflict resolution. In some theories a super-ordinate organizational goal is postulated, for example, profit maximization. Through a conflict procedure a decision is reached that, in the light of this supreme goal, one alternative proposal advocated by one group will move the firm further toward its goal than will other alternatives. Two further assumptions are contained in such models. First, it is necessary to assume that a joint preference ordering system exists within the firm, and; second, that the firm will act on the basis of this ordering. This sort of behavioral theory retains the advantage of holistic theory for, although it seems to scrutinize the decision-making process more closely, it makes the same sorts of final judgments about goals, alternatives, and outcomes. This type of theory advances the notion of competing groups within the firm, each with its own alternative, and each of which is vying to have its choice selected. Out of this conflict a choice of alternatives is made, with the successful one being that which conforms most closely with the super-ordinate organizational goal. Unfortunately, although this sort of theory is tractable and simplifies the view of conflict resolution within the firm, it also suffers from a lack of realism. There is no evidence for the assumption that a super-ordinate business goal is stable or consistent. Nor is it clear that the formal establishment of broad organizational goals is very meaningful for resolving conflicts or for selecting among competing alternatives under conditions of uncertainty.

Many behavioral theories, as we have seen in earlier chapters, are designed to produce some sort of conflict resolving mix that is much more complex than the assumption that best alternatives are consistently selected according to the criterion set by super-ordinate organizational goals. The problem with many of these theories is that they are not powerful predictive devices. Usually they are descriptive and realistic, but not analytic.

The differences between holistic and behavioral theories of business behavior, then, may often be subsumed under the general problem of tractability versus realism in theory. Holistic theories typically are computationally simple, but they are not often realistic. Behavioral theories, on the other hand, tend to be most frequently descriptive and detailed, but are not tractable. Some business theorists, as we shall observe later in this chapter, are currently trying to solve this dilemma by establishing computer models that give to more descriptive, realistic, behavioral theories a degree of tractability. Because the electronic computer can handle a large number of variables it seems likely that tractability can be obtained with little loss of realism.

Common Elements

Most theories of business behavior contain similar broad categories of assumptions. Only a few, for example, fail to assume goal-oriented behavior. All theories postulate some sort of environment for action; most involve choice processes. Not a sufficient number of theories are constructed in such a fashion that they encourage—or even permit—empirical tests.

The majority of theories that have their foundation in the traditional economic theory of the firm assume a single organizational goal. Other theories, not stemming from this tradition, also seem implicitly to assume one goal, or at least one goal that is of primary importance to the firm. A few theories, such as some of those in Chapters 5 and 8, assume multiple goals, or a primary goal that is at least restrained in some way by secondary considerations.

One of the chief differences between major theoretical classes can be observed in the type of goals that are given. Traditionally oriented theories most often postulate fixed super-goals toward which business actions and decisions are directed. Behavioral theories more often treat goals that vary; that require less heroic assumptions about decision makers. Thus, one of the major clashes in business theory occurs between that school that adheres to maximization and that which maintains that satisficing behavior must form one basis for theories of behavior. The latter theories, reinforced by studies from the behavioral sciences—from sociology, psychology, and even anthropology—buttressed by theoretical apparatus such as aspiration levels and by empirical evidence, appear to be gaining more and more support among students of business.

The environment within which business choices are made often forms an integral part of business theories. The most formal environments are, of course, those found in the conventional economic theory of the firm. Most organizational theories of business behavior, on the other hand, consider the relevant environment to be that which is contained within the firm. Societal and cultural theories construe the environment in its broadest sense, as any parameter that impinges upon the decision-making process. In learning theory the pertinent environment consists of the sequence of prior trials in a series. The personality of the decision maker enters into some theories of choice. Finally, in several theories the state of information is of prime importance, for example, decisions made under uncertainty conditions may require procedures and result in outcomes substantially different from ones in those theories where certainty is assumed to exist.

Most theories of business behavior, other than the economic model, are not really too explicit about the environment, and do not emphasize a range of variables both internal and external to the firm that enter into the decision process. As a result it is sometimes difficult to know the conditions surrounding choice that are considered relevant in the theory. One of the beneficial consequences of the trend toward mathematical model building has been that parameters and variables have had to be explicitly and carefully set forth.

Similarities and Differences:
An Overview

It would be misleading and, in the light of the discussions in earlier chapters, somewhat ridiculous to claim that there were no differences, or few differences, between theories of business behavior. When one theory emphasizes profit maximization, another sales maximization (subject to a profit constraint, of course), and still a third stresses satisfactory profits, the differences are obvious. In fact, the variety of theories speaks perhaps too eloquently, so that the similarities and relationships between many of the theories are often obscured.

Knowledge accumulates in business as in other fields. Many of the theories discussed in this book are built upon the foundation of earlier theoretical structures; many utilize concepts and fragments developed by others, and piece these parts together, perhaps adding a new connecting link here or a new component there, or perhaps simply consisting of a new combination of known variables. The relations between homeostasis and cybernetics; between aspiration levels and satisficing theories such as those by Margolis and Simon; between the theory of games and decision theory and other similar connections seem clear. That theories of business behavior are related should not, furthermore, be too surprising, for even to the uninitiated it is evident that the relevant variables are limited, that is, in any theory of behavioral choice only the decision maker and the situation are involved. The nature of the decision maker, whether individual or organization, is of course complex, and the situation may be made up of historical and future patterns of events, as well as those existing at the time of the decision. The fact that the number of possible variables is finite, therefore, does not necessarily mean that theories need be simple, or that they will not conflict. It does mean, however, that these theories will often be related, will often use common elements or approaches, and frequently will resemble one another.

In the next part of this chapter we shall examine two theories that might be classified as indigenous to business. As we shall observe, these theories draw upon many of the theoretical constructs we have examined in earlier chapters.

BUSINESS THEORIES

This book has aspired to present theories of business behavior and certain allied theoretical concepts from the behavioral sciences so that the student may gain an understanding of the importance of theory in business studies, and thus be able to obtain some notion of the ferment that is currently affecting this field. The construction of theories to explain and predict business behavior is a difficult task, but yet there have been advances, and we seem to be approaching a better understanding of the underlying structure of decision-making processes in business. Our comprehension of behavior has not only been broadened by the evolution of new theories and by the interdisciplinary mixes that have taken place in recent years. This broadening process has also resulted in a deepening of our knowledge and understanding of business behavior. The deepening and broadening processes, to some extent, are illustrated by the business theories presented in this section.

A Managerial Theory of the Firm

Sherrill Cleland has recently attempted a sketch of what he calls "the managerial theory of the firm."[1] We shall discuss the outline of his model, and attempt to fill in some parts by drawing upon the work of others, or by pointing out the relationships between this model and other theories.

A managerial theory of business behavior contains as its key element the centrality of the manager, or decision maker. Cleland bases his model upon the parameters that limit the decision-making process, and upon the variables that enter into it. He argues that the parameters consist of the external (outside the firm, for example, markets) environment and the internal, or organizational, environment. The major variable upon which decisions are based is the communications system through which information flows to and through the organization. The parameters in this model are not necessarily fixed, and the firm—through pressures upon prices or wages, for example—may at times affect these limits on the scope of its actions.

Given these environmental, organizational, and informational components, Cleland sets forth five assumptions which he believes are implicit in the managerial theory of the firm. These are:

1. The motivational assumption—the goals and purposes of the firm are assumed to be satisficing or minimaxing ones.
2. The informational assumption—it assumes that the normal information system is unorganized, distorted, and full of noise, and that the acquisition and dissemination of relevant information to the firm and within the firm are problems that must be solved internally.
3. The organizational assumption—it assumes that the decision process is determined by the organizational structure of the firm which in turn determines the information system.
4. The growth assumption—it assumes that the wants, resources, state of technology, and body of knowledge are changeable and changing.
5. The influence assumption—it assumes that wants, resources, state of technology, and body of knowledge are not independent of one another and can be influenced by the actions of the firm.[2]

Cleland assumes satisficing and minimaxing rather than maximizing behavior. He believes that his motivational assumption provides a framework wherein the so-called uneconomic decisions of industry (for example, community affairs or gifts to institutions) may be understood, explained, and even predicted.[3] He argues that the assumption of satisficing or minimaxing motivations conforms more suitably with the decisions that have been observed whereby firms try to change or reduce uncertainty, or to protect themselves from its effects. In other words, Cleland would agree with Herbert Simon that satisficing models are richer than those that advance the maximizing hypothesis.[4]

The emphasis in Cleland's model is on the decision maker, who becomes the prime element of control. As in Margolis' theory of the deliberative firm, the manager operates under conditions of uncertainty, and consequently is forced to be less than perfectly rational. He must as a result, rely upon company habits and business conventions to a considerable extent. The reason for such reliance is the noise and excess capacity of information. Operating procedures and organization act as filters to treat information as efficiently as possible, and to reduce the amount of irrelevant bits of information that enter into the decision-making process. The organization also serves as a constraint on the activities of subordinates. Cleland, therefore, defines the managerial firm as "an economic structure organized under an agent with authority who must develop a control and coordination system and an informational system." [5]

Without going further with Cleland's theory, we can observe that, because the decision maker is the central figure in it, information is required about the characteristics of the manager, not merely about his environment, and about the relations between the two. In fact, had Cleland proceeded to fill out his theoretical framework he undoubtedly would have become more involved with many of the psychological, organizational, and cultural theories we described in earlier chapters. However, even though Cleland's theory is incomplete, it is interesting as an approach that closely resembles other theories, especially those of Simon and Margolis, and to a lesser extent those of Chamberlain and Boulding.

A Behavioral Theory of the Firm

One of the most elaborate theories of business behavior has recently been presented by Richard M. Cyert and James G. March.[6] This work is the outgrowth of a great deal of research into the firm, conducted by the authors and others at the Graduate School of Industrial Administration, Carnegie Institute of Technology. The focus of the Cyert and March theory is on the organizational decision-making process, with the prediction of decisions on price, output, and resource allocation the subject of particular attention. In the development of their theory, the authors construct four major subtheories: (1) A theory of organizational goals that explains how goals are formed, how they are altered, and their influence on organizational behavior. (2) A theory of expectations that explains the search procedure and information-gathering behavior of organizations. (3) A theory of choice to treat the organizational selection of alternatives and the decisions made among them. (4) A theory of control to explain the differences that occur between decision making and implementation.[7] We shall examine these four subtheories in the following paragraphs.

Cyert and March view the business firm as a coalition of individuals, some of whom are also organized into subcoalitions. This concept, which conforms well with such formulations as game theory, the theory of teams, and the inducement-contributions framework, requires that any goal theory take into account potential conflicts between coalition members. Cyert and March argue that goals are best conceived as constraints on business behavior, and that they are established through a bargaining process among coalition members.[8] Organizational goals, furthermore, are inconsistent; they change over time, and they are multiple rather than single. Thus, in their model, five major goals of the firm—production, inventory, sales, market share, and profit—are identified and isolated. Most importantly, goals are attainable, that is, they are satisficing rather than maximizing constraints, and Cyert and March assume that they shift with the changes in aspiration levels.

Decisions made within organizations depend upon the expectations formed within the organization and upon the information possessed by it. Cyert and March specify a hierarchy of search activities by the firm. Search activity will tend to be standardized at some level. If this sort of routinized activity fails to produce satisfactory solutions that satisfy organizational constraints and obtain coalition support, the search will proceed at a higher, more intensive level. There is no effort, however, to secure perfect information. Decisions are based on a relatively small number of alternatives and the firm ordinarily looks only at a few anticipated consequences of their decisions. The firm also includes in its expectations such factors as bias and the aspirations of organizational subunits. As a result, its expectations may be unreliable, although often bias is recognized and corrected for prior to the decision.

Cyert and March summarize their theory of organizational choice and control in four points:

1. Multiple, changing, acceptable-level goals. The criterion of choice is that the alternative selected meet all of the demands (goals) of the coalition.
2. An approximate sequential consideration of alternatives. The first satisfac-

tory alternative evoked is accepted. Where an existing policy satisfies the goals, there is little search for alternatives. When failure occurs, search is intensified.

3. The organization seeks to avoid uncertainty by following regular procedures and policy of reacting to feedback rather than forecasting the environment.

4. The organization uses standard operating procedures and rules of thumb to make and implement choices. In the short run these procedures dominate the decisions made.[9]

Much of the Cyert-March model, then, ties in closely with many of the theories we have examined in earlier chapters of this book. The model contains elements, in fact, found in every chapter. In this theory the firm becomes an adaptive organization, resolving, at least in part, conflicts between the individuals that inhabit it; avoiding uncertainty by reliance upon feedback and rules; learning from its past experience; and searching for satisfactory rather than optimal solutions to its problems.

The advance in business theory observable in this model, therefore, does not occur because of its individual components, most of which are not unique. Rather, this advance takes place because of the manner in which these elements are put together into a theoretical entity, and also because Cyert and March have utilized this theory as a framework wherein they have simulated and predicted the behavior of business organizations. Through the use of computer programs they have been able to obtain evidence that corroborates their general behavioral theory of the firm. Although the evidence is not conclusive, it is consistent with the model they have constructed, and the results are most promising. It appears, therefore, that the ability of the computer to handle a large number of variables and a great deal of datum will enable behavioral theories of business behavior to possess a high degree of tractability, so that more realistic theories (such as that advanced by Cyert and March) may be readily tested.

SUMMARY

In this book we have traveled a long—and perhaps tortuous—route through the intricacies of business theory. We have examined a large number of theories and explored a variety of social disciplines. We have not uncovered that omniscient theory that will explain all business activity or that will predict the outcome of every business decision. Nor was it expected that we would do so. Nevertheless, we have learned a great deal about theory construction, types of theories, and about theories of business behavior. We have also seen that theories of business behavior have drawn upon, and are founded in, economics and the behavioral sciences. We have observed that, despite their differences, there are many similarities between these theories.

The search for business theories continues. More than this, it progresses. From theories with considerable naivete we have moved to theories with considerable sophistication. From theories of the utmost simplicity we have gone toward theories of increasing complexity. We have tended toward greater realism but, through the computer and the growth of knowledge about higher mathematics, have sacrificed but a small degree of tractability. We have, in short, tended to develop better and more complete theories of business behavior.

Notes and References

1. Sherrill Cleland, "A Short Essay on a Managerial Theory of the Firm," in Kenneth E. Boulding and W. Allen Spivey, eds., *Linear Programming and the Theory of the Firm* (New York: The Macmillan Company, 1960).
2. *Ibid.*, p. 209.
3. *Ibid.*, p. 210.
4. Herbert A. Simon, "Theories of Decision-Making in Economics and Behavioral Science," *The American Economic Review,* Vol. XLIX, No. 3 (June, 1959), p. 263.
5. Cleland, *op. cit.*, p. 213.
6. Richard M. Cyert and James G. March, *A Behavioral Theory of the Firm* (Englewood Cliffs, N. J.: Prentice-Hall, Inc., 1963).
7. *Ibid.*, p. 21.
8. *Ibid.*, p. 43.
9. *Ibid.*, p. 113.

INDEX

INDEX

A

Acculturation, 224
Achievement:
  motive, 212
  scale, 212
Achieving society, the, 203
Ackoff, Russell L., 136
Action, theory of, 26
Act of cooperation, 31
Adams, Donald K., 219
Adaptation:
  to environment, 106
  psychological and social, 226
Adler, Alfred, 198
Administrative man, 32
Adoption, by environment, 106
Ainu, 224
Albert, Robert, 189
Alchian, Armen A., 106, 108, 111, 185
Alderson, Wroe, 42, 218
Allen, R. G. D., 41, 69
Allport, F. H., 199
Allport, Gordon W., 199, 215, 216, 217
Alpha press, 201
Alternatives, sequential consideration of, 253
American character, the, 231
Analysis, defined, 4
Anderson, N. H., 220
Ansbacher, H. L., 217
Ansbacher, Rowena R., 217
Anthony, Robert N., 82, 88
Anthropologist, social, 230
Anygal, Andras, 202, 219

Apache Indians, 231
Apel, Hans, 71, 88
Arensberg, Conrad M., 230, 241, 242
Arrow, Kenneth J., 38, 136, 243
Aspiration level, 97, 109, 211-14
Assumptions, realism of theoretical, 8-11
Atkinson, John W., 212-13, 221
Attneave, F., 137
Average cost curve, 61
Average revenue, 62

B

Bach, George L., 87
Bacon, Francis, 4
Bales, F. L., 191
Bales, Robert F., 190
Baratta, P., 137
Bargaining theory of business behavior, 103-104
Barnard, Chester I., 33, 43-44, 175
Barnard-Simon model, 175-78
Barnett, H. G., 233-34, 244
Barriers, in field theory, 201
Bateson, Gregory, 242
Baumol, William J., 44, 91-92, 109, 136, 159
Bavelas, A., 170, 189
Beer, Stafford, 136
Behavioral concept of the firm, features of, 27
Behavioral concepts, defined, 18
Behavioral decision theory, 210-14
Behavioral and holistic, differences between, 28
Behavioral theories, 247-48

Bendix, Reinhard, 7
Benedict, Ruth, 230, 242
Benne, K. D., 191
Bennion, E. G., 158
Bentham, Jeremy, 66
Bernoulli, Daniel, 121
Bernstein, Peter L., 68
Beta press, 201
Beveridge, W. I. B., 5, 14
Bierman, H., Jr., 158
Binary choice experiment, 207
Bio-dynamics, 17
Biological needs, 229
Biological theories of business behavior, a critique of, 107-108
Bishop, R. L., 70
Blau, Peter M., 188
Boaz, Franz, 228, 230
Bober, M. M., 69
Bock, Kurt, 189
Boddewyn, Jean, 233, 243
Bodenhorn, Diran, 34, 39, 44, 67, 89
Borel, Emil, 39, 139, 158
Borgatta, Edgar F., 190
Borko, Harold, 220
Boulding, Kenneth E., 39, 41, 74, 86, 103-104, 107, 110, 135, 158, 200, 252, 255
Bowen, Howard R., 15
Bowman, Mary Jean, 114, 135
Brand, H., 215
Breakeven analysis, 98
Bronfenbronner, Martin, 69
Bross, Irwin D. J., 135
Brown, Alvin, 187
Brunswik, E., 215
Buchanan, Norman S., 68
Bureaucracy:
  dysfunctional aspects of, 29
  "ideal-type," 29-30
Bureaucratic concepts of the firm, 28-30
Bureaucratic structure, 165-67
Burns, Lee S., 110
Business practices, in France, 237
Bush, Robert R., 220
Bushaw, D. W., 66

C

Cannon, Walter B., 41, 102, 110
Cantril, H., 219
Captain of industry, 238
Cardinal utility index, 122
Carter, C. F., 132, 137
Cartwright, Dorin, 189, 218
Cattell, R. B., 199, 217
Centrality of manager, 251
Certainty and choice, 112
Chamberlain, Neil W., 44, 87, 103-104, 107, 110, 182, 252
Chamberlin, Edward, 23

Chance device, employed to find saddle point, 144
Chapple, E. D., 232, 242
Choice, a theory of, 253
Clark, R. A., 221
Clarkson, G. P. E., 184, 192
Clawson, Joseph, 42, 218
Cleland, Sherrill, 251, 252, 255
Clemence, Richard V., 72
"Closed-loop" control systems, 24
Clower, R. W., 66
Coase, R. H., 39
Coefficient of optimism, 127
Cohen, Morris R., 4, 14
Cohesiveness, 169
Combs, A. W., 219
Commercial bank behavior, theory of, 93
Common purpose, 31
Communication nets, 171
Communism, evolution of, 225
Competition:
  perfect, defined, 19
  pure, 62-63
Concept of the firm:
  economic, 18-20
  in theory of games, 21-24
Concepts of the firm, parallels and differences, 37-38
Configuration, 230
Configurational approaches to culture, 230-31
Conflict procedure, 248-49
Confucius, 238
Conscious cooperation, 20
Conspicuous consumption, 238
Constant-sum game, described, 22
Constraints, in programming, 115-16
Control:
  as a profit constraint, 77
  a theory of, 253
Constructs, scientific, 3
Contiguity theory, 206-209
Convex body, 152
  defined, 160
Coon, C. S., 242
Cooper, W. W., 41, 93, 96, 109
Cooperative games, 151-154
Cooptation, 168
Corner rule, 117, 136
Cost:
  accounting, 49
  alternative, 49
  curves, 59-61
  defined, 49
  doctrine, opportunity, 49
  long-run, 50
  short-run, 50
  total, 57
Costs of production, defined, 56
Cournot, Antoine A., 23, 72

INDEX

Covert (latent) needs, 201
Cox, Reavis, 42, 218
Crum, W. L., 67
Culture:
    configurational approach to, 230-31
    defined, 224
    functional approaches to, 229-30
    historical theories of, 228-29
    mainsprings of, 231
    patterns of, 230-31
    self-interest in, 236-37
    a systems approach, 229-30
Cultural change, theories of, 233-36
Cultural evolution, theories of, 227-28
Cultural lag, 235
Cultural regularities, 223
Cultural traits, 228-29
Cybernetic cycle, 24
Cybernetics, 18
    concept of firm in, 24-25
Cyert, Richard M., 67, 184-86, 192, 208-209, 220, 252, 254-55

D

Dahl, Robert A., 189
Dale, H. C. A., 221
Dantzig, George B., 136
Darwin, Charles, 4, 225
Darwin, F., 14
David, Henry P., 216
Davidson, D., 221
Davis, R. M., 53, 68
Dean, Joel, 88
Death instincts, 197
Decision making:
    under certainty, 115-19
    under risk, 119-24
    under uncertainty, 124-34
Degree of belief, 133
Deliberative business firm, 97
Deliberative model of business behavior, 96-101
Deliberative model of the firm, 34-35
Dembo, T., 220
Demand curves, kinked, 63-65
Demand function, 62
Demand, imagined, 63-64
Derived needs, 229
Descartes, René, 4
Design theories, 166
de V. Graaff, J., 89
DeVoto, Bernard, 36, 44
Dewey, John, 4
Dickson, William J., 164, 187-88
Diffusion, of innovations, 234-35
Direction field, 173
Dollard, J., 219
Dominance principle, 127
Dorfman, Robert, 39, 135-36

Drever, James, 215
Drieser, Theodore, 37, 45
Due, John, 69
Dysfunctional aspects of bureaucracy, 29
Dysfunctional elements in organization, 167-68

E

Earley, James S., 84-85, 89
Economic choice, 46-47
Economic environments, 62
Economic goal of the firm, 47-48
Economic goods and services, 49
Economic man, 46, 181
Economic theory of the firm, summary of, 47
Economizing, 46-47
Edgeworth, F. Y., 23
Edwards, Ward, 40, 133, 137, 220-21
Eels, Richard, 79, 88
Efroymson, C. W., 72
Ego:
    defined, 197
    wants, 36
Ego goal enlarged, 36
Eiteman, Welford J., 71, 81, 88
Ellertson, Norris, 189
Ellis, H. S., 69
Ellsberg, Daniel, 133, 137
Empire building, 79
Enke, Stephen, 41, 89, 105-106, 111
Entrepreneur:
    as the firm, 20, 53
    in concept of the firm, 19
Entrepreneurial activity, 75
Entrepreneurial function, the, 238-39
Entrepreneurial functions, 55
Entrepreneurial role, 19, 20
Environment, discussed, 226
Environmental theory of innovation, 233
Equilibrium:
    of balance sheet items, 25
    in Barnard's theory, 31
    in cybernetics, 24-25
    long-run, 65
    role structures, 179
Estes, W. K., 207-209, 219
Enthnographic survey, 228
Ettlinger, H. J., 219
Etzioni, Amitai, 190
Evolution, cultural, 227-28
Excellently managed firms, 84
Expansion path, the, 71
Expectations, a theory of, 253
Expected value, 120
Eysenck, H. J., 199, 217

F

Factor analysis, 199
Facts of science, 3-4

Failure avoidance, 213
Farnsworth, Paul R., 220
Faxen, Karl-Olof, 39
Feasible solutions in programming, 116
Feather, N. T., 137
Feedback process, 24
Feldman, Julian, 206, 209-10, 220
Feldman's problem-solving model, 209-10
Fellner, William, 68, 78, 87
Fenichel, O., 216
Festinger, Leon, 189, 220
Field theory, 26, 200-201
Fixed-cost curve, 60
Focus outcomes, 130-31
Follett, Mary Parker, 175, 190
Force, in field theory, 200
Forde, C. Daryll, 226, 241
Fouraker, Lawrence E., 158
Frame of reference, 17
Frechet, Maurice, 39, 159
French business practices, 237
Freud, Sigmund, 196, 198, 216
Freudian system, 197
Freud's concept of the firm, 42
Friedman hypothesis, 7-11
Friedman, Milton, 7-11, 14, 84, 108
Friendliness, level of, 172
Fromm, Erich, 198, 217
Functional approaches to culture, 229-30
Functional bias, 166
Full-cost doctrine, 81

G

Galanter, Eugene, 200, 217
Galileo's law, 6
Gambler's fallacy, 209
Game:
 extensive form of, 142
 normal form of, 142
 rules of the, 140
 terminology, 21, 140-42
 theory:
  contributions of, 156-58
  development of, 139-40
  promise of, 139
Games, m x n
Gardner, Burleigh B., 32, 43
Garrett, H. E., 218
Geertz, C., 241
Gemeinschaft, 225
Geographic determinism, 226
Gerth, H. H., 42, 188
Gesellschaft, 225
Gestalt, 28
Gibson, Mark, 201, 218
Gilden, John, 216
Gilfillan, S. C., 244
Gillin, John P., 242

Goals, multiple, changing, acceptable-
 level, 253
Goldstein, Kurt, 202, 219
Golembiewski, Robert T., 169, 189
Gordon, R. A., 69, 82, 89
Gore, William J., 38, 43
Gorer, Geoffrey, 242
Gouldner, Alvin W., 7, 43, 167, 188
Governors, unformational, 24
Grand theory, comments on, 164
Grant, D. A., 220
Gregory, Davis, 189
Gross, Llewellyn, 188
Gross, Neal, 35, 44, 191
Gross profit, 50
Group dynamics, 169-70
Growth assumption, 251
Guetzkow, Harold, 171, 189
Gulick, Luther, 187
Guthrie, E. R., 207, 220

H

Haberstroh, Chadwick J., 187
Hailey, Lord, 228, 241
Haire, Mason, 184, 189, 192
Hake, H. W., 220
Haley, Bernard F., 39, 69
Hall, Calvin S., 195, 215
Hall, R. L., 81, 88
Hansen, A. H., 71, 88
Hare, A. Paul, 190
Harmony of interest theme, 165
Harsanyi, J. C., 160
Harsh, Charles M., 216
Hart, A. G., 114, 135
Hart, Hornell, 243
Haskins, Caryle P., 225, 240
Hawthorne experiment, 164
Hedonism, 66
Henderson, A. M., 43, 188
Henderson, James M., 67
Hermann, Cyril, 134, 137
Hero theory of innovations, 233
Herskovits, Melville J., 238, 240, 244
Hickman, C. A., 219
Hicks, J. R., 86
Hierarchy:
 of needs, 202
 of offices, 166
Higgins, Benjamin, 86
Hilgard, Ernest R., 205, 219
Hill, Walter, 159
Historical theories of culture, 228-29
Hitch, C. J., 81, 88, 136
Holistic concepts:
 characteristics of, 18
 defined, 18
Holistic theories, 247-48
Homans, George C., 35-36, 44, 171-72, 189

INDEX

Homans-Simon theory of small groups, the, 171-75
Homeostasis, 24, 32, 102-105
  of the balance sheet, 102
Homeostatic equilibria, 103
Horney, Karen, 198, 217
Hornseth, J. P., 220
Hughes, Everett C., 35, 44
Hughes, James W., 191
Human relations, 163-65
Hunt, J. McV., 220
Huntington, Ellsworth, 226, 241
Hurst, Paul M., 221
Hurwicz criterion, the, 127-28
Hurwicz, Leonid, 39, 127, 136, 139, 156, 158-60
Huxley, T. H., 4
Hypothesis, defined, 4-5
Hypotheses, verification of, 6

I

Id, defined, 197
Id goals, 36
Ideal adult Freudian personality, 197
Ideal type of bureaucracy, 166
Imitation by firms, 106
Imperatives, three levels of cultural, 229
Implicit restrictions, 116
Imputation, 155
Incentive function, 19
Independence-of-path assumption, 207
Individual vs. organizational decision making, 247-48
Inducement-contribution balance, 165, 175-78
Inductive empiricism, 4
Inferences, scientific, 3
Inferiority complexes, 198
Influence assumption, the, 251
Informational assumption, the, 251
Innovation, 55
  as mutation, 106
  sources of, 234
  theories of, 233-36
Inputs:
  fixed, 50
  variables, 50
Integer programming, 117
Interaction, rate of, 172
Introspection, 11
Invention, 234
Irwin, Frances W., 134, 137, 221
Iso-profit lines, 116-17, 136

J

Jaedicke, Robert K., 158
James, H. M., 41
Jarvik, M. E., 220

Joint preference ordering system, 248
Johnson, Charles E., 68
Johnson, Harold L., 38, 45
Jones, Ernest, 216
Jones, M. R., 221
Jung, Carl G., 198, 216

K

Katona, George, 10-11, 15, 87
Kelley, Harold H., 189
Keynes, J. M., 7
Kimball, S., 230, 242
Kinked revenue function, 100
Kluckhohn, Clyde, 35, 44, 218, 223, 231-32, 240, 242
Knauth, Oswald, 103-104, 107, 110
Knight, Frank H., 48, 53-54, 67, 69, 113, 135
Koopmans, Tjalling C., 38, 89
Kroeber, A. L., 224, 240
Kropa, E. L., 158
Krupp, Sherman, 5, 9, 14-15, 165, 188
Kulen, M. H., 219
Kuznets, Simon, 243
Kwakiutl Indians, 237
Kwang, Ching-Wen, 135

L

Lagrange multipliers, 70
Landes, David S., 237, 244
LaPiere, Richard T., 241
Laplace criterion, the, 125-26
Lasswell, Harold D., 38
Latent functions, 28
Lauterbach, Albert, 45
Law of diminishing returns, 58, 61-62
Lazarus, Richard S., 216
Learning, defined, 205
Learning function, 205
Learning theory, 205-10
  fundamental concepts in, 205
Least cost argument, the, 81-82
Leavitt, H. J., 189
Lecky, Prescott, 202, 219
Leeper, Robert W., 42, 218
Leftwich, Richard H., 67
Leibenstein, Harvey, 178-79, 190
Leisure and income, 75
Lerner, Daniel, 14, 38, 243
Lester, Richard A., 80-81, 87-88
Level of group activity, 172
Lewin, Gertrude W., 218
Lewin, Kurt, 26, 42, 169, 201, 203, 211, 218, 220
Life instincts, 197
Life space, 200
Lindzey, Gardner, 195, 215-16
Linear programming, 115-18

Linton, Ralph, 179, 191, 224, 229, 240, 244
Liquidity:
  and the maintenance of control, 93-96
  restraints, 93
Lippitt, R., 170
Littig, L. W., 134, 137
Littman, R. A., 215
Locomotion, 170
London, I. D., 218
Long-run period, 50
Loomis, G. P., 240
Lowell, E. L., 221
Luce, R. Duncan, 159, 206, 219
Lundberg, G. A., 41
Lunt, P. S., 242

M

Machlup, Fritz, 69, 80, 84, 89
Mainsprings of culture, 231
Malinowski, Bronislaw, 229-30, 241-42
Managerial theory of the firm, a, 251-52
Mandelbaum, David G., 242
Manifest functions, 28
March, James G., 41, 43, 67, 175, 178, 184-85, 190, 192, 208-209, 220, 253-55
Marchal, Jean, 67
Marginal analysis, 56-57
  the subjective approach to, 84
Marginal controversy, the, 80-81
Marginal cost curve, 61
Marginal functions, 56, 59
Marginal product, 59
Marginal revenue, 56
  discontinuous function, 64
Margolis, Julius, 34, 44, 89, 97, 110, 182, 250, 252
Market behavior, 20
Market structures, 62-64
Marschak, Jacob, 38, 114, 135, 184
Marshall, Alfred, 101, 110
Marx, Karl, 225
Maslow, A. H., 202-203, 219
Mason, Ward S., 44, 191
Mass media, as societal bond, 225
Materialism, 47
Mathematical programming, 115-18
Maximax criterion, the, 126-27
Maximum, in the theory of games, 22
Mayo, Elton, 42, 163-67, 178, 187-88
McBride, Dorothy, 189
McCary, J. L., 195, 215
McClelland, D. C., 203-204, 217, 221
McCracken, H. L., 157, 160
McEachern, A. W., 44, 191
McGuire, Joseph W., 188, 218
McNemar, Alga, 220
McNemar, Quinn, 220
McVoy, E. C., 243
Mead, G. H., 179, 190

Mead, Margaret, 231, 242
Melanesia, 228
Merton, Robert K., 7, 29, 43, 167, 188
Methods and materials of science, 2-7
Metcalf, Henry C., 190
Meyer, John R., 87
Miller, George A., 200, 217
Miller, N. E., 219
Mills, C. Wright, 42, 188
Minimax, 22
  strategy, 143
  theorem, 140
Minimum cost mix, the, 58-59
Mitchell, Wesley C., 233, 243
Mixed strategy, defined, 141
Monogamous marriage practices, 225
Monopoly, defined, 19
Monney, James D., 187
Moreno, J. L., 169
Morgan, Clifford T., 218
Morgenstern, Oskar, 22, 39, 122, 136, 139, 142, 149, 151, 153-55, 157-59, 161
Mosteller, Frederick, 123, 136, 220
Motivational assumption, the, 251
Motivational determinants of risk-taking behavior, 212
Move, defined in game theory, 140
Multiple goals, 74, 108, 185
Munroe, Ruth L., 217
Murad, Anatol, 70
Murray, Henry A., 35, 44, 201, 218, 231-32, 242

N

n-achievement, 202-204
Nagel, Ernest, 4, 9-10, 15
Nash, J. F., 40, 160
National Bureau of Economic Research, 243
Needs, types of, 229
Negotiation set, 153
Neiman, Lionel J., 191
Neo-freudians, 198
Net inducements, 31
Nettl, J. P., 76, 86
Nichols, N. B., 41
Nogee, Phillip, 123, 136
Noncooperative games, 149-51
Nonlinear programming, 117
Nonoscillatory movements to equilibrium, 94-95
Northrup, F. S. C., 14-15
n-person game, 154-56

O

Observations, scientific, 3-4
Obtuse demand curve, 64
Odbert, H. S., 199, 217

Ogburn, William F., 235, 244
Oligopoly, 63-66
Oliver, Henry M., Jr., 82, 89
Olmstead, Michael S., 170, 189
Operations research and the theory of the firm, 118
Opler, Morris, 231, 242
Optimum combination of inputs, 59
Organismic psychology, 202
Organization:
  as a coalition, 185
  dysfunctional elements in, 167-68
Organizational assumption, the, 251
Organizational concepts of the firm, 30-34
Organizational decision making, 184-86
Organizational dissatisfaction, 177
Organizational equilibrium, 176-77
Organizational goals, a theory of, 253
Organizational learning process, 208-209
Organizational viability, 163
Oscillatory movements to equilibrium, 94-95
Overt needs, 201

P

Papandreou, Andreas G., 26, 39, 41, 89, 237, 239, 244
Pareto locus, 153
Pareto optimal set, 152
Pareto optimum, 153
Parsons, Talcott, 26, 35, 42, 43, 188
Pathology, 17
Patterns of culture, 230-31
Payoff:
  defined, 113
  function, 141
  matrix, 113, 125, 141
Pearson, E., 241
Pearson, Karl, 3, 14
Pederson-Krag, Geraldine, 216
Penrose, Edith T., 107, 111
Perfect competition, 72
Personality:
  definition of, 195
  the holistic schema of, 196
  theory, 195-205
  scope of, 195
Phenomenological approaches to personality, 200-202
Phenomenology, 17-18
Phillips, Almarin, 118, 136, 242
Phillips, R. S., 41
Physiological theories, 26
Pigou, A. C., 54-55, 69
Polanyi, Karl, 241
Policy, business, 2
Popper, Karl R., 5, 14
Potential surprise function, 129-30
Potlaches, 237

Prediction as a test for theory, 8-11
Preference function, 93
Preference-function maximization, 39
Preferred cash position, 93
Preferred profit position, 93
Preplay messages, 151
Preston, M. G., 137
Pribram, Karl R., 200, 217
Primary focus outcomes, 131
Primary needs, 201
Principle of insufficient reason, 126
Prisoners dilemma, the, 150
Problems in theory construction, 246-48
Production function, the, 58
Profit:
  constraint, 91, 109
  vs. control, 77-78
  defined, 48
  maximization, conditions for, 56-57
  streams, 68
  theories, 48-56
    functional, 54-55
    profit per se, 48-52
  windfall, 55
Profits:
  consumption of, 76
  as a distributive share, 52-54
  exante, 52, 54-55
  expost, 52, 54
  institutional, 53
  maximization of, 56-57
  from monopoly, 55
  as one variable, 91
  personal, 53
  as a residual, 54
  and uncertainty, 54
Programming:
  feasible solutions in, 116
  goals of, 118
Projected balance, 103-104
Propriate functions, 199
Protocol, 209
Psychoanalysis, 197
Psychological health, 202
Psychology, objectives of, 194
Pure competition, conditions for, 62
Pure profit, 50
Pure strategy, defined, 141

Q

Quandt, Richard E., 67
Quasi-rents, 55

R

Radcliffe-Brown, Alfred R., 229-30, 242
Raiffa, Howard, 159
Rapaport, A., 184
Rate of return, 51

Rationalistic deduction, 4
Rationality:
  bounded, 33, 181-82
  economic, 56
  in culture, 236-38
  in economic theory, 19
  in organization theory, 180-82
Reaction patterns, 23
Realism:
  vs. predictability, 7-11
  vs. tractability, 246
Rectangular game, 146-49
Reder, Melvin W., 77, 87
Reflex curve, 65
Reinforcement effects, 212
Reissman, Leonard, 191
Regret:
  defined, 22, 40
  matrix, 129
Regret criterion, the, 128-29
Resultant motivation, 212
Riesman, David, 239, 242, 244
Rigid prices, 63
Risk, defined, 114, 119, 123
Robinson, Joan, 23
Roby, T. B., 6, 14
Roethlisberger, Fritz J., 164, 187-88
Rogers, Carl R., 202-203, 219
Rohrer, John H., 189
Role, definition of, 179
Role theory, 35, 178-80
Rose, Edward, 243
Rosen, E., 215
Rothschild, G. H., 189
Rothschild, K. W., 78, 87
Rotwein, Eugene, 9, 15, 89
Rubenstein, Albert H., 187
Ruch, Floyd L., 215

S

Saddle point, 143
Safety margins, 78
St. Petersburg Paradox, 121
Sales maximization, 91-92
Salvation, as a goal, 47
Samuelson, Paul A., 7, 10, 15, 39, 139
Sapir, Edward, 230, 242
Satisficing, 33, 97, 247, 250
  vs. maximizing, 182-84
Satisficing man, 182
Saunders, D. R., 217
Savage, L. J., 40, 128-29, 136-37, 158
Schacter, Stanley, 189
Schneider, D., 218
Schoen, M., 217
Schrickel, Harry G., 216
Schumpeter, Joseph A., 69, 233, 239, 243-44
Science, defined, 3

Scientific management, 26-27, 163
  method, 2-3
Scientific observations, 3-4
Scitovsky modification, the, 75-76
Scitovsky, Tibor, 75-76, 86
Sears, P. S., 220
Secondary needs, 201
Secure profits, 78
Self-actualization, 202
Self-assertion, drive for, 198
Self-interest, in culture, 236-37
Self-theory, 202
Selznick, Philip, 7, 28-29, 43, 188
Selznick's theory of organization, 167-68
Servosystem, analogy with firm, 24
Shackle criterion, the, 129-32
Shackle, G. L. S., 129-31, 136
Sheats, P., 191
Sheriff, Muzafer, 189, 196, 216, 219
Shibutani, Tamotsu, 179, 191
Shils, Edward S., 42
Short-run period, 50
Short-run planning period, 98-99
Shubik, Martin, 40, 156, 158, 160-61
Side conditions in programming, 115
Siegal, Sidney, 160, 211, 220-21
Silander, Fred S., 38, 42-43
Simon, Herbert A., 10, 11, 15, 32-34, 40-41, 43-44, 171-72, 175, 178, 181-82, 189-91, 221, 250, 252, 255
Simplification, defined, 4
Sioux Indians, 237
Small group theory, 35-36, 168-75
Smith, Adam, 236, 244
Smith, S. B., 158
Snygg, D., 219
Social anthropologist, 230
Social contract doctrine, 225
Social equilibrium, 165
Social responsibilities, 79
Social science theory, the complexities of, 7-13
Society, defined, 225-26
Sociometric analysis, 170-71
Sociostasis, 41
Solow, Robert, 39, 136
Spencer, R. F., 241
Spier, Leo, 188
Spivey, W. Allen, 135, 255
Staehle, Hans, 88
Stafford, Alfred B., 243
Standard gamble technique, 122
State of nature, defined, 113
Status systems, 32
Stauss, James H., 39, 53
Stern, William, 196
Steward, Julian H., 233, 241, 243
Stewart Amer, 241
Stewart, John B., 134, 137
Stigler, George J., 39, 67, 72, 80, 88, 158

Stochastic models, 206
Stogdill, Ralph M., 180, 191
Stone, Richard, 145, 159
Stouffer, S. A., 191
Strachey, J., 216
Strodbeck, Fred L., 189
Strategies, in decision theory, 113
Strategy:
  defined, 40, 140
  in theory of games, 21
Structural-functional analysis, 168
Subculture, 233
Subjectively expected utility, 211
Subjective probability, 133-34, 211
Success achievement, 213
Sullivan, Harry Stack, 198, 217
Superego, defined, 197
Superego wants, 36
Super-ordinate organizational goal, 248
Suppes, P., 221
Svennilson, I., 135
Sweezy, Paul M., 72
Synthetic needs, 229
Systems approach to culture, 229-30

T

Taft, Ronald, 195, 215
Taussig, F. W., 67
Taylor, Frederick W., 26-27, 29, 42, 163, 166, 187
Technological change, 235
Theobald, Robert, 240, 244
Theodorson, George A., 243
Theories:
  conflict between tradition and change, 7
  discrimination between, 6
Theory:
  attributes of, 6, 7
  common elements in, 248-50
  defined, 5
  local validity of, 6
  normative, 11-12
  positive, 11-12
  predictability of, 8, 9
  realism of, 8
  in the social sciences, 7-13
  statistical validity of, 6-7
  subjunctive validity of, 6
  types of validity of, 6, 7
Thermostat, as a cybernetic device, 24
Thibant, John W., 189
Thomas, Merlin, 216
Thompson, Laura, 229, 241
Thurnwald, Richard, 241
Thurstone, L. L., 219
Time, as a factor in cost, 49-50
Tintner, Gerhard, 39
Tolman, E. C., 45, 218
Tonnies, 225, 240

Topology, 200
Total cost curve, 60
Toulmin, Stephen, 6, 14
Trade position, 103, 107
Traditional theories, power of, 7
Traits:
  common, 199
  cultural, 199, 228-29
Transformation unit, 51, 57
Trees in forest, analogy to growth of firm, 101
Triffin, Robert, 53, 68
Turner, Ralph H., 179, 191
Tuttle, C. A., 69
Two-by-n zero-sum game, 146-49
Tylor, E. B., 241

U

Uncertainty:
  defined, 54
  and profit maximization, 83
Unit-cost curves, 61
Universal evolution, 228
Urwick, L., 187, 190
Utility, and money, 121-22
Utility of money, measurement of, 121-22
Uzawa, H., 136

V

Variable-cost curve, 60
Veblen, Thorstein, 238, 244
Vector payoff functions, 183
Viability analysis, 105, 107
Viability, in organization theory, 34
Vining, Rutledge, 38
Von Bracken, Helmut, 216
Von Neumann, John, 39, 122, 136, 139-40, 142, 144, 149, 151, 153-55, 157-59

W

Wagner, Harvey M., 160
Wald, Abraham, 40, 126, 136
Warner, W. Lloyd, 230, 242
Watson, G., 242
Weak law of large numbers, the, 120
Weber, Max, 7, 28-29, 42, 163, 165, 168, 188
Weiner, Norbert, 41
Westermarck, 225
Weston, J. Fred, 54, 68
Wheeler, John T., 89
White, Leslie A., 170, 227, 241
Whitehead, Alfred North, 234, 243
Whiting, John, 242
Whyte, William F., 43, 189
Whyte, William H., Jr., 239, 244

Wiles, P. D. J., 67, 68, 87
Williams, J. D., 156, 159
Wilson, E. Bright, Jr., 14
Wissler, Clark, 229, 241
Wright, H. F., 218
Wu, Yuan-Li, 135

Z

Zander, Alvin, 189
Zener, K. E., 218
Zero-sum, two-person games, 142-46
Zuni Indians, 237

70
71
72
74
75
76
77
81
83
89